THE
CROWN

THE
CROWN

THE INSIDE HISTORY

ROBERT LACEY

Published by Blink Publishing
3.08, The Plaza,
535 Kings Road,
Chelsea Harbour,
London, SW10 0SZ

www.blinkpublishing.co.uk

facebook.com/blinkpublishing
twitter.com/blinkpublishing

Hardback – 978-1-911274-98-8
Special – 978-1-911274-99-5
Ebook – 978-1-911600-22-0

A CIP catalogue of this book is available from the British Library.

Designed by Emily Rough
Printed and bound by Rotolito Lombarda, Italy

1 3 5 7 9 10 8 6 4 2

Blink Publishing is an imprint of the
Bonnier Publishing Group
www.bonnierpublishing.co.uk

HOUSE OF W

FAMILY TR

PHILIP MOUNTBA
B.1921

ANDREW OF GREECE   =
1882–1944

LOUIS OF BATTENBURG   =
1ST MARQUESS OF
MILFORD HAVEN
1854–1921

LOUIS IV OF HESSE   =
1837–1892

PRINCE ALBERT
SAXE-COBURG-G
1819–1861

QUEEN ELIZABETH II
B.1926

KING GEORGE VI   =   ELIZABETH BOWES LYON
1895–1952   1900–2002

YOUNGER BROTHER OF
KING EDWARD VIII
DUKE OF WINDSOR
1894–1972

KING GEORGE V   =   MARY OF TECK
1865–1936   1867–1953

KING EDWARD VII   =   ALEXANDRA OF DENMARK
1841–1910   1844–1925

QUEEN VICTORIA
1819–1901

THE
CROWN

What is real? And what is imagined? What is truth, and what is fiction? What happened? What did not? It's become clear that many viewers, while watching *The Crown*, did so while scrolling through the pages of Wikipedia, searching for answers to these questions.

It was an extraordinary pleasure to write *The Crown*, to anatomise the many vivid characters and events that make up the story in the years 1947–1955. But it was sheer agony to condense ten dramatic event-filled years of history into just ten hours of television. So I was delighted by the suggestion that the royal historian Robert Lacey should take up the challenge to clear things up and separate fact from fiction – while telling us a great deal more. So, let me hand you over to Robert to take you back to 1947, when the King realizes he is gravely ill and his eldest daughter, the shy, 21-year-old Princess Elizabeth is about to marry a handsome but fractious young foreigner of whom nobody seems comfortably sure…

1
WOLFERTON SPLASH

Love and marriage

1

'Buckingham Palace, 1947' reads the caption, and Episode 1 of *The Crown* takes us straight inside it – to discover the cancer-stricken King George VI leaning over a lavatory bowl, painfully coughing up his life's blood. The King is dying, make ready for the Queen . . . Kneeling in the palace throne room is Lieutenant Philip Mountbatten RN, lean and threadbare in his wartime uniform, ready to be ennobled before his wedding to Princess Elizabeth the next day. The Lord Chancellor, the Earl Marshal and a row of stern establishment faces look on as the ailing monarch takes hold of the sword that will transform his future son-in-law from commoner to royal, their eyes darting with alarm as the King starts to stutter. Then George VI gamely clenches his jaw, twists his tongue around Philip's trio of titles, and rounds off the list with the highest honour in his gift, the Order of the Garter, with which Edward III first knighted his fighting companions in 1348. 'His Majesty has been pleased to authorise the use of the prefix "His Royal Highness"

The newly ennobled Philip Mountbatten sports his Order of the Garter sash (left) following his dubbing in Buckingham Palace by King George VI on 19th November 1947, the eve of his wedding day. Meanwhile, (right) back in Whitehall, this 1947 photo shows young Lt. Mountbatten still working at his day job in the Admiralty.

LIEUT.
PHILIP MOUNTBATT

by Lieut. Philip Mountbatten,' reported *The Times* next day, 20th November 1947, 'and to approve that the dignity of a Dukedom of the United Kingdom be conferred upon him by the name, style and title of Baron Greenwich of Greenwich [a tribute to Philip's naval background], Earl of Merioneth [a nod to Wales] and Duke of Edinburgh [a traditional royal dukedom and a compliment to Scotland] . . . The King touched Lieut. Mountbatten on each shoulder with a sword as he knelt before him in the ceremony of the accolade of knighthood, and invested him with the insignia of the Order of the Garter.'

Which is all pretty much as we see things on the screen. The foreigner had been made familiar – with just one difference. As a prelude to the investiture scene we watch 'His Royal Highness Prince Philip of Greece and Denmark' renounce his Greek nationality 'and all foreign titles' to become a British citizen. The obscure and dubious foreign prince becomes a brave British war hero in front of our eyes.

In reality, however, Philip had already become a British citizen earlier that year via the routine, form-filling legal process, and certainly not inside Buckingham Palace. History records that Prince Philip of Greece renounced his Greek titles to receive his British citizenship on 18th March 1947 under the British Nationality and Status of Aliens Act – so he went by the name of plain Lieutenant Philip Mountbatten RN for a full eight months before his father-in-law ennobled him that November.

You are watching an historical drama, dear reader, not a history documentary. *The Crown* is a work of creative fiction that has been inspired by the wisdom and spirit of real events. To understand Philip, we need to witness his renunciation of his foreign royal status at the very moment we first meet him, the better to savour his full entry into the House of Windsor the next day. What you see on the screen is both truth and invention – in the age-old tradition of historical drama. Friedrich Schiller's revered and much translated *Maria Stuart,* first staged in 1800, is often cited as the classic example of a history play, depicting the

The Viking Spirit . . . In 1935 Prince Philip of Greece (aged 14) played Donalbane in Shakespeare's Macbeth **as a pupil at Gordonstoun, the progressive academy in northern Scotland established by the Jewish educationalist Kurt Hahn, after he fled Nazi Germany.**

bitter clash of personalities when Mary Queen of Scots came face to face with Queen Elizabeth I – except that in history the two women never met.

As this book will demonstrate, *The Crown* is based on meticulous factual research. But it is also a TV show, an artfully arranged assemblage of pixels whose purpose is to entertain, to explore great characters and themes in the life of a nation, and to winkle out the meaning of extraordinary events. The ultimate power of the ancient and modern British monarchy lies in its capacity to generate heartfelt emotion, sometimes angry and hostile, but more usually curious and admiring – and always sentimental to an extraordinary degree. 'Of the various forms of government that have prevailed in the world,' wrote the historian Edward Gibbon, 'an hereditary monarchy seems to present the fairest scope for ridicule.'

These are the paradoxes that Peter Morgan seeks to address in *The Crown* – whose drama revolves around two very real people, Elizabeth Windsor and Philip Mountbatten, and the extraordinary lifetime's adventure on which they embark together. It's the dramatisation of a seven-decade relationship – a love story that is both simple and highly complicated. So that is why Episode 1 of the series does not begin with the accession of Queen Elizabeth II in February 1952, nor with her solemn crowning in June the following year, grand constitutional landmarks though both events were. We first meet Elizabeth half a decade earlier – on the eve of her wedding to Philip. In reality, neither of the couple has ever

> *'The King touched Lieut. Mountbatten on each shoulder with a sword as he knelt before him.'*

been quite sure precisely where and when they first met. But they do recall exactly when they first took serious notice of each other. 'We may have met before,' wrote Princess Elizabeth in 1947, trying to be helpful in response to a court correspondent's request, 'at the Coronation [of George VI in May 1937] or the Duchess of Kent's wedding [in November 1934].' As direct descendants of Queen Victoria, Elizabeth and Philip were both children of the glamorous and fading miasma of 19th-century European royalty that still gathered for such events. But 'the first time I *remember* meeting Philip,' wrote Elizabeth – heavily underlining the word 'remember' – 'was at the Royal Naval College, Dartmouth, in July 1939, just before the war.'

The meeting had been masterminded by George VI's cousin, Lord Louis 'Dickie' Mountbatten, who, like the King, had trained at Dartmouth as a naval cadet. The Mountbatten destiny had been intertwined with that of the House of Windsor since the reign of Queen Victoria. Dickie, like George VI, was one of her great-grandchildren, and his father Louis had been First Lord of the Admiralty at the outbreak of the First World War. But though this elder Louis had risen to First Lord on merit after 46 years of patriotic naval service, he was German by birth, and less than three months after hostilities started he had been hounded out of office during the popular witch-hunt against all things Teutonic, from German sausages to sausage dogs. The ties between Windsor and Mountbatten had been bound yet closer by this younger Louis who had been with the new George VI on the sad evening in December 1936 when the two men had stood

KING GEORGE VI

(1895–1952)

PLAYED BY JARED HARRIS

The VC (Victoria Cross) is Britain's supreme award for battlefield bravery. In September 1940, at the height of the Blitz, King George VI created the George Cross for civilian valour – and it became an apt metaphor for his life. With his infant legs strapped in to painful splints to prevent the public dishonour of knock knees, while enduring daily correction from his gruff father George V, it was small wonder that 'Bertie' had developed a stammer by the age of eight. Between them, his wife, Elizabeth Bowes Lyon, and his Australian speech therapist, Lionel Logue, restored self-belief to his heart and tongue. 'I broke down and sobbed like a child,' confessed the new King privately over the 1936 abdication of his brilliant, overshadowing elder brother. But in public, the stoicism with which George VI battled his evident shyness and speech handicap showed monarchy with a fallibly human face. Winston Churchill's funeral tribute to the King was a wreath of white lilies and carnations in the distinctive shape of a George Cross.

and watched the recently abdicated Edward VIII pack his bags to go into exile. 'Dickie, this is absolutely terrible,' Mountbatten recalled the new King saying, close to tears. 'I'm only a naval officer. It's the only thing I know about.'

'That is a very curious coincidence,' Lord Mountbatten replied, 'for my father once told me that when the Duke of Clarence died [in 1892], your father [the future George V] came to him and said almost the same things that you have said to me now, and my father answered: "George, you're wrong. There is no more fitting preparation for a king than to have been trained in the Navy."' In 1939 at Dartmouth, the two cousins shared the pleasure of reliving their naval training, while two more distant and younger cousins, Elizabeth and Philip, got to know each other over a game of croquet.

Born on the island of Corfu in June 1921, Philip, Prince of Greece, ash-blond and angular like a Viking, had not a drop of Greek blood in his veins. He was a Dane, one of the exports to Greece of the most successful exporting dynasty of modern times, the Danish royal house, known to genealogists as the Schleswig-Holstein-Sonderburg-Glücksburgs. 'You don't look like a bloody Greek to me,' said Mike Parker, a young Australian who met Philip when they both served on naval convoy duty during the war, and would later become his close friend and private secretary. 'I'm part-Danish, part-German and part-Russian,' explained Philip. 'I can go to practically any country in Europe and there's a relation there I can stay with.' He needed the hospitality. His father Prince Andrew was exiled from Greece in December 1922 in one of the frequent ups and downs of Greek politics, and the family fled Corfu in a British warship, carrying the 18-month-old

Philip in an orange box. Philip's mother was Alice, the beautiful, deaf daughter of Queen Victoria's granddaughter, Victoria of Hess, who had married Louis of Battenberg, the ill-treated sea lord and first of the Mountbattens. This mixture from the gene pool of European royalty lay at the root of Philip's self-assurance, which he displayed at that first meeting in Dartmouth, to the evident liking of Princess Elizabeth. 'She is shy and he is not,' explained one of their friends. 'That is the fundamental dynamic of their relationship. He gives her "ginger".'

After that 1939 encounter and through his years of wartime naval service, Philip wrote letters to Elizabeth 'from here and there' on what he later described as 'kind of family relationship terms', always downplaying suggestions of any romantic understanding with his younger cousin. 'I thought not all that much about it . . .' he told his official biographer, Basil Boothroyd. 'We used to correspond occasionally.' But Cousin Elizabeth saw things very differently. Nearly 20 years later Sir John Wheeler-Bennett published his official biography of her father George VI, a work commissioned and scrutinised word for word by Queen Elizabeth II, and although it might have been politic for such a biographer to play down any impression of infatuation on the part of the Queen at such an early age, Sir John's royally approved verdict was emphatic on the subject of Prince Philip of Greece: 'This was the man with whom Princess Elizabeth had been in love from their first meeting.'

Old Queen Mary, Elizabeth's grandmother, was taking a close interest. The couple had been 'in love for the last eighteen months, in fact longer I think,' she confided in 1944 to her lady-in-waiting, the Countess of Airlie. The old Queen

26th October 1946: Philip and Elizabeth had just become secretly engaged when they attended the wedding of Uncle Dickie's daughter Patricia Mountbatten to John Brabourne at Romsey Abbey, Hampshire, not far from the Mountbatten home at Broadlands.

had a soft spot for Philip, remembering him as 'a nice little boy with very blue eyes' who had come to tea when she lived in Buckingham Palace. From the start of the war she had honoured him with a place on her knitting list, one of the favoured relatives for whom she crocheted woollen scarves.

The Princess's mother, Queen Elizabeth, was not so sure. She would have welcomed more evidence of reticence to balance Philip's bumptiousness, and she didn't like his politics, which veered 'too far to port' (leftwards), in her opinion, in the subversive tradition of his Uncle Dickie. War's isolation had left her daughter unqualified to make such a major commitment at an early age, she felt, and she took to inviting well-born young Guards officers to Windsor for the weekends – the future Dukes of Grafton and Buccleuch, and Henry Herbert, Lord Porchester, the future Earl of Carnarvon.

These handsome heirs to ancient estates had the style the Queen thought suitable for her daughter, and the Princess enjoyed their company. Several of them did indeed become staples of her social circle in later years – particularly Henry Herbert, 'Porchey', with whom the Princess had already established a friendship based on their shared love of horses. But none of the Queen's 'First XI', as intimates slyly called them, had the bounce and excitement of Philip.

'Everyone was starting to say that he could be the one,' remembered Edward Ford, later one of Elizabeth's assistant private secretaries. 'But he wasn't deferential or ingratiating. He behaved with all the self-confidence of a naval officer who'd had a good war . . . He wasn't in the least afraid to tell Lord Salisbury [the senior Conservative politician] what his own opinions were.' 'The Salisburys and the hunting and shooting aristocrats around the King and Queen did not like him at all,' remembered Mike Parker. 'And the same went for [Tommy] Lascelles and the old-time courtiers. They were absolutely bloody to him.' But the groundswell only made Elizabeth the more determined. In the summer of 1946 Philip took a few weeks' leave from his teaching duties to join the royal family's annual Scottish holiday and there, according to legend, in a picturesque spot in the hills overlooking Balmoral, he formally proposed and was accepted. Elizabeth would be 21 on her next birthday, and she had waited, as her parents had requested. But she knew whom she loved and whom she wanted.

'I suppose one thing led to another,' Philip later explained to his biographer, determinedly downplaying the romance, '… It was sort of fixed up.' Practicalities ruled when it came to making the news public. Buckingham Palace had two priorities in the aftermath of victory – to thank the countries of the Empire for their support in the war and to restore the overtaxed health of the King – and the two objectives were neatly combined in a family tour to South Africa scheduled for the spring of 1947. George VI had set his heart on this sunny foreign foray by the family unit he liked to call 'us four', and there was no room in this picture for a son-in-law.

A compromise was reached. The King consented to his daughter's engagement, but it must remain a secret until after the tour. That October Elizabeth and Philip attended the wedding of Lord Mountbatten's daughter Patricia in the parish church of Romsey in Hampshire, and they played the game of keeping a public distance from each other. 'When I come back,' said Elizabeth to her grandmother's old friend Lady Airlie, thanking her

for an early twenty-first-birthday present, 'we will have a celebration – maybe two celebrations.' The South African tour was a triumph for Elizabeth, culminating in her coming-of-age dedication, broadcast on the evening of 1st April 1947: 'I declare before you all,' she enunciated in her clear, young voice, 'that my whole life, whether it be long or short, shall be devoted to your service and the service of our great Imperial Commonwealth to which we all belong. But I shall not have the strength to carry out this resolution unless you join in it with me, as I now invite you to do; I know that your support will be unfailingly given.'

The broadcast had been drafted by Tommy Lascelles, George VI's severe and traditional Private Secretary, whose own summing up of the tour gave pride of place to Elizabeth: 'She has come on in the most surprising way, and all in the right direction . . .' he noted in his diary. 'When necessary, she can take on the old bores with much of her mother's skill, and never spares herself in that exhausting part of royal duty. For a child of her years, she has got an astonishing solicitude for other people's comfort.' This consideration for the convenience of others, noted the private secretary, who had served George V, Edward VIII and George VI, not to mention Queen Mary and the apparently charming Queen Elizabeth, 'is not a normal characteristic of that family'. Princess Elizabeth had come of age. She was ready – and she needed to be. When George VI returned from his 1947 tour of South Africa, he was looking and feeling dreadful. In his twelve weeks away he had lost 17lb in weight. He suffered from painful cramps in his legs and his secretaries would find him in his study kicking his feet against the desk to try to restore circulation – signs of the arteriosclerosis that came from his smoking and the restriction of blood flow to his lower limbs.

LORD LOUIS 'DICKIE' MOUNTBATTEN

First Earl Mountbatten of Burma

(1 9 0 0 – 7 9)

PLAYED BY GREG WISE

The leanly handsome, charming and shamelessly pushy Louis Mountbatten could take some credit for his nephew Philip's jackpot marriage – and he frequently did. Born royal, but not *very* royal, 'Uncle Dickie' got even closer to the inner circle in his later years as mentor and 'honorary grandfather' to Prince Charles. In fact, he had no Richard among his names, having been christened Louis Francis Albert Victor Nicholas – the family explanation was that 'Dickie' had been an alteration of the last of these to distinguish him from his Uncle Nicky, Tsar Nicholas II. His wartime naval career won him distinction in Burma (modern Myanmar), but his greater achievement came in 1947–48 as the last Viceroy of India, where his energies reduced at least some of the killing in the bloodthirsty partition of India and Pakistan. The IRA thought they'd scored a famous victory when they blew up Uncle Dickie on a family fishing expedition off County Sligo in August 1979, but the bombers actually handed him the hero's farewell, of which he could only have dreamed. The most grudging critics of Mountbatten's ego had to admit it was his due.

19th November 1947.
The stag party for the
recently ennobled HRH
Baron Greenwich of
Greenwich, Earl of
Merioneth and Duke
of Edinburgh, Knight
of the Garter, aka
Lieutenant Philip
Mountbatten (centre),
was conducted in the
finest naval tradition
by his uncle Lord Louis
'Dickie' Mountbatten
(second from right
with cigar).

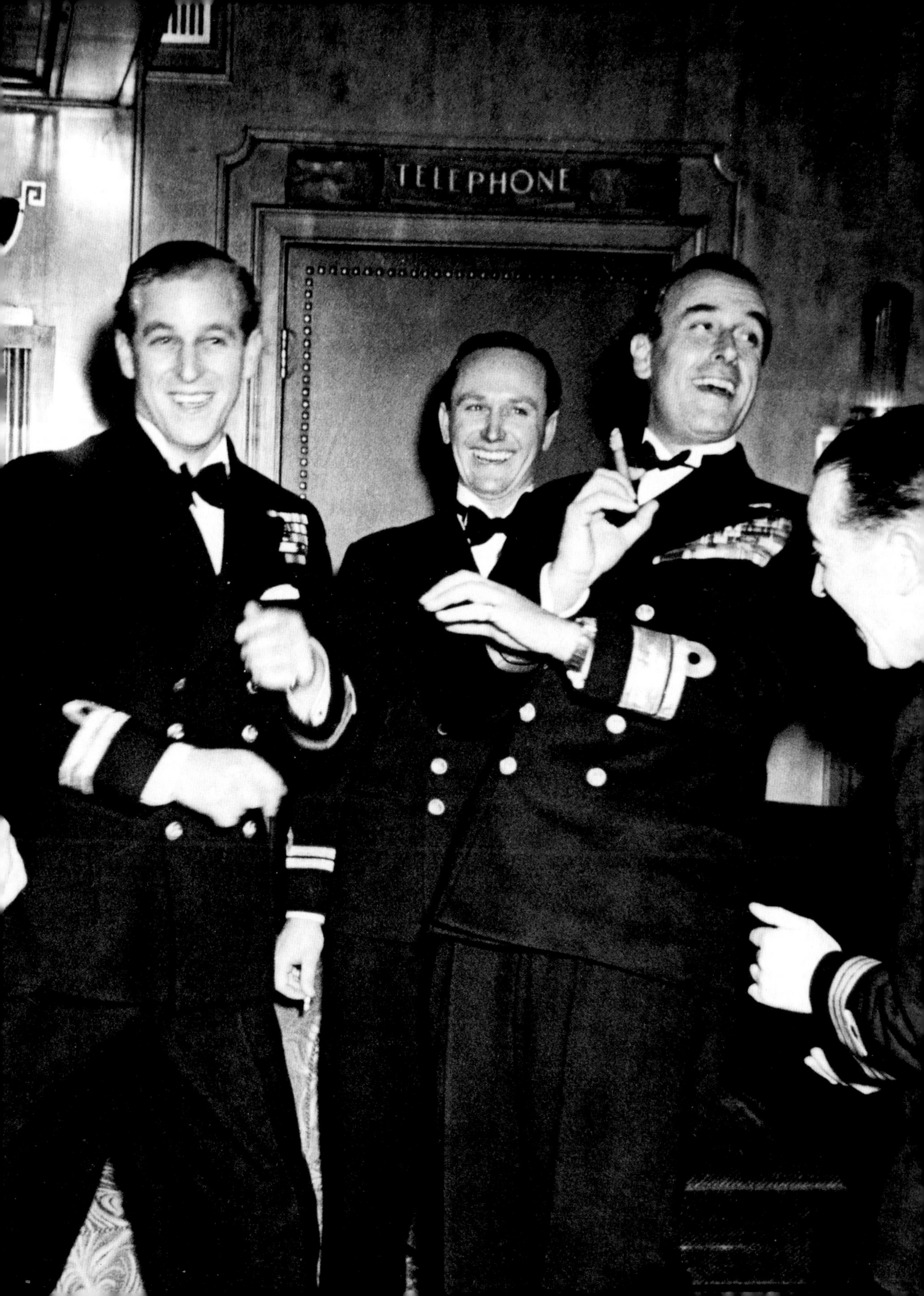
TELEPHONE

The King's immediate symptom was a peppery temper that was fiercer than ever – and an obstinate refusal to accept that the time had finally come for his daughter to marry Philip.

Elizabeth and Philip, for their parts, were more in love and more determined than ever. Early in June 1947 Philip wrote assuagingly to his prospective mother-in-law to concede that delaying their plans until after the South African tour had been correct. But now he and the Princess wanted to start their new life together. Elizabeth's personal conviction was the decisive factor. Whatever her parents' doubts, she herself had none, and she was now 21 – an adult who declined to accept further delay. The dutiful daughter finally put her foot down and, faced with her resolve, her parents bowed to the inevitable. 'She has known him ever since she was 12,' wrote the still worried Queen on 7th July 1947 to her sister May, *'very secretly'* (underlined in both black and red). 'I think she is really fond of him, and I do pray that she will be very happy.' Three days later, the secret was revealed. 'It is with the greatest pleasure', read a statement from Buckingham Palace, 'that the King and Queen announce the betrothal of their dearly beloved daughter the Princess Elizabeth to Lieutenant Philip Mountbatten RN . . . to which union the King has gladly given his consent.' 'They both came to see me after luncheon looking radiant,' wrote a delighted Queen Mary, who gave

'The monarchy's work has got to be done well.'

her granddaughter some family jewellery. Mabell Airlie was impressed by how Philip's worn uniform reflected the country's current austerity – 'the usual "after the war" look . . . I liked him for not having got a new one for the occasion, as many men would have done, to make an impression.'

Life was tough in post-war Britain. Wartime rationing restrictions still applied. Clothing, like food, could only be purchased with coupons from a government-issued ration book, and the officially encouraged atmosphere of make do and mend raised tricky questions about the proper scale of the forthcoming royal wedding. For Princess Elizabeth, sharing her joy with the nation meant sharing its grumbling as well. The cost and style of royal celebrations would provide a theme of national fractiousness throughout her reign, though it was Aneurin Bevan, the beating heart of Labour's left wing, who put the controversy in context. 'As long as we have a monarchy,' he declared, 'the monarchy's work has got to be done well.' That proved to be the national consensus by the time the wedding day rolled around on 20th November 1947. The list of over 1,500 wedding gifts displayed extraordinary generosity from ordinary members of the public, with many women saving up their ration coupons to send the Princess the most coveted feminine asset of the times: '351 – Mrs David Mudd: a pair of nylon stockings. 352 – Miss Ethel Newcombe: a piece of old lace. 353 – Mrs E. Klarood: a pair of nylon stockings.' People who had been running for their lives into bomb shelters a few years earlier could now celebrate and laugh in the streets. It was, in the words of the historian Ben Pimlott, 'a kind of victory parade for liberty' – and for the constitutional monarchy as well. 'Affection for a King's person and family,' wrote G. M. Trevelyan in the official programme to the wedding, 'adds warmth and drama to every

man's rational awareness of his country's political unity and historic tradition. It is a kind of popular poetry in these prosaic times.'

The wedding helped the family reconcile their differences. 'I was so proud of you and thrilled at having you so close to me on our long walk in Westminster Abbey,' wrote the King to his daughter after the ceremony. 'But when I handed your hand to the Archbishop, I felt that I had lost something very precious . . . I am so glad you wrote & told Mummy that you think the long wait before your engagement & the long time before the wedding was for the best . . . I can see that you are sublimely happy with Philip, which is right, but "don't forget us" is the wish of Your ever loving and devoted PAPA.' All was forgiven as far as Elizabeth was concerned. 'Darling Mummy,' she wrote on the second day of the couple's honeymoon at Broadlands, the Mountbatten estate in Hampshire, 'I don't know where to begin this letter, or what to say, but I know I must write it somehow because I feel so much about it . . . I think I've got the best mother and father in the world, and I only hope that I can bring up my

children in the happy atmosphere of love and fairness which Margaret and I have grown up in.' The arrival of a healthy son and heir within less than a year completed the family and the national joy. Prince Charles was born on 14th November 1948, and Princess Anne less than two years later – 'heavenly little creatures' according to their doting grandmother: 'I can't tell you what a difference it makes having [them] in the house – everybody loves them so, and they cheer us up more than I can say. Thank you very very much for letting them come.'

The reason why the baby prince and princess were staying with their grandparents at Royal Lodge in Windsor Great Park at the start of 1951 was because their mother was abroad enjoying an interlude unlike any other in her life, the closest she would ever come to everyday existence. Philip's naval career, which both he and the Palace felt he should continue to pursue, had taken him to the Mediterranean island of Malta on active service, and Elizabeth went along too. For three spells that added up to nearly a year, she could do relatively ordinary things, such as sunbathe and swim off a beach, drive her own car and visit Tony's hairdressing salon in Shema every ten days for a six-shilling shampoo and set. On Saturday nights, the Princess and the Duke would join other naval couples for dinner dances in the ballroom of the Hotel Phoenicia, where Philip enjoyed Duke Ellington ('Take the "A" Train') while Elizabeth shook a lively leg in the samba.

The Duke of Edinburgh and his new wife walk down the aisle at Westminster Abbey on 20th November 1947. 'I was so proud of you . . .' wrote the King to his daughter after the ceremony. 'I can see that you are sublimely happy with Philip, which is right, but "don't forget us" is the wish of Your ever loving and devoted PAPA.'

Princess Elizabeth and the Duke of Edinburgh posing in Buckingham Palace on 20th November 1947 with their wedding guests, including their best man, Philip's cousin, the Marquess of Milford Haven (front row, next to the bride and to the left of Princess Margaret holding flowers); Queen Elizabeth the Queen Mother (front row with sash, fourth from right); Queen Mary (behind and between the bride and

groom); and the delighted mastermind of the whole event, Lord Louis 'Dickie' Mountbatten (back row, third from left). The guest list did <u>not</u> include any of Philip's sisters from Germany, because of post-war sensitivities in Britain. The husbands of three of his sisters had been prominent Nazis.

1951 – Malta. Lieutenant Commander Philip Mountbatten (front left) rows stroke for his frigate HMS Magpie, leading his crew to victory in the British fleet's annual regatta in which Magpie won six of the ten boat events. 'Dukey', as he was known behind his back, impressed his crew with both his rowing and his seamanship skills.

Not surprisingly after all their Balmoral evenings, the couple both excelled at the Eightsome Reel. 'They were so relaxed and free, coming and going as they pleased . . .' recalled John Dean, Philip's valet, of these Malta adventures. 'I think it was their happiest time.'

Philip, meanwhile, had achieved his long-standing ambition to captain a ship of his own. After a few months as first lieutenant on HMS *Chequers*, a C-class destroyer, he was given command of HMS *Magpie*, a frigate in Britain's still considerable Mediterranean fleet. 'Dukey', as he was known behind his back, soon impressed his crew with his seamanship skills, negotiating difficult shallows or turning the ship with precision. Philip made clear to his men that royal titles were never to be used, and he impressed still more when he stripped to the waist to row stroke in one of the

frigate's whalers, leading his crew to victory in the fleet's annual regatta in which *Magpie* won six of the ten boat events. In February 1951, Dukey and his wife, a frequent visitor to the ship, were said to be investigating married quarters ashore with a nursery, so they could bring their two children out to live with them.

But back in London George VI's health was worsening. When he opened the Festival of Britain exhibition on the south bank of the Thames in May 1951, the 55-year-old King looked worn beyond his years and had to retire to bed soon afterwards, suffering from what appeared to be an attack of flu. X-rays revealed a shadow on his left lung which his doctors told him was 'pneumonitis', a less severe form of pneumonia which could be treated with penicillin injections. The King was a good patient, taking careful notes of his symptoms to help his conversations with his doctors. He was a particular believer in the homeopathic prescriptions of his beloved Dr. Weir, and had even named one of his racehorses, Hypericum, after a homeopathic remedy that Weir had prescribed him.

But as the weeks went by, the monarch remained reluctantly bedridden, unable to 'chuck out the bug' as he put it, and Elizabeth returned from Malta to help with the traditional royal duties of the summer. Early in June, she read the speech of welcome at the banquet to honour the visiting King Haakon of Norway, then took her father's place at his official birthday celebration, Trooping the Colour on Horse Guards Parade, riding Winston, a 16-hand chestnut gelding that George VI had ridden in previous years. 'It must have been an ordeal for her,' wrote Queen Mary to the King, 'but she was so calm & collected all through the Ceremony, it was really a pleasure to watch her.' Towards the end of July, Philip returned to Clarence House, the London family

and office headquarters that he and Elizabeth had renovated for themselves on the Mall. 'It will be a long time before I want those again,' he said regretfully as he watched his valet unpack and hang up his white naval uniforms. The couple were due to tour Canada in the autumn, and it already looked likely that they would have to take the place of the King and Queen on the long royal tour to Kenya, Ceylon, Australia and New Zealand that was scheduled for the following year. The hope had been that some winter months in the sun would fortify the King's health, but he still was not able to shake off his cough. Further tests in September confirmed the doctors' worst fears, and an operation was recommended. 'If it's going to help me to get well again, I don't mind,' said the King, 'but the very idea of the surgeon's knife . . .' Going into hospital would only intensify the royal hyper-anxiety, so his surgeons decided to create an exact replica of Westminster Hospital's principal operating theatre inside the Palace, moving an adjustable operating table, gas and oxygen

cylinders, high-intensity lighting and sterilising equipment into the high-ceilinged Buhl Guest Suite on the first floor looking out onto the Mall. To ensure peace and quiet for their patient, they asked for the daily changing of the guard ceremony in the front courtyard outside to be moved down to St James's Palace, both during the operation and for the several weeks of bed rest that followed. The King was told that 'structural changes' had necessitated the removal of his entire left lung and he did not enquire what those changes might be.

But Winston Churchill, getting ready to fight a general election the following month, asked his own doctor, Charles Moran, why the specialists had spoken in such vague terms. 'Because,' replied Moran, 'they were anxious to avoid talking about cancer.' The C-word was never mentioned to the King or the Queen, nor to anyone else in the royal family, though the process of removing the left lung on 23th September made clear to the surgeons that the right lung was now infected as well. On the brightest prognosis, George VI had only a few months left to live. On the evening of the operation – during which a crowd of more than 5,000 people had stood in silent vigil outside Buckingham Palace – the diarist Harold Nicolson received a phone call from Wilson Harris, the editor of the *Spectator*, asking him to write an obituary of the King on the basis of Charles Moran's suspicions. Moran would later tell Wilson that 'even if the King recovers, he can scarcely live more than a year.'

'The King [is] pretty bad,' noted Nicolson the following day. 'Nobody can talk about anything

Deputising for her father, the ailing King George VI, Princess Elizabeth took the salute for the first time at the Trooping the Colour ceremony on Horse Guards Parade on 7th June 1951, riding 'Winston', a chestnut-coloured police horse. 'She was so calm and collected . . .' wrote her grandmother, Queen Mary. 'It was really a pleasure to watch her.'

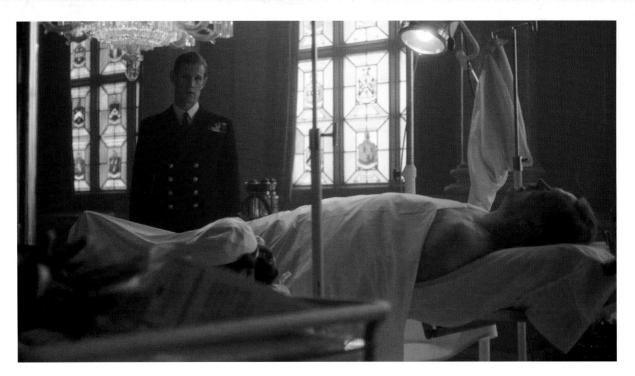

else – and the Election is forgotten. What a strange thing is Monarchy!' Early in October the King was still not strong enough to get out of bed to attend the Privy Council meeting that was necessary to approve the formalities proroguing Parliament prior to the election. So, on 5th October, a small delegation of Privy Councillors gathered round his bedroom door while the Lord President read out the order of business. Speaking with difficulty, George VI muttered the word 'Approved', while Lascelles took the necessary documents to his bedside for a shaky royal signature.

As events turned out, the narrow election victory on 25th October of his old friend and wartime companion, Winston Churchill, seemed to re-galvanise the monarch. When Churchill submitted his list of proposed ministerial appointments in his new cabinet, George VI's sharp eye spotted that Anthony Eden's title of Foreign Secretary was followed by the words 'Deputy Prime Minister' – Churchill's sop to pacify his ambitious no. 2. The King struck out the words of this title imperiously, since they infringed, in his opinion, on his royal prerogative to choose a successor in the event of the

Prime Minister dying in office or resigning, and as the weeks went by, his own recovery continued. On 14th November, he was fit enough to attend Prince Charles's third birthday party, being photographed on a sofa sitting happily beside his grandson. A pre-ordained political succession might be taboo, but the royal succession flourished.

That December, George VI was able to write and pre-record his annual Christmas broadcast before heading out to Sandringham for the traditional Christmas festivities with his family. The sportsman sovereign seemed back to his old self as he enjoyed several energetic weeks of the midwinter shooting that he loved so well. But when his daughter and her husband set off for Kenya on the last day of January 1952, ready to start on the long southern odyssey that the King and his wife had been due to carry out, Princess Elizabeth's private secretary, Martin Charteris, carried sealed envelopes containing a draft Accession Declaration in his briefcase, together with a message to both Houses of Parliament.

SIR JOHN WEIR

Homeopathic Doctor

(1879–1971)

PLAYED BY JAMES LAURENSON

The bedside manner of Sir John Weir, physician to George VI and Queen Mary, relied on a pocket notebook of 'pawky jokes' and 'wee stories' that he would relate to his patients in his Scottish accent. But their faith in him rested primarily on a shared belief in homeopathy, the alternative medicine that seeks to use the body's own abilities to heal itself. Homeopathy, Weir liked to argue, 'is no religion, no sect, no fad, no humbug'. Its small doses of often herbal remedies 'merely stimulate the vital reactions of the patient, and this causes him to cure himself'. Courtiers like Dermot Morrah, the royal historian, dismissed Weir as an 'old menace' whose 'quack' remedies did his royal patients more harm than good. But Queen Elizabeth the Queen Mother and Princess Alice, Duchess of Gloucester, were two of Weir's patients who lived comfortably beyond their hundredth birthdays – with Queen Elizabeth II and Prince Charles also faring quite healthily as later recruits to the cause of homeopathy.

'No religion, no sect, no fad, no humbug.'

The Order of
the Boot

WINSTON CHURCHILL
IN OPPOSITION

Winston Churchill made his entrance to Westminster Abbey with exquisite timing at the royal wedding of 20th November 1947. The former prime minister was late (a sheer accident, according to his friends; deliberate calculation, in the view of his critics) – and the entire congregation rose to its feet in salute. 'Everyone stood up,' reported the diarist Sir Henry 'Chips' Channon, 'all the Kings and Queens.' It was difficult to believe this was the man whom the British electorate had flung out of power little more than two years earlier. 'Has Winston no shame?' asks 'Bobbety', Marquess of Salisbury, in Episode 1 of *The Crown*, as Peter Morgan imagines how Churchill's principal Conservative critic might have expressed his disdain. 'He's outrageous,' responds Anthony Eden, Churchill's not-so-loyal lieutenant and nominal deputy. 'But you have to admire him . . . Poor old Attlee . . . No one got up for *him*.'

The Winston Churchill whom we first meet at the beginning of *The Crown* is theoretically a beaten man, no longer prime minister but the Leader of His Majesty's Opposition. As the Second World War had drawn to a close in the spring and summer of 1945, the cross-party coalition government which Churchill had so successfully headed since the dark days of 1940 had started to fracture. The European war had been

triumphantly won, and, though Japan fought on, the coalition's deputy leader, Clement Attlee, felt the time had come for the Labour Party to strike out on its own again.

In the general election that followed, the British electorate resoundingly agreed. They wanted a fresh start, handing Labour a massive 146-seat majority to implement its programme to build a bright new cradle-to-grave 'Welfare State', featuring a free National Health Service along with a massive programme of nationalisation. King George VI offered his departing prime minister the knighthood of the Garter, but Churchill declined. 'How can I accept the Order of the Garter,' he said a few months later, 'when the people of England have just given me the Order of the Boot?'

By October 1951, however, after six years of Socialist government, Britain had come to view Churchill and Conservatism more kindly. Clement Attlee's great reforming administration seemed exhausted by its efforts, and life remained drab for many people, with many items of daily existence, from sweets to tobacco, still rationed. Labour's promised brave new world had not dawned.

As a general election loomed, the Conservatives seemed to offer fresh energy and practical competence, with a commitment to build 300,000 new homes per year – and inside the party some influential voices argued for finding a new young leader to match. Since 1945 'Bobbety' Cecil (he became Marquess of Salisbury in 1947) had led a cabal of disaffected younger Tories plotting how to persuade their revered but ageing leader to resign, or at least delegate day-to-day control of the party to Anthony Eden, the well-respected foreign secretary whom Churchill himself acknowledged to be his designated successor.

But the old man would have none of it. He angrily repulsed at least two approaches from his colleagues, while Eden declined to be party to any coup – so it was Winston Churchill who took up residence again in Downing Street on 26th October 1951 after the electorate narrowly handed victory to the Tories.

Yet the smiles on many Conservative faces were forced. Labour had easily won the popular vote (by 48.8 to 44.3 per cent), and it was only the first-past-the-post constituency system that had given a shaky 17-seat majority to Churchill. Bobbety Salisbury and a growing number of his Conservative colleagues had no doubt that the party's first order of business in victory would be to map out a retirement schedule for their 76-year-old leader now that Churchill had managed to win what he described as 'the last prize I seek'.

'How can I accept the Order of the Garter...'

Ousted from Downing Street in 1945 by Clement Attlee's Labour Party, Winston Churchill's reinforced his reputation as a 'war monger' with his 1946 speech at Fulton, Missouri, where he coined the phrase 'Iron Curtain': 'From Stettin in the Baltic to Trieste in the Adriatic, an iron curtain has descended across the Continent.' This article described how the Tory Leader of the Opposition was trying to soften his image and win back power – as he did in October 1951.

Collier's

September 22, 1951 ● Fifteen Cents

Helen Hayes Picks
The 10 Most Memorable
Stage Performances

Richard Deane Taylor

WINSTON CHURCHILL
And His Fighting Young Men

HERBERT HOOVER:
Power Politics at the Peace Table

Sporting Monarch

KING GEORGE VI, COUNTRY GENTLEMAN

Whenever the royal train rolled across East Anglia's windswept fens towards his family's Norfolk estate at Sandringham, King George VI would talk of 'going home'. He had been born at Sandringham in December 1895, and 57 years later he would die there, having spent some of his happiest hours striding the Norfolk countryside in his tweed cap and plus fours, a gun in the crook of his arm, scanning the high skies for partridge, coot or mallard. Born Prince Albert of York and known to his family as 'Bertie', the stuttering King played diverse roles in his life – knock-kneed naval cadet, the last Emperor of India, father of Queen Elizabeth II, steady prop to the post-abdication monarchy, and dogged wartime leader. His secret to managing all these parts was that he remained consistently in style and at heart a Norfolk country gentleman.

Wolferton Splash was his special pride. On 19th January 1915, the Sandringham estate was surprised by one of the first German airship raids on Britain. The Zeppelins had also bombed the nearby towns of King's Lynn and Great Yarmouth, and there can be little doubt that the German objective at Sandringham was a direct hit on the British royal family. The raiders had previously targeted (and failed to hit) the Belgian royal family at Antwerp.

But the bombs only succeeded in cratering the sandy salt marshes along the Wash, and one such crater near the village of Wolferton, the site until the 1960s of the Sandringham railway station, filled up with water and became an attraction for visiting wild duck. That meant that the pond also became an attraction for keen-eyed duck hunters, so when George VI took charge

Aged 27 in 1922, the future King George VI remained at heart a Norfolk country gentleman.

To the end of his life, the sporting monarch loved ranging the hedgerows with his gun dogs.

In the years that followed, the royal game book came to document a tally which, to the non-sporting outsider, can only look like the most indiscriminate slaughter. But shooting is the preserve of the countryman, and as such George VI became noted for moving the Sandringham agenda away from the formal battues of slow-moving, overfed pheasants that passed for sport in Edwardian times, followed by a marquee lunch served by footmen. He loved rough forays with the estate workers, ranging the countryside to hunt up the hedgerows, pausing only for a quick sandwich and swig from a whisky flask behind a handy haystack – and he was no fair-weather sportsman. 'Snow and very cold east wind,' he noted in his gamebook one January. 'I spent four hours in a hide in a kale field.' Modest and generous to his guests, George VI also abandoned his father's and grandfather's tradition whereby the King took the best place at every stand throughout the day.

of the estate in 1937 he had Wolferton Splash enlarged, and it became a favourite destination for his winter expeditions.

The young Prince Albert of York had started his shooting career near Wolferton at the age of 12, noting the details on the opening page of his brand-new game book: 'December 23rd, 1907. Sandringham Wolferton Warren. Papa, David and myself. 1 pheasant, 47 rabbits. My first day's shooting . . .' Papa was his father, George V, who inculcated him with his passion for field sports; David was his elder brother, the future Edward VIII, who soon came to find shooting a bore. 'I used a single barrel muzzle loader with which Grandpa [King Edward VII], Uncle Eddy [Albert Victor, Duke of Clarence] and Papa all started shooting. I shot 3 rabbits.'

His last ever day of shooting on 5th February 1952 took the form of his beloved end-of-season rough forays, and the details were not recorded in the game book. But his Norfolk neighbour and fellow sportsman Aubrey Buxton described the scene – 'the wide arc of blue sky, sunshine and long shadows, a crispness underfoot and the call of mating partridges ringing clearly across the broad fields. They were all there, the King's men – his staff, some friends, the keepers, the estate workers, some local policemen and visiting gamekeepers.' And so they set off to hunt the hedgerows . . .

In August 1943, the Royal Family walked the fields of Sandringham which had been turned over to agricultural production in aid of the war effort. Princess Elizabeth, 17, and Princess Margaret, just 13, carried the dog leads.

2
HYDE PARK CORNER
The King is dead

2

On 5th February 1952 King George VI, the last Emperor of India and first Head of the Commonwealth, stepped out for a bracing expedition of late-season rough shooting through the woods and marshes of his beloved Sandringham. Ever the marksman, he killed three hares with his final three shots and came home a happy man. A few hours later, at the age of 56, he was dead.

The King's valet could not rouse him in the morning. The King had suffered a thrombosis in the night, the aftermath of the drastic lung removal operation he had undergone the previous September in a vain attempt to check the progress of cancer. Outside the circle of royal physicians, only Winston Churchill had been aware of how truly poor the King's health was, but when news of the death reached him on the morning of 6th February in Downing Street, sitting up in bed in his pyjamas smoking a cigar and surrounded by state papers, the 77-year-old prime minister burst into tears.

Early February 1952. Princess Elizabeth and the Duke of Edinburgh admiring the view from a bridge in the grounds of Sagana Lodge, Kenya, their first stop on what they expected to be a long royal tour from Africa onwards via Ceylon (modern Sri Lanka) to Australia and New Zealand. But then came the bad news – 'Hyde Park Corner'.

'Bad news?' he growled. 'The worst!'

'I tried to cheer him up by saying how well he would get on with the new Queen,' recalled his private secretary John Colville in his diary. 'But all he could say was that he did not know her and that she was only a child.'

The King's death triggered a series of procedures bearing the code name 'Hyde Park Corner', starting with a message cabled out to the British High Commission in Nairobi, Kenya, where Princess Elizabeth had arrived with her husband the Duke of Edinburgh five days earlier. Deputising for the ailing King, the couple had just completed the first stage of a Commonwealth tour that was due to take them on from Africa to Ceylon (modern Sri Lanka), Australia and New Zealand.

Episode 2 of *The Crown* depicts the thrilling and quite dangerous final hours that Elizabeth enjoyed in Africa as a princess, surrounded by trumpeting wild elephants as she made her way with her husband to the legendary Treetops Hotel, built 35 feet up in the spreading boughs of a giant fig tree in Kenya's Aberdare National Park. Many viewers might have imagined that the sequence sprang from the imagination of *The Crown*'s creator, Peter Morgan. But it was, in fact, based on the memories of Colonel Jim Corbett, the British hunter who accompanied the royal couple on the trip.

'In the course of a long lifetime I have seen some courageous acts,' Corbett later recounted, 'but few to compare with what I witnessed on that fifth day of February [1952]. The princess and her companions, who had never previously been on foot in an African forest, had set out that glorious day to

The legendary Treetops Hotel, built in 1932 in the boughs of a giant fig tree in Kenya's Aberdare National Park. Elizabeth went up a Princess and came down a Queen.

go peacefully to Treetops and, from the moment they left, their ears had been assailed . . . by the rampaging of angry elephants.'

The royal couple were walking along a narrow jungle track that had been beaten out – and was still used constantly – by rhinos, buffalo and elephants. The only human escape routes were ladders that had been nailed to occasional trees along the track.

'In single file, and through dense bush where visibility in places was limited to a yard or two,' continued Corbett, 'they went towards those sounds, which grew more awe-inspiring the nearer they approached them. And then, when they came to the bend in the path and within sight of the elephants, they found that they would have to approach within ten yards of them to reach the

safety of the [Treetops Hotel] ladder.'

A large cow elephant was standing guard over her offspring. 'I was sweating blood,' said one of the rangers later. But, covered by guns, Elizabeth and her husband crossed the glade and climbed the ladder. One minute later the Princess was up on the balcony with her cine camera filming the elephants.

And so it was, in the small hours of 6th February 1952, that Elizabeth II became Queen while sitting in the branches of a giant fig tree. The moment is marked in *The Crown* by the flight of a magnificent African fish eagle that appears out of nowhere, hovering and swinging in the air above the Princess, an eerie omen of her fate. This sequence is based on another contemporary memory, from Commander Michael Parker, the

Private Secretary Martin Charteris hurries from the British press centre to break the news of her father's death to the unsuspecting Elizabeth II, readying herself for the next stage of her tour – which would now have to be cancelled.

MARTIN CHARTERIS

(1 9 1 3 – 9 9)

PLAYED BY HARRY HADDEN-PATON

> ### *'I simply fell in love with her when I met her.'*

The wry and quizzical Martin Charteris saw the function of the monarchy as fun – 'to unroll the carpet of national happiness' – and the former lieutenant colonel (King's Royal Rifle Corps) brought the same sense of sprightly joy to his work as private secretary to Elizabeth II both as Princess (1950–52) and Queen (1972–77), with a 20-year stint in between as loyal subordinate to Tommy Lascelles and Michael Adeane. 'I simply fell in love with her when I met her,' he later confessed. 'She was so young, beautiful, dutiful, the most impressive of women.' The royal speeches became more humorous the day Charteris took over, with the new speechwriter displaying the gift of putting his mistress's thoughts into words. That is what made the post-retirement interview he gave to the *Spectator* so fascinating: in it he called Prince Charles – 'whiney', Princess Margaret – 'the wicked fairy', the Queen Mother – 'a bit of an ostrich' and Sarah Ferguson – 'vulgar, vulgar, vulgar!' Soon after the interview appeared, both the Queen and the Queen Mother invited dear Martin to lunch.

Duke of Edinburgh's naval friend and private secretary, who had persuaded the couple to watch the sun rise over the jungle and was struck by the majesty of the huge bird of prey as it hovered in apparent salute.

'I never thought about it until later,' he wrote. 'But that was roughly the time when the King died.'

By a strange quirk, however, the new Queen was one of the last people in the world to hear the news of her own accession. When the crucial 'Hyde Park Corner' telegram reached Nairobi early on the morning of 6th February, the High Commissioner had already left Nairobi with most of his staff, heading for Mombasa where he was due to bid farewell to his royal guests as they left for Ceylon – and he had taken the official code book with him. (Also in Mombasa, packed and ready for the voyage, were many of the items in Elizabeth's formal wardrobe, including the black mourning outfits that travel everywhere with royalty. A telegram to Buckingham Palace ensured that a black hat would be discreetly brought on board the royal plane next day when the Queen got back to London.)

'He looked as if you'd dropped half the world on him.'

As the cables piled up in Government House, it was Elizabeth's private secretary, Martin Charteris, who first got wind that something was amiss when he was summoned to a phone in the British press centre. There in the booth he found a journalist looking dazed and white – blankly turning a packet of cigarettes over and over in one hand, Charteris later remembered. The Reuters wire had just passed on the momentous news from London

that the government felt they could keep secret no longer. It was Parker who, alerted by Charteris from the press centre, had to break the news of the King's death to Philip at Sagana Lodge. 'He looked as if you'd dropped half the world on him', Parker recalled. 'I never felt so sorry for anyone in all my life.'

Philip took his wife away from everyone else. 'He took her up to the garden', Parker remembered. 'And they walked slowly up and down the lawn while he talked and talked and talked to her.'

When Charteris arrived at Sagana, he found the couple back alone together in the lodge, with Philip lying flat on a sofa, holding a copy of *The Times* over his face like a tent. The new Queen's cheeks were flushed, but there was no sign of tears. 'She was sitting erect, fully accepting her destiny', recalled Charteris, struck by the composure with which Elizabeth insisted on personally drafting the telegrams of apology to those awaiting her on the next stages of the now-cancelled tour. When the private secretary asked her how she wished to be known as Queen – her regnal name – she answered briskly: 'Oh, my own name – what else?'

Elizabeth II left Sagana in the blue jeans she had worn at Treetops, requesting that the three press photographers present should not take any photographs. 'We stood silently outside the lodge as the cars drove away in a cloud of dust,' recalled one of them, John Jochimsen, 'not one of us taking a shot at that historic moment. Seeing the young girl as Queen of Great Britain as she drove away, I felt her sadness as she just raised her hand to us as we stood there silent, our cameras on the ground.'

On the long, 19-hour overnight flight back to London, Philip's valet John Dean noticed how the new Queen left her seat once or twice. When she returned, he thought she looked as if she had been crying. But no one saw any tears. Philip's cousin Pamela Mountbatten, who had come on the trip as a lady-in-waiting, remembers Elizabeth apologising for spoiling the exciting South Pacific voyage to which everyone had been looking forward. 'I'm so sorry that we're all going to have to go home,' she had said as they left Sagana.

Elizabeth II's reluctance to play the top potato would prove a defining characteristic of her low-key style as monarch – along with her dry sense of humour. As the aircraft finally taxied to a halt at Heathrow airport, she looked out of the window at the line of large, black official cars waiting.

'Look,' she said. 'They've sent the hearses.'

A memorable scene in Episode 2 of *The Crown* shows the interior of the royal DC-4 (a propeller plane) as it taxis to a halt beside the waiting line of bare-headed dignitaries in the early evening dusk of 7th February at London airport. Tommy Lascelles has come aboard to take charge of the protocol, and he blocks the Duke of Edinburgh as Philip moves forward to accompany his wife down the air stairs to the tarmac.

'No, sir. If you don't mind', says Lascelles. 'The Crown takes precedence.'

Did it happen exactly like that? The details are not recorded. But that, or some similar process of discussion, produced the moving image of the young Queen – not Elizabeth Mountbatten or Elizabeth Windsor, but now a newly minted person, Elizabeth Regina, Elizabeth the Queen – dressed in black and descending the stairs quite alone to meet her prime minister and government.

It was, observed the diplomat Sir Evelyn Shuckburgh, 'the 20th-century version of [Lord] Melbourne galloping to Kensington Palace, falling on his knees before Victoria in her nightdress'.

When Elizabeth arrived back at Clarence House, her first visitor was her grandmother Queen Mary who had come straight round from Marlborough House next door. All her life, Elizabeth had curtseyed to her grandmother, but now their roles were reversed.

'Her old granny and subject,' declared Queen Mary with pride and sorrow, 'must be the first to kiss her hand.'

The following day, 8th February 1952, the new Queen's first official act was to meet with her Accession Council in St James's Palace.

'By the sudden death of my dear father,' she told them, 'I am called to assume the duties and responsibilities of sovereignty . . . My heart is too full for me to say more to you to-day than that I shall always work, as my father did throughout his reign, to uphold constitutional government and to advance the happiness and prosperity of my peoples, spread as they are all the world over. I know that in my resolve to follow his shining example of service and devotion, I shall be inspired by the loyalty and affection of those whose Queen I have been called to be . . . I pray that God will help me to discharge worthily this heavy task that has been laid upon me so early in my life.'

7th February 1952, London Airport. Dressed in mourning, the young Queen – no longer plain Elizabeth Mountbatten or Elizabeth Windsor, but now a newly minted person, Elizabeth Regina, Elizabeth the Queen – descends the aircraft stairs quite alone to meet her waiting prime minister and government.

'The Queen's entrance', wrote the future prime minister Harold Macmillan in his diary, 'the low bows of her councillors; the firm, yet charming voice in which she pronounced her allocution and went through the various ceremonious forms of the ritual produced a profound impression on us all.'

Britain was still in the grip of post-war austerity, and Macmillan thought that the assembled politicians in their dark coats and striped trousers presented 'rather a scruffy, scrubby appearance . . .' He also noted that while the new monarch was being proclaimed 'Queen Elizabeth the Second, by the Grace of God Queen of this Realm and of all Her Other Realms and Territories', the Scots would argue that she was, in fact, only Queen Elizabeth the First of Scotland,

> ## 'I could hardly control my emotions.'

since Scotland did not join the Union until 1603. (Churchill later compromised on this dilemma by deciding that the royal style in Scotland would be ER, for Elizabeth Regina.)

'There must have been nearly two hundred Privy Councilors present,' recalled Oliver Lyttelton, Secretary of State for the Colonies. 'The door opened, and the Queen in black came in. Suddenly the members of the Privy Council looked immeasurably old and gnarled and grey. The Queen made one of the most touching speeches to which I have ever listened, and I, like many others, could hardly control my emotions.'

Convened only once at the start of every reign, the Accession Council is made up of Privy

6th February 1952. Newspapers announce the death of King George VI. 'In the end,' declared Winston Churchill, 'death came as a friend, and after a happy day of sunshine and sport, and after "good night" to those who loved him best, he fell asleep as every man or woman who strives to fear God . . . may hope to do.'

Councillors (many of them former or current cabinet ministers), Great Officers of State, the Lord Mayor and Aldermen of the City of London, some senior civil servants and representatives of the Commonwealth. Its principal role is to prepare and sign the Accession Proclamation to be read out from the balcony of St James's Palace and at other spots around the country.

'It was a very moving occasion', wrote Vincent Massey, the new Governor-General of Canada. 'A slight figure dressed in deep mourning entered the great room alone and, with strong but perfectly controlled emotion, went through the exacting tasks the Constitution prescribes. Her speeches were perfectly delivered. After this, Prince Philip

. . . stepped forward quietly and went out of the door with her.'

Behind the scenes, meanwhile, Churchill's mutinous cabinet considered the political implications of the change of monarch. Led by Foreign Secretary Sir Anthony Eden, a cabal of senior Conservatives felt that the 77-year-old prime minister was losing his faculties, and should be replaced by a younger, more dynamic leader – Eden himself, in fact. On the day following the King's death, Churchill had overslept and failed to chair the cabinet meeting that he himself had

8th February 1952. The new Queen's first official act was to meet with her Accession Council.

SECOND SUPPLEMENT TO

The London Gazette

EXTRAORDINARY

OF WEDNESDAY, 6th FEBRUARY, 1952

Published by Authority

Registered as a Newspaper

FRIDAY, 8 FEBRUARY, 1952

At the Court at *St. James's*, the 8th day of *February*, 1952.

PRESENT.

The QUEEN'S Most Excellent Majesty in Council.

Her Majesty, being this day present in Council, was pleased to make the following Declaration:—

"Your Royal Highnesses, My Lords, Ladies and Gentlemen:

By the sudden death of my dear Father, I am called to assume the duties and responsibilities of Sovereignty.

At this time of deep sorrow, it is a profound consolation to me to be assured of the sympathy which you and all my Peoples feel towards me, to my Mother, and my Sister, and to the other members of my Family. My Father was our revered and beloved Head, as he was of the wider Family of his subjects: the grief which his loss brings is shared among us all.

My heart is too full for me to say more to you to-day than that I shall always work, as my Father did throughout his Reign, to uphold constitutional government and to advance the happiness and prosperity of my Peoples, spread as they are all the world over. I know that in my resolve to follow his shining example of service and devotion, I shall be inspired by the loyalty and affection of those whose Queen I have been called to be, and by the counsel of their elected Parliaments. I pray that God will help me to discharge worthily this heavy task that has been laid upon me so early in my life."

Whereupon the Lords of the Council made it their humble request to Her Majesty that Her Majesty's Most Gracious Declaration to Their Lordships might be made public, which Her Majesty was pleased to Order accordingly.

F. J. Fernau.

At the Court at *St. James's*, the 8th day of *February*, 1952.

PRESENT,

THE QUEEN'S MOST EXCELLENT MAJESTY.

His Royal Highness The Duke of Gloucester.
His Royal Highness The Duke of Edinburgh.
Lord Chancellor.
Archbishop of York.
Prime Minister.
Lord President.
Mr. Speaker of the House of Commons.
Lord Privy Seal.
Earl Marshal.
Master of the Horse.
Duke of Buccleuch and Queensberry.

11th February 1952. Borne by a guard of honour, the coffin of King George VI arrives in London's King's Cross Station from Sandringham, where it had lain in Sandringham Church for two days.

summoned – 'being much tired,' according to Harold Macmillan, 'with the emotion of yesterday'. Anticipating that the accession of the new young Queen would show up the old warrior's frailties, his critics looked forward to the broadcast that he had to prepare at short notice in praise of the late King, confident that he would mix up his words or forget his lines.

At one point during the speech their hopes seem justified. 'My friends, no Minister', declared Churchill in his live BBC radio broadcast of 7th February 1952, before pausing and appearing to stumble '– I suppose no Minister – I am sure no Minister – saw so much of the King during the war as I did.'

In fact, Churchill's human hesitation only added to the strength of his heartfelt tribute to the dead monarch and his emotional evocation

of the new Elizabethan age. His speech, which he entitled 'For Valour', the motto of the Victoria Cross, Britain's highest award for bravery, proved a triumph, ranking alongside the great perorations with which he had rallied the country during the darkest days of the Second World War.

The final scenes of 'Hyde Park Corner' depict Churchill's critics – Eden and Robert 'Bobbety' Cecil, the fifth Marquess of Salisbury and Leader of the House of Lords, along with Clement Attlee, the former Labour prime minister and Leader of the Opposition – as they digest the quivering brilliance of the prime minister's oratory. Churchill

11th February 1952. Elizabeth II (left), Queen Mary and Elizabeth the Queen Mother. Three queens in mourning attend the lying-in-state of King George VI in Westminster Hall. Queen Mary herself passed away less than two months later on 24th March.

was secure as the leader of Elizabeth II's first government, for the time being at least, as he conjured up the memory of the father that she, and the nation, had lost.

'During these last months', he declaimed into the microphone, 'the King walked with death as if death were a companion, an acquaintance whom he recognised and did not fear. In the end death came as a friend, and after a happy day of sunshine and sport, and after "good night" to those who loved him best, he fell asleep as every man or woman who strives to fear God and nothing else in the world may hope to do . . .

'My friends, no Minister – I suppose no Minister – I am sure no Minister – saw so much of the King during the war as I did. I made certain he was kept informed of every secret matter, and the care and thoroughness with which he mastered the immense daily flow of State papers made a deep mark on my mind . . .

'For fifteen years George VI was King. Never at any moment in all the perplexities at home and abroad, in public or in private, did he fail in his duties. Well does he deserve the farewell salute of all his governments and peoples.

'It is at this time that our compassion and sympathy go out to his consort and widow [Queen Elizabeth, now the Queen Mother] . . . that valiant woman, with famous blood of Scotland in her veins, who sustained King George through all his toils and problems, and brought up with their charm and beauty the two daughters who mourn their father today. May she be granted strength to bear her sorrow . . .

'Now I must leave the treasures of the past and turn to the future. Famous have been the reigns of our queens. Some of the greatest periods in our history have unfolded under their sceptre. Now that we have the second Queen Elizabeth, also ascending the Throne in her twenty-sixth year, our thoughts are carried back nearly four hundred years to the magnificent figure who presided over and, in many ways, embodied and inspired the grandeur and genius of the Elizabethan age.

'Queen Elizabeth II, like her predecessor, did not pass her childhood in any certain expectation of the Crown. But already we know her well, and we understand why her gifts, and those of her husband, the Duke of Edinburgh, have stirred the only part of our Commonwealth she has yet been able to visit. She has already been acclaimed as Queen of Canada. We make our acclaim too . . . and tomorrow the proclamation of her sovereignty will command the loyalty of her native land and of all other parts of the British Commonwealth and Empire.

'I, whose youth was passed in the august, unchallenged and tranquil glories of the Victorian era, may well feel a thrill in invoking once more the prayer and the anthem, "God save the Queen!"'

11th February 1952. After her return from Africa on 7th February, the new Queen Elizabeth II travelled up to Sandringham to be with her grieving mother and sister. There she was driven behind the coffin of her father to the local church, where local villagers and estate workers paid their respects, before the late King was taken on his final journey to London, from Wolferton Station, Norfolk, where Elizabeth (right) followed him.

Nearly a third of a million mourners queued for four hours or more to shuffle slowly past the body of the late King George VI as he lay in state in Westminster Hall. On 15th February 1952, the entire country observed two minutes' silence as the King's coffin was transferred to Windsor to be lowered into the ground in St George's Chapel. Fifty years later in March 2002, the Queen Mother would similarly lie in state in Westminster Hall before her funeral in the Abbey, followed by her burial beside her husband in Windsor.

Tobacco

THE FATAL ROYAL CURSE

Stricken by lung cancer, **King George VI** was the fourth British monarch of the 20th century to die of smoking-related causes.

His grandfather 'Bertie', **King Edward VII**, was a passionate devotee of tobacco, doing much as Prince of Wales to popularise the smoking of cigars and helping to endorse the remark of his acquaintance the playwright Edward Bulwer-Lytton: 'a good cigar is as great a comfort to a man as a good cry is to a woman'. In 1878 the Prince, who smoked 12 large cigars and 20 cigarettes a day, gave the London tobacconists Benson & Hedges their first royal warrant. His mother Queen Victoria disapproved greatly. Throughout her long reign cigars, pipes and cigarettes were strictly banned at court, so it was with unabashed delight at the end of dinner on the evening following his mother's death on 22nd January 1901, that Bertie declared, 'Gentlemen, you may smoke!' Aged 59 when he came to the throne, the massively overweight Edward VII was dogged by ill health, suffering from emphysema, chronic bronchitis and a series of heart attacks, finally dying of pneumonia in 1911 at the age of 69.

His less flamboyant son **King George V** shared his father's fondness for cigarettes, and was often taken for the bearded sailor depicted on the packets of Player's Navy Cut cigarettes. Suffering for much of his life from bronchitis and numerous lung

Holding his pipe, King George VI visits the Natal National Park during the royal tour of South Africa in April 1947 with his daughter Princess Elizabeth.

problems, he died in January 1936 of a viral respiratory infection, aged 68.

Edward VIII, George V's eldest son and short-lived successor who abdicated in December 1936, was seldom pictured without a cigarette dangling elegantly from his lips or fingers. As Duke of Windsor he resisted the efforts of advertising companies who wanted him to endorse their products, but as Governor of the Bahamas in the Second World War he did not stand in the way of his wife, who lent her name to a promotion campaign by Chesterfield cigarettes. 'Our records show,' wrote the Duchess of Windsor from the United Services Canteen in Nassau in 1943, 'that day in and day out smokers show a preference for Chesterfield over all other brands by a margin of four to one.'

'The American-born Duchess', explained Chesterfield, was working hard at the Nassau canteen to entertain both American and Allied troops. 'She takes an active part in making her service guests feel at home – [she] cooks eggs and bacon, carries trays and hands out cigarettes.' The Duke of Windsor died of throat cancer at the Villa Windsor outside Paris in 1972, with the Duchess following him 14 years later, having suffered from poor blood circulation, dementia and eventually loss of speech.

George V's widow **Queen Mary**, an inveterate smoker, died of lung cancer in 1953 at the age of 85, and **Princess Margaret**, who smoked 30 cigarettes a day for many years and suffered from migraines, laryngitis, bronchitis, hepatitis and pneumonia, died of a heart attack aged 71. Contemplating this sorry medical record, Prince Charles, a resolute non-smoker, is thought to have been behind the removal in the 1990s of the royal warrant from Gallagher, the 20th-century producers of Benson & Hedges, Silk Cut, Kensitas, Senior Service and other brands. At her son's suggestion, Queen Elizabeth II cancelled the supply of all smoking products to the royal households. So, in the year 2000, after 122 years, the royal coat of arms finally disappeared from the packets of any British tobacco, cigars or cigarettes.

As Prince of Wales, the future King Edward VIII was seldom pictured in the 1920s without a cigarette dangling elegantly from his lips or fingers.

In 1943, the Duke of Windsor and his wife were happy for the Duchess to be featured in this glowing testimonial for Chesterfield cigarettes.

The American-born Duchess of Windsor presides in person at the United Services Canteen in the beautiful old Bahamian Club in Nassau. She takes an active part in making her service guests feel at home—cooks eggs and bacon, carries trays and hands out cigarettes.

IN NASSAU
AT THE *Duchess of Windsor's*
UNITED SERVICES CANTEEN WHERE OUR SOLDIERS
AND OUR ALLIES MEET

Chesterfield
is the Smoker's Choice

GOVERNMENT HOUSE
NASSAU

June 17, 1943

Liggett & Myers Tobacco Co.,
630 Fifth Avenue,
New York, N. Y.

Dear Sirs:
Answering your inquiry as to what cigarettes we have here at the Canteen, I can say that we carry all the leading American brands.

Our records show that day in and day out smokers show a preference for Chesterfield over all other brands by a margin of four to one.

Of course, most of the Service men who come to the Canteen are British and American, but there are representatives of all the other Allied Nations.

It never occurred to me to ask any of the men why they preferred Chesterfields, but it's quite evident that Chesterfields are what 80% of them want.

Sincerely,
Wallis Windsor

Yes, and it's Chesterfield at canteens, ship stores, post exchanges and everywhere that smokers want a milder, better-tasting smoke.

The basic difference between Chesterfield and other cigarettes is in the tobaccos we use and the way they are blended in the *right combination* to give you what you want in a smoke. They really SATISFY.

Copyright 1943, LIGGETT & MYERS TOBACCO CO.

Queen Alexandrina, King David and two King Alberts

BRITAIN'S MONARCHS WHO MIGHT HAVE BEEN . . .

QUEEN VICTORIA (1837–1901)

Elizabeth II's decision to take her own name for her title – her so-called 'regnal name' – was quite unusual in the modern history of the British monarchy.

Her great-great-grandmother **Queen Victoria (1837–1901)** was christened Alexandrina Victoria, after her godfather Tsar Alexander I and her mother Marie Louise Victoire. She was known to her family as 'Drina' in her early childhood, and the accession documents prepared on the first day of her reign proclaimed her as Queen Alexandrina Victoria. But the new monarch insisted on Victoria alone because she had developed a strong personal fondness for the second name – a choice in which she had been encouraged by her uncle and predecessor King William IV, the 'Sailor King'. William thought the navy would like it: sailors would tattoo Victoria's face and name on their arms, he suggested, imagining that their Queen had been named after Nelson's famous flagship HMS *Victory*.

Elizabeth's great-grandfather **King Edward VII (1901–11)** was named after his high-minded but disapproving father, Albert the Prince Consort. It was as a signal of his respect as a son, the new King suggested to his Accession Council in 1901, that the name of 'Albert the Good' should henceforward be allowed to 'stand alone'. But modern biographers of the fun-loving monarch have suggested quite the opposite – that 'Bertie' could not wait to step clear of the father who had never found him good enough.

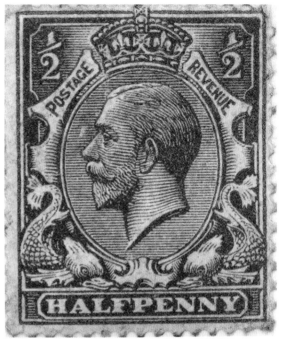

KING EDWARD VII (1901–11)　　　　GEORGE V (1911–1936)

Elizabeth's grandfather **George V (1911–36)** was unique among the Queen's modern predecessors in choosing to reign under the first name by which his family called him as a child.

Edward VIII (1936) was baptised Edward Albert Christian George Andrew Patrick David, the last four of his names being those of the patron saints of England, Scotland, Ireland and Wales. His parents chose to call him David – in fanciful reference, perhaps, to the fact that he would become Prince of Wales. He took the trouble to learn a little Welsh when he was invested as Prince of Wales in 1911, but as both Prince and King, David took the more historic name of Edward.

regnal *(adjective, from the Latin 'regnum': kingdom, kingship or royalty)*

of a sovereign, reign or kingdom

designating any year of the sovereign's reign calculated from the date of his or her accession

designating the chosen name of a sovereign (or pope), usually followed by a regnal number traditionally written as a Roman numeral (George VI rather than 6)

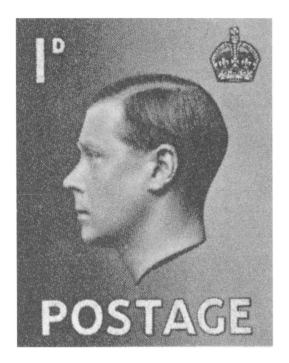

EDWARD VIII (1936)

GEORGE VI (1936–1952)

Elizabeth's father **George VI (1936–52)**, previously Prince Albert Duke of York, was known to his family as 'Bertie', like his grandfather Edward VII. But when the time came to choose his regnal name in the troubled aftermath of the abdication, it was considered wise to emphasise continuity with his popular and solid father (and founder of the House of Windsor), King George V.

It is generally assumed that Queen Elizabeth II's successor, christened Charles Philip Arthur George, will, in due course, be proclaimed His Majesty King Charles III. But it is not impossible that he might choose to pay tribute to his grandfather (and to his great-grandfather) by adopting the regnal name of King George VII – with Philip and Arthur as two other respectable options.

'Let's not over-complicate matters unnecessarily.'

As she left Sagana Lodge, Kenya, on 6th February 1952, heading back to London, the new Queen Elizabeth II requested that no photographs be taken. 'I felt sadness as she just raised her hand to us as we stood there silent, our cameras on the ground', recalled one of the photographers.

3
WINDSOR
Birth of a dynasty

3

When Britain's Queen Victoria married Prince Albert of Saxe-Coburg-Gotha on 10th February 1840, Saxe-Coburg-Gotha replaced Hanover as the name of the British royal family. The name change was automatic. Its most immediate effect was that Britain's Queen and her future children could now proudly bear the family name of the man she loved – and in 1947 Philip Mountbatten assumed the same would happen when he and Elizabeth Windsor married. The Lord Chancellor of the time, Lord Jowitt, agreed. He examined the proclamation that had changed the royal family's name to Windsor in 1917 and declared that it only applied to male heirs. The rubric did not mention female descendants, so, following the pattern set by Queen Victoria, the Princess and her issue should now take the name of her husband. For the five remaining years of George VI's reign the young couple – plus their children when they arrived – were duly referred to as 'the Mountbattens', and the former Elizabeth Windsor was happy and proud to be known as Elizabeth Mountbatten. This remained the case after the Princess succeeded her father in February 1952. It is not always realised that Queen Elizabeth II came to the throne as Elizabeth

As co-founders of the house of Windsor, King George V and Queen Mary (right) created a new royal brand with which other brands were keen to associate – and to the end of her life, Queen Mary fought to defend the invented identity that had been the saving of the Crown at a time of peril.

CALLARD & BOWSER'S BUTTER-SCOTCH, LONDON.
The design of the "Empire Box."

Mountbatten, and that for eight weeks it was quite true to say, as Lord Louis Mountbatten proudly boasted one night over dinner at Broadlands, 'that the House of Mountbatten now reigned'. But as Episode 3 of *The Crown* reveals, that boast provoked a bitter backlash from Queen Mary and Winston Churchill. When the arguments were over, the reigning house of Mountbatten was no more and Queen Elizabeth II was a Windsor again, with the old name proving more powerful than people expected. 'Windsor' was not just any family surname or title: it was a made-for-purpose brand identity that had been created by history – and by Elizabeth's beloved grandparents, King George V and Queen Mary, one of whom remained alive in 1952 to defend what she had helped to fashion 35 years earlier.

'Windsor' had, at the outset, been the product of war – the Great War of 1914 whose official declaration George V aged 49, had had to sign on 28th July 1914. 'It is a terrible catastrophe,' the King noted in his diary that night, 'but it is not our fault.' He and his wife threw themselves immediately into war work, with the King travelling to France that November to visit the troops. 'I cannot share your hardships,' he told them, 'but my heart is with you every hour of the day.' Queen Mary, meanwhile, vigorously encouraged voluntary sewing and knitting campaigns, only to discover that she was provoking unemployment – her prolific consignments of free socks and shirts led to women getting dismissed from mills and clothing factories. Perplexed, she turned for advice to a prominent trades unionist, Mary Macarthur, inviting her to Buckingham Palace – to the horror of her ladies-in-waiting – for a meeting that proved to be the first of many. 'The Queen does understand and grasp the whole situation from a Trade Union point of view,'

Macarthur reported back to her colleagues. 'I positively lectured the Queen on the inequality of the classes, the injustice of it. . . Here is someone who *can* help and *means* to help!'

Queen Mary's willingness to embrace the radical stemmed from the misfortunes of her youth. Her parents, Prince Francis and Princess Mary of Teck, were the laughing stock of the Victorian royal family, literally outcasts because they were driven abroad to flee their debtors – living 'in Short Street', as their industrious eldest daughter would put it in later life. Born in 1867 and christened 'May', the teenage princess took advantage of her parents' exile in Florence in the 1880s to add Italian to the English, French and German that she already spoke.

When her parents came back to England, May expanded her studies to include history and the social problems of an industrial society, putting her interests into practice by visiting poor houses, asylums and ragged schools. Statuesque and strong-featured, Princess May of Teck would have made the ideal wife for any socially concerned European prince or aristocrat – if she had not been born of 'morganatic' blood.

The morganatic marriage, *die morganatische Ehe*, was an aristocratic Germanic device to prevent a nobleman or woman passing on their nobility to a spouse of lesser rank, so-called because all that the lesser-born partner could receive from the marriage was the *morgengeba*, the morning gift or dowry on the day after the wedding. It was social inequality enshrined in law, since the dowry might involve money, jewellery or property, but carried no precedence or succession rights – thus preserving the 'purity' of the family title, while also consigning the morganatic partner and their

Numb. 30186.

The London Gazette.

Published by Authority.

The Gazette is registered at the General Post Office for transmission by Inland Post as a newspaper. The postage rate to places within the United Kingdom, for each copy, is one halfpenny for the first 6 ozs., and an additional halfpenny for each subsequent 6 ozs. or part thereof. For places abroad the rate is a halfpenny for every 2 ounces, except in the case of Canada, to which the Canadian Magazine Postage rate applies.

*** *For Table of Contents, see last page.*

TUESDAY, 17 JULY, 1917.

BY THE KING.

A PROCLAMATION

DECLARING THAT THE NAME OF WINDSOR IS TO BE BORNE BY HIS ROYAL HOUSE AND FAMILY AND RELINQUISHING THE USE OF ALL GERMAN TITLES AND DIGNITIES.

GEORGE R.I.

WHEREAS We, having taken into consideration the Name and Title of Our Royal House and Family, have determined that henceforth Our House and Family shall be styled and known as the House and Family of Windsor:

And whereas We have further determined for Ourselves and for and on behalf of Our descendants and all other the descendants of Our Grandmother Queen Victoria of blessed and glorious memory to relinquish and discontinue the use of all German Titles and Dignities:

And whereas We have declared these Our determinations in Our Privy Council:

Now, therefore, We, out of Our Royal Will and Authority, do hereby declare and announce that as from the date of this Our Royal Proclamation Our House and Family shall be styled and known as the House and Family of Windsor, and that all the descendants in the male line of Our said Grandmother Queen Victoria who are subjects of these Realms, other than female descendants who may marry or may have married, shall bear the said Name of Windsor:

And do hereby further declare and announce that We for Ourselves and for and on behalf of Our descendants and all other the descendants of Our said Grandmother Queen Victoria who are subjects of these Realms, relinquish and enjoin the discontinuance of the use of the Degrees, Styles, Dignities, Titles and Honours of Dukes and Duchesses of Saxony and Princes and Princesses of Saxe-Coburg and Gotha, and all other German Degrees, Styles, Dignities, Titles, Honours and Appellations to Us or to them heretofore belonging or appertaining.

Given at Our Court at *Buckingham Palace*, this Seventeenth day of *July*, in the year of our Lord One thousand nine hundred and seventeen, and in the Eighth year of Our Reign.

GOD SAVE THE KING.

1917. The Saxe-Coburg-Gotha's don a new British uniform. 'Do you realise,' Lord Rosebery congratulated the King's private secretary who came up with the name, 'that you have christened a dynasty!'

When the arguments were over, the reigning house of Mountbatten was no more.

descendants to a permanently inferior social status. May's morganatic taint came from her grandfather, a duke who had married a mere countess, thus disqualifying his descendants from marriage into many of Europe's royal and noble families.

Queen Victoria, however, had no time for such continental snobberies. She had watched May mature through all her misfortunes in Short Street and she considered the earnest young woman, now 25, to be the ideally solid partner for her wayward grandson Eddy, the elder son of the future King Edward VII, and thus a future heir to the throne. When flu carried off poor feckless Eddy in January 1892 on the eve of his marriage to May, the family were, perhaps, less inwardly broken-hearted than they outwardly appeared – and who better to pass on to May's care than the new heir in line, Eddy's younger (and significantly less feckless) brother George? The young man duly proposed and was accepted, and the couple were married in the Chapel Royal, St James's, on 6th July 1893. This more-than-semi-arranged marriage of Georgie and May (they became George and Mary on his accession to the throne in 1910) produced a strong emotional bond, particularly under the strains of the war that the King took so personally.

'Very often I feel in despair,' he wrote in one of the daily letters that he and his wife exchanged when their war duties took them apart, 'and if it wasn't for you I should break.' Mary responded warmly, but with regretful rebuke at her husband's face-to-face formality: 'What a pity it is,' she replied, 'that you cannot <u>tell</u> me what you write, for I should appreciate it so enormously.'

Forty-four-years-old when he came to the throne, George V had spent much of his youth as a naval officer, and his stiff, quarterdeck upper lip was part of his style. Having sent his eldest son David to the Western Front, the King dispatched his second son Bertie to a succession of postings

on naval warships where the young midshipman – checked off daily as 'Mr Johnson' on the ship's roll call – learned to shovel coal, sling his hammock in the communal mess room, and eventually saw action in a gun turret at the Battle of Jutland in the summer of 1916.

In London, Queen Mary was seeking to fashion her own response to the appalling toll of war. Jutland had seen 6,000 British deaths in a single battle; 57,470 had died on the first day of the Battle of the Somme, 1st July – more than had been killed in the Crimean and Boer wars put together. That August colourful 'street shrines' started appearing on the brick walls of terrace houses in the East End of London, folk memorials created by locals to honour those from the neighbourhood who had lost their lives.

The names of the local casualties were framed by flags, flowers and ribbons, as well as by pictures of military leaders and members of the royal family. When Queen Mary appeared in Hackney that August, walking quite informally and with no obvious security from shrine to shrine, huge crowds gathered to cheer. The Queen bowed her head and laid a posy beside each of the ten rolls of honour, talking at length to those who had gathered in grieving. Men and women wept openly. It was difficult to imagine any princess of

August, 1916. Queen Mary visits Hackney's 'street shrines', folk memorials created in London's poorest areas to honour locals killed in the war. The Queen bowed her head and laid a posy beside each.

Germany, Austria or Russia getting such a warm and welcoming response from their people – if, indeed, any of them would have dreamed of mingling with their subjects in the street.

But events in faraway St Petersburg changed the tone. 'Bad news from Russia,' noted George V in his diary on 13th March 1917, 'practically a Revolution has broken out in Petrograd.' Two days later came the news that his cousin Nicky, Tsar Nicholas II, had been compelled to abdicate: 'I am in despair.' The Russian Revolution struck a chill into monarchies all over Europe. Within 18 months, two other emperors had vanished, along with eight ruling sovereigns – all victims of military defeat – and even the monarchies of victorious countries felt the difference: 'I have noticed, since the news came to hand of the Russian revolution,' noted Colonel Unsworth, a Salvation Army officer from Essex, 'a change has come over a certain sector of the people in respect to their attitude towards the King and the royal family. In the streets, trains and buses, one hears talk . . . A friend of mine saw written in a second-class railway carriage, "To hell with the King. Down with all royalties."' Railway second-class carriages were the equivalent of business class in aeroplanes today. So, Unsworth was wondering, might the slogans in the third-class carriages be even more disloyal?

In June 1917 George V's financial adviser, Lord

These British 'patriots' who attacked German shops in Poplar in the East End of London in May 1915 were typical, said Prime Minister Herbert Asquith, of 'a feeling of righteous indignation among all classes in this country.' But what were the patriots to feel about their King and royal family who were also German?

GAOL IS THE HOME FOR THE HUN IN WAR TIME.

DAILY SKETCH.

GUARANTEED DAILY NETT SALE MORE THAN 1,000,000 COPIES.

No. 1,927.   LONDON, THURSDAY, MAY 13, 1915.   [Registered as a Newspaper.]   ONE HALFPENNY.

Clear Out The Germans, Say The People.

For the anti-German scenes which took place in London and all over England yesterday the German Government alone is responsible. In the words of Mr. Asquith, in the House of Commons, " No one could be surprised that after the progressive violation by the enemy of the usages of civilised war and the rules of humanity—culminating *for the moment* in the sinking of the Lusitania—there had arisen a feeling of righteous indignation among all classes in this country for which it would be difficult to find a parallel." The above pictures were taken during attacks on shops in Poplar, which was the scene of fierce anti-Teuton outbursts.—(*Daily Sketch* Photographs.)

Revelstoke, wrote to the King's private secretary, Lord Stamfordham, suggesting that the King should be better briefed on the anti-monarchical and republican sentiment in the country – to the indignation of the private secretary. 'I can unhesitatingly say,' he responded, 'that I do not believe there is any Sovereign in the World to whom the truth is more fearlessly told by those in his immediate service, and who receives it with such goodwill – and even gratitude – as King George. There is no Socialist newspaper, no libellous rag, that is not read and marked and shown to the King if they contain any criticisms, friendly or unfriendly, of His Majesty and the Royal Family.'

The truth of Stamfordham's claim resides today in the Royal Archives, in a file entitled 'Unrest in the Country'. Inside are the carefully marked articles from radical publications – and the project went beyond clippings. Stamfordham assembled a 'floating brains' trust of experts who were felt to have their fingers on the pulse of the country. Part intelligence network, part think tank, their deliberations and reports are also included in the files.

'I may be uninspiring, but I'll be damned if I'm an alien.'

One such gathering took place at the end of April 1917 when the chief talking point was an inflammatory letter that the novelist H. G. Wells had sent to *The Times* calling for the creation of 'A Republican Society for Great Britain', designed to show that 'our spirit is warmly and entirely against the dynastic-system that has so long divided, embittered, and wasted the spirit of mankind'. In a much-quoted exchange, Wells had made

no secret of his contempt for George V's 'alien and uninspiring court' – to which the King had famously retorted, 'I may be uninspiring, but I'll be damned if I'm an alien.'

The word 'alien' hit a particularly sensitive spot in the spring of 1917. The Zeppelin airships that had erratically bombed East Anglia and Sandringham in 1915, creating Wolferton Splash, had been supplemented by a far more formidable threat – heavily armed German 'battleplane' bombers manufactured by the Gothaer Waggonfabrik factory that was located, of all places, in Gotha, the southern section of the duchy from which the British ruling family took their name. The first Gotha bombing raid killed 95 people in and around Folkestone on the south coast in Kent, with a June raid on London killing 162, and in the next 16 months Gotha battleplanes would carry out a total of 22 raids on England, dropping 186,830 pounds of explosives. But the numbers were less important than the popular bewilderment that this dreadful destruction should be raining down from enemy aircraft that bore part of the King's family name.

The issue of the royal family's Teutonic origins and links had been on the agenda since the beginning of the war, when Dickie Mountbatten's father, Prince Louis of Battenberg, had been hounded from the admiralty by the witch-hunt against all things Germanic. But with the arrival over London of the Gotha battleplanes, the issue became serious, and Stamfordham discussed the problem with another member of the 'Unrest

in the Country' think tank, the former prime minister Lord Rosebery.

In a letter of 15th May, Stamfordham had come up with an idea of an English surname – 'Tudor-Stewart' was his suggestion – that could be used by the entire royal family, Battenbergs and Tecks included. At a meeting two days later, Roseberry suggested 'Fitzroy', and over the weeks that followed 'Plantaganet', 'York', 'Lancaster' and even 'England' were canvassed. After some discussion, the Tecks (Queen Mary's family) and Battenbergs chose to go their own way, the Battenbergs becoming Mountbatten while the Tecks became Cambridge, leaving Stamfordham with the dilemma of Saxe-Coburg-Gotha. Pondering all the alternatives one day – he was said to have been looking out of the window at the famous Round Tower at the time – the private secretary hit upon 'Windsor'. It clicked immediately. 'Do you realise,' Rosebery congratulated him, 'that you have christened a dynasty!'

It was an extraordinary leap of imagination. Just saying the word 'Windsor' conjured up the benevolent solidity of the stone Round Tower rising on the mound first built beside the Thames by William the Conqueror. No monarchy in history had done as such before. Newcomers and usurpers had taken over old names. But for an ancient clan coolly to reinvent itself with a fresh identity plucked from the air reflected hard-eyed realism – plus a certain measure of fear. On 17th July, the Privy Council announced the change, along with the royal family's renunciation of all 'German degrees, styles, dignitaries, titles, honours and appellations'. A new dynasty had been created to meet public demand. The decree gave no explanation for the reinvention, but the reason was obvious, and would become the guiding principle

of the new House of Windsor – survival at any price. In Germany, the Kaiser remarked that he was looking forward to the next performance of 'The Merry Wives of Saxe-Coburg-Gotha'.

George V, Queen Mary and their 'Unrest in the Country' advisers had understood the changes that mass industrialisation had wrought. The still-feudal monarchies of Germany, Austria and Russia, with their morganatic marriages and class-based barriers, saw themselves as the summit of a social pyramid in which the monarchy stood on the shoulders of the nobility, below whom were stacked the merchant middle classes, with the common people below that. Hierarchy mattered.

It was Stamfordham's analysis – and the instinct of the King and Queen – that hierarchy was out of date. They had the same vision, in fact, as Karl Marx – that power in the modern world lay at the true foundation of the pyramid, with the people.

'Are we going to keep the king?' a left-wing activist had asked at a socialist summer camp in 1913. 'Of course, we are,' came the answer, displaying the wobbly logic of which both socialists and monarchists are capable. 'In England, the King does what the people want. He will be a

A new dynasty had been created to meet public demand.

entering St Paul's Cathedral for the service of thanks presented the latest iconography of the Royal House of Windsor, which featured by that date the little princesses Elizabeth and Margaret Rose. The girls were taken out on the balcony of Buckingham Palace at the end of that day for their first experience of the crowds surging and cheering in their thousands against the Palace railings, in spontaneous acclamations that swelled up every night for the rest of the following week. 'I had no idea they felt like that about me,' declared the 69-year-old King. 'I'm beginning to think they must really like me for myself.'

This was the history that fuelled the outrage of the 84-year-old Queen Mary early in February 1952, when Ernst August of Hanover brought her the news of Louis Mountbatten's toast down at Broadlands to the new reigning 'House of Mountbatten'. She angrily summoned Jock Colville, Churchill's private secretary, to take instant action, and the prime minister responded at a cabinet meeting that same day. Churchill shared the old Queen's historical memories

socialist King.' A still more emphatic answer came at the Labour Party conference a few years after the war in 1923, when votes were invited on the proposition 'That the Royal Family is no longer necessary as part of the British Constitution.' Three hundred and eighty-six thousand votes supported the motion; 3,694,000 voted against. General affection for the monarchy survived across Britain through the 1920s and 1930s, little shaken by the hardships of the Great Depression, and on 6th May 1935 the Silver Jubilee of George V's 25 years on the throne was marked by celebrations all over the country. A spectacular panoramic oil painting by Frank Salisbury of the royal family

6th May 1935. Frank Salisbury's panoramic painting of the royal family entering the west door of St. Paul's Cathedral for the Silver Jubilee Service celebrating King George V and Queen Mary's 25 years on the throne. Behind the King and Queen can be seen the little princesses Elizabeth, 9, and Margaret Rose, 4, between their Uncle David, the Prince of Wales, and their parents Bertie and Elizabeth, the Duke and Duchess of York.

'I'm the only man in the country not allowed to give his name to his children.'

and indignation. There were war criminals and German finance contributions to discuss, but to the very top of the agenda for 18th February 1952 went 'Name of the Royal Family'. 'The Cabinet's attention was drawn to reports that some change might be made in the Family name of the Queen's Children and their descendants,' read the cabinet minutes. 'The Cabinet was strongly of the opinion that the Family name of Windsor should be retained, and they invited the Prime Minister to take a suitable opportunity of making their views known to Her Majesty.'

Within two days Churchill had passed on the government's unanimous verdict to the Queen – provoking a domestic explosion. 'Philip was deeply wounded,' recalled his naval comrade Mike Parker 50 years later, still shaking his head at the memory of the ructions that ensued. 'I'm just a bloody amoeba,' the injured husband famously complained. 'I'm the only man in the country not allowed to give his name to his children.' Philip sat down immediately to write a paper arguing his case, and also suggesting a compromise – that

his children might take the name of Edinburgh and that the royal house might now be known as the House of Windsor and Edinburgh. Churchill was unimpressed – in fact, he flew into a rage when presented with the paper. He instructed the Lord Chancellor, the Lord Privy Seal, the Home Secretary and the Leader of the House of Commons – the biggest legal guns in his government – to spend two long meetings with Colville stamping every breath of life out of Philip's proposals.

The grievance would rumble on for years. The Conservative politician R. A. Butler later said that the only time he saw the normally equable Elizabeth II close to tears was when confronted by the troubled issue of the family surname. But in the short term the issue was settled by a proclamation of 7th April 1952 declaring the Queen's 'Will and Pleasure that I and My children shall be styled and known as the House and Family of Windsor, and that My descendants, other than female descendants who marry and their descendants, shall bear the name of Windsor.' The proclamation had been prepared and taken to the Queen's study in Buckingham Palace by her private secretary 'Tommy' Lascelles, a confirmed pro-Windsor and anti-Mountbatten man, and as Elizabeth II bent her head to sign the document, he later related with grim satisfaction, he stood over her like 'one of the Barons of Runnymede'.

SIR ALAN 'TOMMY' LASCELLES

(1887–1981)

PLAYED BY PIP TORRENS

'**He** is the most attractive man I have ever met,' declared Alan 'Tommy' Lascelles (pronounced to rhyme with 'tassels') as he joined the staff of Edward, Prince of Wales in 1921. Eight years later, Lascelles resigned in disgust at his master's incorrigible womanising and neglect of his royal duties, and his sense of betrayal infused the rest of his career with a dark and holy anger. Lascelles fumed in his diary against Edward VIII as 'the most tragic might-have-been in history', and even when he located the principles that he valued in George VI and his daughter, he saw himself as more their tutor than their Private Secretary (1943–52 to the king, 1952–53 to Elizabeth II). It was for Lascelles to teach them their job and enforce the Faustian bottom line of modern monarchy: that kings and queens must 'abide by the rules of conduct expected of them by those who put them there', since those who put them there are the people who pay for them.

'The most tragic might-have-been in history.'

QUEEN MARY

(1 8 6 7 – 1 9 5 3)

PLAYED BY EILEEN ATKINS

'I played with Lilibet in the garden making sand pies!' wrote Queen Mary delightedly in her diary for 14th March 1929. 'The Archbishop of Canterbury came to see us and was so kind and sympathetic.' Less than three years old, the future Elizabeth II was already learning lessons from her grandmother who, as co-founder with George V of the House of Windsor, helped develop the blend of grandeur with accessibility that lies at the heart of the modern popular monarchy. Queen Mary taught her granddaughter the value of an upright posture; the helpfulness of high heels and fancy hats for a lady of limited stature; and the over-arching importance of putting Crown before self. She also passed on a special Windsor trick for dealing with over-intimate remarks and presumptuous questions: to keep smiling levelly at the perpetrator as if you are hearing absolutely nothing – then move on smartly.

The Duke and
the Cry Baby

'What a smug stinking lot my relations are . . . You've never seen such a seedy worn out bunch of old hags . . .' Whenever family business brought him to London, the exiled Duke of Windsor liked to let his feelings rip, and in February 1952 the notes that he wrote to his wife about the funeral of his brother George VI were especially direct: 'Cookie & Margaret feel most.' ('Cookie' was the couple's nickname for Queen Elizabeth the Queen Mother). 'Mama [Queen Mary] as hard as nails but failing. When Queens fail, they make less sense than others in the same state . . .

'*Mountbatten*. One can't pin much on him but he's very bossy & never stops talking. All are suspicious & watching his influence on Philip.' The ex-King's only kind words were for his niece the new Queen ('Shirley Temple' in the Windsor code) who invited him to lunch with her husband in Clarence House: 'Informal & friendly. Brave New World. Full of self-confidence & seem to take the job in their stride.'

In Episode 3 of *The Crown*, Peter Morgan introduces the former King Edward VIII to the drama, starting with a flashback to his abdication in December 1936 – 'A few hours ago, I discharged my last duty as King and Emperor' – while we watch the little princesses play unsuspectingly with their corgis and bicycles. Later in the episode we follow the Duke, played by Alex Jennings, as he arrives in London in February 1952, mingling his role at his brother's funeral with his manoeuvrings to save the £10,000 annual pension that George VI had been paying him while he was alive. We see the Duke triumph on screen at the end of the episode, working out a deal with Winston Churchill that also helps resolve the impasse over the royal family name. In reality, the Duke of Windsor did *not* retrieve his £10,000 pension – Cookie and Mama made sure of that. But the dynamics of the plot are based on an intriguing strand of history: that Edward VIII was an old friend of Winston Churchill, and that Churchill nearly destroyed his own political career when he took the King's side in 1936 and tried to save him from having to abdicate. The two men became close in the summer of 1919

when the 25-year-old Prince was due to deliver a speech at a banquet for the victorious Allied war leaders after the First World War. The 34-year-old Churchill, Secretary of State for War and Air in Lloyd George's post-war coalition, sent the young man some speaking advice – that he should not feel ashamed to read out his speech, but that if he did go the written route, he should 'do it quite openly, doing it very slowly and deliberately'. It would be better, of course, to memorise his text, or to speak with only glancing reference to notes, and in this event Churchill recommended creating an improvised lectern from the table glassware and crockery – a fingerbowl placed on top of a tumbler, with a plate on top of that as a mini-platform for your notes. 'But one has to be very careful,' he warned, 'not to knock it all over, as once happened to me.' In the event, the young Prince of Wales committed his 1919 speech to memory and delivered it entirely without notes – to Churchill's approval. 'You are absolutely right to take trouble with these things,' he wrote. 'With perseverance, you might speak as well as anybody in the land.'

'…as necessary to his happiness as the air he breathed.'

As abdication loomed 15 years later, Churchill instinctively took the King's side. He was a royalist – 'the last believer in the divine right of kings', as his wife Clementine once put it despairingly. He was also a romantic, defending Wallis Simpson, Edward VIII's much-reviled American sweetheart, to be 'as necessary to his happiness as the air he breathed'. With pressure and publicity mounting in December 1936, the King turned to Churchill, long out of office but rebuilding his reputation through his sturdy opposition to German Rearmament and a founder member of

'Focus', a cross-party group that spoke out against Fascism. Churchill's advice to the King was to play for time, hoping for some sort of solution short of abdication – a German-style morganatic marriage, perhaps, whereby Mrs Simpson might become his wife, but not his Queen, renouncing royal status for herself or any children. This proposal received short shrift, not least from the prime minister, Stanley Baldwin. 'Is this the sort of thing I've stood for in public life?' he asked disgustedly. Ernest Bevin was even firmer on behalf of the Labour Party: 'Our people won't 'ave it,' he said.

On Friday 4th December Churchill went to dine with Edward VIII in Fort Belvedere, the King's castellated residence near Sunningdale on the fringe of Windsor Great Park. The King must keep up his strength, Churchill insisted with emotion. He suggested the King must see a doctor, and that he should on no account go abroad. Above all, the King must play for time and ask for as long as he needed to make up his mind – 'there is no force in this country,' he declared, 'which would or could deny it you.' Parliament would be debating the subject shortly, and Churchill felt confident that the so-called 'King's Party' would prevail. 'Good advances on all fronts,' he wrote to the King the following day, claiming success with his lobbying activities. There were 'prospects of gaining good positions and assembling large forces behind them.'

But Churchill had gravely mistaken the mood of the country. That weekend MPs canvassed opinion in their constituencies, and when they returned to Westminster on Monday they strongly backed the intransigence of Baldwin and Bevin.

1919. Winston Churchill and the Prince of Wales share cigars and conversation after a luncheon party at the House of Commons to honour US airmen who had flown the Atlantic during the Great War.

The King could not have it both ways – he would have to renounce Mrs Simpson if he wanted to keep the throne. When Churchill rose to his feet in the Commons on Tuesday to plead the King's cause, 'filled with emotion and brandy' (according to one observer), he was brutally shouted down. The once-respected former minister begged his colleagues not to rush to judgement and to give the King more time – to be ridiculed by an overwhelmingly hostile House.

'It was,' wrote *The Times* the next day, 'the most striking rebuff in modern parliamentary history.' Robert Boothby, Churchill's loyal ally in his stand against Hitler, was devastated. 'In five fatal minutes,' he wrote, the Focus crusade against appeasement had 'crashed into ruin'. Like Violet Bonham Carter and Churchill's other allies, Boothby was appalled by this latest 'Churchillian' error in judgement. 'No one will deny Mr. Churchill's gifts,' editorialised the *Spectator* gloatingly, 'but a flair for doing the right thing at the right moment – or not doing the wrong thing at the wrong moment – is no part of them . . . He has utterly misjudged the temper of the country and the temper of the House, and the reputation, which he was beginning to shake off, of a wayward genius unserviceable in council, has settled firmly on his shoulders again.' Staggered by the unanimous rejection, Churchill shuffled out of the Chamber humiliated. 'What happened this afternoon,' wrote Boothby in fury to his former hero, 'makes me feel that it is almost impossible for those who are devoted to you personally to follow you blindly (as they would like to do) in politics. Because they cannot be sure where the hell they are going to be landed next.'

In the days that followed, Churchill helped Edward VIII frame the eloquent words of the abdication speech that was now inevitable, and he also fought his friend's corner in the deeply bitter negotiations over the pension that George VI reluctantly agreed to pay his brother. It was hardly surprising that when Britain's desperate wartime situation eventually brought Churchill out of the wilderness, initially as First Lord of the Admiralty in 1939 and then into Downing Street in May 1940, George VI had his reservations – 'I cannot yet think of Winston as P.M.,' he noted in his diary. And Churchill ruefully described in his memoirs how he had been 'smitten in public opinion . . . It was the almost universal view that my political life was ended.' 'I have defended you so many times,' says Churchill in Episode 3 to the Duke of Windsor. 'Each time to my cost and in vain.'

There was much to recall when Churchill and the Duke of Windsor met again in London in the run-up to George VI's funeral in February 1952, and the tears welled up in the old prime minister's eyes. 'Nobody cried in my presence,' the Duke reported home to Wallis. 'Only Winston as usual', prompting the Duke and his wife to devise and bestow another of their clever nicknames upon the great war hero – 'Cry Baby', which said more about them than it did about him. After a few glasses of brandy, the Duke liked to deliver an after-dinner parody of the Fort Belvedere meeting when Churchill had pleaded with him not to abdicate, complete with a spoofed-up Churchillian accent: 'Suhrrr, we must fight . . .' As 'Tommy' Lascelles wrote sadly in 1944, Churchill's sentimental loyalty to the Duke was 'based on a tragic false premise – viz that he (Winston) really *knew* the D of W, which he never did'.

6th October 1945. Almost nine years after his abdication in December 1936, the former King Edward VIII, now Duke of Windsor, visited London to see his mother, Queen Mary, who made little attempt to hide her feelings. 'You did not seem able to take in any point of view but your own . . .' she wrote in response to his request in a letter to tell him her true feelings. 'I do not think you have ever realised the shock which the attitude you took up caused your family and the whole Nation. It seemed inconceivable to those who had made such sacrifices during the war that you, as their King, refused a lesser sacrifice . . .'

Clarence House

1952

Clarence House is tacked on to the side of St James's Palace like a brightly iced Christmas cake. Designed and built by John Nash, the architect of Regency London, the white stuccoed mansion was the home of the Duke of Clarence, who later became King William IV (1830–37), and it has traditionally been the perch of retired royals or of royals-in-waiting: Queen Elizabeth the Queen Mother lived there for nearly half a century until her death in 2002, to be succeeded by Prince Charles as he restarted his married life with his new wife Camilla. But early in 1952 Clarence House seemed destined for a higher purpose, as the principal home base of Queen Elizabeth II and her young family – a new perch for a new monarch, with the huge royal standard fluttering overhead. 'Thank you for all this,' says Elizabeth at the opening of Episode 3 of *The Crown*, looking appreciatively around the renovations that her husband has been supervising. 'It looks splendid.' 'This is the first proper home I've ever had,' responds Philip contentedly, leaning down to kiss his wife's cheek as the family breadwinner sets off on her daily commute to Buckingham Palace – no longer a royal residence, just a very grand office.

Lacking a single modern bathroom or a proper electrical system when the royal couple first inspected it in October 1947, Clarence House had emerged from the war in a mournfully derelict state, with bomb-damaged ceilings and a leaking roof. Lighting was provided by

An engraving of Clarence House around 1874, showing the large covered carriage porch, or porte-cochère, and how the white stucco building was connected directly to the red brick walls of St James's Palace on the right, with the two royal homes sharing the same long garden alongside the Mall.

surface wiring on cleats tacked on to the wall by the Red Cross, the principal occupants after 1942, along with a temporary department of 200 Foreign Office civil servants concerned with the welfare of British prisoners of war. Parliament voted £50,000 for restoration, despite protests that the money could be better spent on public housing, and the work was completed in a speedy 18 months (and a cost overrun of £28,000), with Elizabeth and Philip visiting as often as twice a day. Elizabeth helped to mix the soft 'Edinburgh Green' shade of paint for the dining room – 'Put a bucket of hay in there,' she said when someone complained about the smell, 'and that'll take it away' – while Philip delighted in bringing back

gadgets and labour-saving devices from the Ideal Home Exhibition. His office boasted the latest intercom, telephones and switchboard, along with a fridge for cold drinks, while his wardrobes could magically eject any uniform or shirt he wanted at the press of a button. The young Duke had picked up many of his ideas from his gadget-crazy uncle, Dickie Mountbatten, though he did not go in for the latter's ultimate time-saving contrivance – a 'Simplex' shirt with built-in Y-fronts.

'The Duke' developed an unconventional reputation among the 11 staff, each of whom had their own carpeted bedroom and radio, and a 'sleek, white, very futuristic television set' in the servants' hall, a wedding present from the Mountbattens: word circulated that their boss did not own a single pair of pyjamas! 'Never wear the things,' he said to one valet, while another reported him totally unembarrassed to be discovered one morning naked in bed with the Princess (who always wore a silk nightgown). Sir Frederick 'Boy' Browning, Treasurer of the Duke's Household, tracked the Duke down to the Palace pool across the road one day to find Philip giving his children swimming lessons stark naked. The Clarence House emphasis was on informality – light, serve-yourself lunches in the relaxed style that had impressed the Duke of Windsor on his 1952 visit, with casual dishes such as bangers and mash for supper. They almost lived

like 'ordinary people . . .' recalled John Gibson, the nursery footman in charge of polishing and pushing Prince Charles's pram, 'a lot less formal than some people I came across – people much further down the social scale'. Both Elizabeth and Philip loved playing with their children in the extensive garden that Clarence House shared with St James's Palace.

As the couple confronted the unexpected challenge of taking up their new royal duties in February 1952, both of them were attracted by the prospect of continuing to operate from their purpose-designed and cosy home base, defying tradition and the expectation of the royal

Renovated at a cost of £78,000 in 1948–49, Clarence House became the home base of Princess Elizabeth, the Duke of Edinburgh and their two children, Prince Charles, aged 2, and Princess Anne, aged 1, photographed in the garden after their parents' return from Malta in the summer of 1951.

establishment that they would move down the road to the grandeur of Buckingham Palace. Philip and Elizabeth decided that they did not, in fact, want to live 'above the shop'. Staying in Clarence House would avoid the disruption of a move, and Philip, so happy in the up-to-date setting he had worked so hard to fashion, had developed a particular aversion to the cold formality of the Palace, headquarters of what younger courtiers called the 'old codgers', headed by 'Tommy' Lascelles, whose disapproval he could sense. As a precedent, the very first occupant of Clarence House had continued living there after he became King William IV in 1830, strolling to work every morning next door in St James's Palace.

Philip set out his case in one of his naval-style position papers with the full support of his wife – and he was able to cite an unexpected ally. Queen Elizabeth, now the Queen Mother, was most reluctant to move out of her long-established quarters in the Palace, and her son-in-law developed this into a longer-term proposition. Looking only 20 years or so into the future, he argued, Prince Charles would require his own residence as Prince of Wales. As the annexe to St James's Palace where so many subsidiary royal gatherings took place, Clarence House was the ideal HQ for the heir to the throne. It would be 'blocked' if the lively and youthful Queen Mother were to be installed there – and that turned out to be precisely what came to pass. Thanks to the Queen Mother's longevity, Prince Charles had to set himself up as a young man in the comparative remoteness of Kensington Palace, and did not move into the St James's Palace complex until 2003 – when he was well into his fifties.

But Philip's pleadings cut no ice with Lascelles and the 'old codgers', who were emphatically supported by Winston Churchill. Buckingham Palace was the long-established focus of royal and national sentiment, insisted the prime minister, and the monarch had no choice but to live there. Elizabeth, Philip and their children went off to Windsor for their Easter holidays early in April 1952, and when they returned to London it was to move into Buckingham Palace – only a few days after the proclamation that had affirmed the enduring primacy of the House of Windsor. In the course of a few months, the Duke of Edinburgh had lost three of his young life's most cherished components – his naval career, his family home and his family name. It did not make for a happy husband.

The Duke of Edinburgh had lost three of his young life's most cherished components.

When Princess Elizabeth was photographed proudly in the drawing room of Clarence House by Baron Nahum, the photographer friend of her husband Philip, in the summer of 1951, she had no inkling that in less than a year she would be moving to Buckingham Palace.

4
ACT OF GOD
The Great Smog of 1952

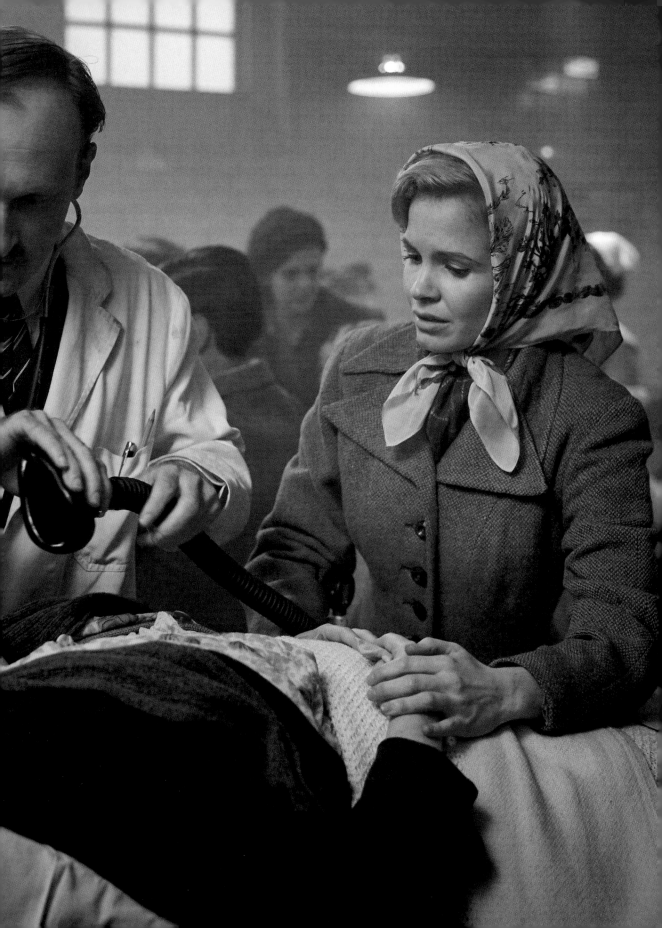

4

On the face of it, there is as much invention as history in Episode 4 of *The Crown*, 'Act of God'. The principal catalyst in this episode, Venetia Scott, Winston Churchill's attractive young secretary who gets killed by a bus, never existed. In the early days of December 1952, the 'Great Smog' was not experienced as a life-and-death crisis by Londoners long inured to the routine of their winter 'pea-soupers'. Nor did Clement Attlee and the Labour Party seek to bring down the Churchill government for its handling of the issue. On the other hand, the heroic Venetia Scott is a carefully researched, true-to-life-and-spirit composite of the remarkable team of women who worked so devotedly for Churchill in Downing Street. The 'Great Smog' (the word was a combination of 'smoke' and 'fog' first coined by newspapers in Edwardian times) did eventually prove the catalyst for Britain's first clean air legislation. And as for Labour not attacking Churchill more strongly, they didn't need to. The ageing leader was undermined by the treachery of some of his own closest cabinet colleagues. Marion Holmes was the youngest

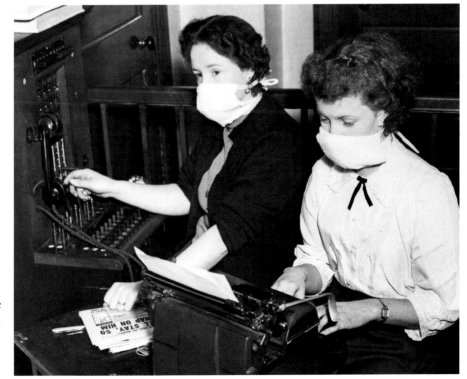

Londoners learned a new word – and developed new health precautions, when the Great Smog struck in December, 1952. This was a new type of struggle for which the Prime Minister, Winston Churchill, was ill-prepared . . .

of Churchill's secretaries, 22, fair-haired and blue-eyed, according to one of her Downing Street colleagues, 'like a fairy' – the most obvious physical model for Venetia Scott. 'That's a damned pretty girl – lovely,' Churchill once remarked to his guests at Chequers (the country residence of British prime ministers), while Marion was out of the room fetching a whisky and soda. 'The sort of girl who'd rather die than have the secrets torn out of her.' 'Oh dear, she's very young,' he said on another occasion to his wife Clementine. 'I mustn't frighten her.'

Fully aware of the knee-quaking effect that his tantrums could have on others, the irascible prime minister tried to adopt a paternal attitude towards the team of half a dozen or more young women who made up his typing pool. Working on a continuous shift and relay system, his secretaries would take his dictation from 8.30 in the morning, while he was having his breakfast – usually in bed – until well after midnight and into the small hours, often in his dressing gown. 'You must never be fright-

ened of me when I "snap",' he once told Marion Holmes. 'I'm not thinking of you. I'm thinking of the work.' Holmes found that Churchill might suddenly go silent, then launch into a long strand of dictation without any warning, unaware of everything and everyone around him as he stalked up and down. He might sound out one tricky phrase to himself as many as 20 times sotto voce, going around and around with it until he got it right – often with the help of a glass of brandy or his beloved Pol Roget champagne. 'You can't make a good speech writer on iced water,' he used to say.

Whenever the prime minister cleared his throat, his secretaries knew they had to get their pencils out and start scribbling their shorthand (they might easily get through an entire notebook in a single session), or else locate one of the so-called 'silent' typewriters that was always nearby and try to type out the words as they flowed. When Churchill returned to Downing Street in 1952, he moved his bedroom upstairs and reserved the room across the hall for his personal secretaries. 'Girl!' he would shout from his bed, and one of them would come running with her pad and pencil at the ready. 'Give me!' was his abrupt instruction when he considered the current document finished, and he would reach out to take the paper as it was peeled off the roller. After the briefest of breaks to look over the words, he would start dictating again.

Phyllis Moir, who joined Churchill's staff in 1932, was the first secretary to document the strange ordeal experienced by Venetia Scott in Episode 1 – taking dictation while her boss splashed around in the bath. The dictating was always done with relative propriety, with the orator's tones being broadcast through a slightly open bathroom door. But occasionally the prime minister would stalk out into the corridor with a towel draped round his expansive midriff, still loudly declaiming the speech he was due to deliver somewhere that evening. Staff took it in their stride in Downing Street, but the rotund and dripping spectacle stalking down a corridor at full volume would 'scare the wits' out of unsuspecting housemaids in country houses, according to Moir, when Churchill went away for the weekend.

During the war his energies never seemed to relent, with dictation continuing full flow on some occasions until 4.30 in the morning. Working for Neville Chamberlain, Churchill's predecessor in No. 10, Marion Holmes had been accustomed to stopping work every day at 6pm. But when Churchill arrived in May 1940, she wrote in her diary, 'it was as if a superhuman current of high-voltage electricity was let loose'. The new PM seemed to relish the blizzard of official papers generated by any crisis, processing each document on the spot and sending it onwards, usually garnished with one of his specially printed red labels demanding 'Action This Day'. 'We must go on and on like gun horses till we drop,' Churchill

'It was as if a superhuman current of high-voltage electricity was let loose.'

Transportation caught the smog headlines to start with – the stories of people sitting on the bonnets of cars or walking in front of them to give directions to drivers. London airport was shut down and air travellers had to travel more than a hundred miles to catch their flights in Bournemouth.

told Elizabeth Nel, who joined his staff in 1941 at the height of the Blitz.

'Fool', 'mug' and 'idiot' were some of the gentler words that the prime minister flung at Nel's head when she mistakenly typed her first memo single-spaced, not with the double spacing that no one had told her he preferred. If frustrated, Churchill would actually stamp his feet like a small child, but the recruit came to accept his frequent 'snaps' as part of the grander project of which she was part. 'Good heavens,' he once said to Nel when he thought he had made her cry, 'you mustn't mind me. We're all toads beneath the harrow, you know.' (The line was Rudyard Kipling's, an allusion to the heavy grid of spikes drawn by farmers across their fields to aerate the soil, doing for any wildlife caught in its path.) Delivered with a cherubic smile, his contrition was irresistible – along with his compelling sense of mission. 'One would have the feeling,' Nel recalled, 'of sharing a tremendous experience with him.' It was this same sense of purpose and urgent loyalty towards her boss that drew the fictitious Venetia Scott to step out into the smog in 'Act of God' – only to be knocked down and killed by a bus.

While Venetia herself was fictional, her fate was not uncommon in London's era of the 'pea-souper'. On 7th December 1952 two railway workers repairing tracks near Norwood Junction, south London, were killed by a suburban train that failed to see them in the fog. The next day, two busy commuter trains were unable to see the warning signals and collided near London Bridge. With 38 ambulances out on emergency calls at one stage, London buses were ordered off the streets, crawling back to their depots in nose-to-tail convoys. But the severest fatalities resulted from the sick and elderly breathing in the toxic fumes and dying at home or in hospital. A windless anticyclone over London had trapped the smoke from the city's coal-burning power stations, blending smoke particles, carbon dioxide, hydrochloric acid and, most lethal of all, some 400 tonnes of sulphur dioxide (as was later calculated) into a deadly cocktail whose principal ingredient was sulphuric acid.

The chemicals came from the low-grade coal burning in the grates and boilers of almost every home in those days before the advent of oil- and gas-powered central heating, and especially from the coal-fired electrical power stations whose towers loomed along the Thames – at Fulham, West Ham and, most substantially, at Battersea. A few hundred yards down the river from Westminster, the four huge towers of the massive Battersea Power Station sprayed out the largest exhaust output of all, so it was no coincidence that Westminster was heavily showered with yellowish black flakes of soot and grit – part oil, part mud – that caused a stinging sensation in the eyes and the lungs. 'The fog itself swirled into the wards and seemed to consist principally of smuts,' recalled Sir Donald Acheson, later Chief Medical Officer of the United Kingdom, then a young doctor at the Middlesex Hospital near Tottenham Court Road, 'so that the wash basins and baths turned darker and darker grey, until it was literally possible to write one's name on them – which I actually did.' The wards of the Middlesex started

> *Drivers abandoned their vehicles in the street to walk to work.*

Health minister Iain Macleod reported that deaths in Greater London had more than doubled in the week ending 13th December – to 4,703 as compared to 1,852 in the corresponding week of 1951, and that 'a large part of these increases must be attributed to fog'.

CLEMENT ATTLEE

Labour Prime Minister

(1883–1967)

PLAYED BY SIMON CHANDLER

'Citizen Clem' was the longest serving leader of the Labour Party and the architect of Britain's 'cradle-to-grave' welfare state. Charitable work in London's East End turned the 23-year-old ex-public schoolboy into a social reformer dedicated to alleviating poverty through state intervention and the redistribution of wealth – 'a right established by law, such as that to an old age pension, is less galling than an allowance made by a rich man to a poor one'. Thrice wounded in the First World War, he was a patriot who did not let his socialist principles prevent him building the free world coalition against Stalin in the 1940s, nor secretly developing Britain's own nuclear deterrent. Slight, reticent and pipe-smoking, Clement Attlee was tap water to Winston Churchill's champagne – a bank clerk to the dog of war. But the nation and the egalitarian consensus he shaped between 1945 and 1951 made him Britain's greatest ever peace-time prime minister.

'…less galling than an allowance made by a rich man to a poor one.'

to fill with middle-aged and elderly patients with breathing difficulties, and after one or two days the young medic called the senior surgeon asking for permission to cancel all routine operations and admissions from the waiting lists. All the available surgical wards, and even the obstetric wards, were filled to overflowing with patients who were displaying the most acute respiratory distress.

This is the scene depicted so graphically in 'Act of God', but it was not the angle projected by the media at the time. Transport problems caught the main headlines – the stories of people sitting on the bonnets of cars or walking in front of them to give directions to drivers, and the closing of London airport. To catch their flights, travellers had to journey from the capital down to Hurn airport near Bournemouth by train – drawn by one of the country's 19,000 coal-fired steam locomotives that were only exacerbating the smog problem. Shipping was halted on the Thames, and drivers abandoned their vehicles in the street to walk to work. 'London has never seemed so empty of traffic since the war years when petrol was drastically rationed,' reported the *Manchester Guardian*.

The cancellation of every sporting fixture in south-east England caught the headlines on the weekend of 6th and 7th December. Britons were 'passionately addicted' to their football, reported the *New York Times:* the dog and horseracing tracks were shut down – and even cinemas were affected. 'Screen visibility nil' warned one manager on a notice outside his theatre; the film could only be seen from the very front rows. On 8th December the audience at the Royal Festival Hall on the south bank of the Thames found that the extra-thick river fog meant they could not see the stage at all. Much worse, and the subject of numerous

lurid headlines, was the increase in what the *Guardian* described as 'footpad crime and burglary . . . The smash-and-grab-men are harvesting fast. The smog made it impossible for the information room at Scotland Yard to direct area wireless cars to 999 calls, and the police are having to use pedal cycles.' When it came to fatalities, the deaths that first caught the headlines were the demise at the Smithfield Show of 11 prize cattle suffering from breathing difficulties, eight of them slaughtered at their owners' request: 'the smoke-laden air of London has proved especially harmful to those cattle from areas where the air is normally cold but dry.'

It was only after winds had dispersed the smog on 10th December that the facts about human illness and death began to be realised, and when the figures were tallied they came as a shock. On 18th December 1952, the health minister Iain Macleod reported to the Commons that deaths in Greater London had more than doubled in the week ending 13th December – to 4,703 as compared to 1,852 in the corresponding week of 1951, and that 'a large part of these increases must be attributed to fog'. A second smog of the month on 27th December, with acrid white clouds swirling through the streets and seeping 'into houses gay with Christmas season decorations', finally brought home the gravity of the situation – with more deaths in the capital, reported the *Lancet*, than the fatalities from the disastrous cholera epidemic of 1886. 'Massacre' was the headline in Lord Beaverbrook's *Evening Standard*, which pointed out how December's full death toll of some 6,000 Londoners matched the 5,957 killed by Nazi bombers in September 1940, the worst month of the Blitz. 'The economic loss – from grounded airplanes, dirt and slowed commerce – runs into millions of pounds,' reported the

PICTURE POST

CONGRATULATIONS!

25 FEBRUARY, 1950   Vol. 46.   No. 8.

52 PAGES

ELECTION SPECIAL

HULTON'S NATIONAL WEEKLY · PRICE FOURPENCE

HARD LUCK!

New York Times '. . . Many Londoners, coughing and feeling vague chest aches, are experiencing a feeling of fright.' From shrugging its shoulders a few weeks earlier, the Churchill government announced that it was now treating the recurring smogs as 'a problem of the very greatest urgency' – the 180-degree change of direction that 'Act of God' dramatises as being provoked within days by the death of Venetia Scott.

Once the facts were known, the process of enquiry and legislation that led to the Clean Air Act of 1956 was relatively bipartisan, reflecting a respect and even affection between Winston Churchill and Clement Attlee that was deeper than the outside world guessed.

Churchill's supposed jibes about the man who defeated him for prime minister in 1945 were well known: 'a sheep in sheep's clothing'; 'a modest man who has much to be modest about'; 'an empty taxi drove up to 10 Downing Street, and out of it stepped Clement Attlee'. But not all these sneers can be traced back to Churchill, and in private he would often defend his laconic opponent as a patriot – 'a faithful colleague who served the country well at the time of her greatest need'. He was referring to the bitter debates inside the Inner War Cabinet on the evening of 28th May 1940 following the ignominious retreat of the British Expeditionary

Clement Attlee was tap water to Winston Churchill's champagne – a bank clerk to the dog of war. But for fifteen years, from 1940 to 1955, the two men took it in turns to occupy 10 Downing Street, and were closer friends than they allowed the world to know.

Force from Dunkirk, when Britain stood alone in what would become known as her 'darkest hour'. Neville Chamberlain and Edward Halifax were urging that some sort of peace deal now had to be attempted with Hitler, outshouting Churchill two to one, until Attlee and his Labour colleague Arthur Greenwood weighed in. The mere suggestion of surrender talks would shatter national morale, they argued, and Churchill never forgot Attlee's staunchness in what Peter Hennessy has described as 'the most crucial two hours in modern Cabinet history'. Even as the rivals later tussled over political issues such as nationalisation and the nature of welfare provision, Churchill would regularly praise the solidity with which the Labour leader – 'an honourable and gallant gentleman' – had served as his loyal and highly efficient deputy in the Coalition cabinet that eventually won the war.

'I hate the Tory party, their men, their words and their methods.'

After the war, Churchill was surprisingly accommodating towards many features of the 'Socialist Commonwealth' that Attlee's Labour government implemented in the years between 1945 and 1951. Thirty years later, radical Conservatives of the Margaret Thatcher era looked back with surprise and regret that when Churchill regained power in October 1951 he had not sought to reverse more aspects of Labour's welfare state – especially the nationalising of transport and energy. But Churchill was never a 'Tory' in the hard-line sense – 'I am an English Liberal,' he wrote in 1903. 'I hate the Tory party, their men, their words and their methods.' He was proud to have introduced the first Unemployment Insurance Scheme as a Liberal frontbencher in 1908, and to have shaped and carried the Widows' Pension and the reduction of the Old Age Pensions from 70 to 65 when he was Chancellor of the Exchequer in 1924. While criticising Attlee's post-war agenda, Churchill came to accept its main framework as Britain's equivalent of Roosevelt's 'New Deal', and his offer to the electorate in October 1951 was not to abolish the welfare state, but to manage it more efficiently – 'houses with red meat, and not getting scuppered'.

When the constituency count narrowly went his way, the re-elected prime minister did not minimise the challenge. 'In the worst of the war I could always see how to do it,' he confessed to Oliver Lyttleton, his Secretary of State for the Colonies. 'Today's problems are elusive and intangible.' He struck a similar note in his tribute to Queen Mary following her death in March 1953. 'It requires not only courage but mental resilience for those whose youth lay in calmer and more slowly moving times,' he declared, 'to adjust themselves to the giant outlines and harsh structure of the twentieth century.' He might have been talking about the giant outline of the Battersea Power Station itself looming up in its angular ugliness out of the smog. Harold Macmillan, his minister of housing, had been partly responsible for the troubles of December 1952 by resisting calls for smoke controls the previous summer, and Macmillan subsequently obstructed the appointment of a commission of enquiry. But once the Committee on Air Pollution started its work under Sir Hugh Beaver in May 1953, progress was rapid. 'Few reports into a social evil have led to such swift action,' wrote Brian Clapp approvingly in *An Environmental History of Britain*. Within ten years of the Clean Air Act becoming law in 1955, industrial smoke emissions had been reduced across the country by some 74 per cent and 'smog' was a stinky relic of history.

Whatever their day-to-day political differences, Churchill and Attlee personally continued to treat each other with respect. Attlee and his wife Violet were invited to all major Downing Street events, both official and private, including Churchill's eightieth birthday party in November 1954 and Clementine's seventieth a few months later. Attlee was on better terms with the Conservative leader, in fact, than some of the leading members of Churchill's own party, who had been trying to dislodge him for nearly a decade.

As early as 1945 a group of Conservatives led by Robert 'Bobbety' Cecil (Viscount Cranbourne, later Marquess of Salisbury) had come up with a plan to put the old warhorse, by then 70, out to pasture in the House of Lords while remaining the nominal head of the party, thus allowing his deputy, Anthony Eden, to fight the day-to-day battles in the House of Commons. Eden was unwilling to push the issue in 1945, but seven years later, with Churchill closer to 80, Bobbety was still trying, and he saw his opportunity on the morning of Friday 22nd February 1952, when Charles Moran, the prime minister's doctor, arrived in his office for a hastily summoned meeting convened by 'Jock' Colville, Churchill's private secretary.

Churchill had suffered a mild stroke the previous afternoon – an arterial spasm – Moran reported. When the prime minister awoke from his regular nap and picked up the telephone, he found his mind had gone blank, temporarily unable to summon any words to utter. He had since recovered his speech, but Moran could only foresee a recurrence of the problem – or worse – in the future. This was surely the moment, Salisbury proposed, for the PM to be moved gracefully 'upstairs', and the other men agreed.

ROBERT CECIL

Fifth Marquess of Salisbury

(1 8 9 3 – 1 9 7 2)

PLAYED BY CLIVE FRANCIS

As a direct descendant of William and Robert Cecil, counsellors to the first Queen Elizabeth, and grandson of Robert Gascoyne-Cecil, Queen Victoria's last prime minister, 'Bobbety' Salisbury prided himself on his service to the monarchy, to the Church of England and to the Conservative Party. An early supporter of Winston Churchill in his fight against appeasement, he took a stand when he could see that the great man's powers were failing – as he later took a stand against Princess Margaret's wish to marry the divorced Peter Townsend. Much-imitated for his difficulty in pronouncing the letter 'r', Bobbety is remembered for the question he put to leading Conservatives in January 1957 when trying to discover whether they favoured 'Rab' Butler or Harold Macmillan to succeed Anthony Eden as prime minister: 'Well,' he enquired, 'is it to be Wab or Hawold?'

' . . . is it to be Wab or Hawold?'

They also agreed that only the Queen could propose such a drastic course of action to Churchill with any chance of success, so they arranged a meeting that very afternoon with Tommy Lascelles at Buckingham Palace. Lascelles concurred with the trio that a mentally impaired prime minister was a serious constitutional problem, and he felt that Bobbety's plan to cajole Churchill sideways might stand some chance of success. But the private secretary adamantly refused to involve the Crown in the matter. He thought that the young Queen, not yet two full months in the job, had not the slightest chance of persuading the prime minister to step aside. If she did broach the subject, Lascelles speculated, Churchill would thank her courteously for her suggestion, then move on imperiously to other business – 'It's very good of you Ma'am, to think of it . . .' were the words that Lascelles suggested to Moran that Churchill might deploy. A botched intervention by the new monarch would damage both her pre-rogative and her relationship with her first prime minister – though it might have been different, added the private secretary, if King George VI had still been alive . . .

So, the old warhorse would stay in harness – until his next stroke, at least – though there is one caveat to make about Lascelles' refusal to raise the question of Churchill's possible resignation with the Queen in February 1952. Only a few days earlier, the private secretary and the prime minister had been conferring together – not to say plotting – to abort the ambitions of the Royal House of Mountbatten and to guarantee the preference of the 'old codgers' in the Palace that the House of Windsor should continue to rule. One good turn deserved another. Lascelles' preservation of Churchill inspired the semi-comical 'non-intervention' scene that Peter Morgan depicts towards the end of 'Act of God', when Elizabeth summons her prime minister to question him on his handling of the smog crisis, only to change course and sidestep confrontation when she sees the sun miraculously breaking through the fog. 'But what if the fog hadn't lifted?' she asks her grandmother Queen Mary afterwards. 'And the government had continued to flounder? And people had continued to die? And Churchill had continued to cling to power and the country had continued to suffer? It doesn't feel right, as Head of State – to do nothing . . . Surely doing nothing is no job at all?'

'It is exactly right . . .' replies the elder woman, drawing on all the experience of her 43 years as Queen. 'To do nothing is the hardest job of all, and it will take every ounce of energy that you have. To be impartial is not natural, not human. People will always want you to smile or agree or frown, and the moment you do, you will have declared a position, a point of view – and that is the one thing as Sovereign that you are not entitled to do. The less you do, the less you say, or agree, or smile . . .' 'Or think? Or feel? Or breathe? Or exist?' interjects the young Elizabeth despairingly. 'The better,' concludes her grandmother with firm and icy decisiveness. It was bitter advice, but Elizabeth II would follow it strictly for the rest of her reign, and the harsh truth it contained would see her safely, if not always happily, through many a foggy crisis ahead.

A second round of smog at the end of December 1952 took London's death toll to some 6,000 – matching the 5,957 killed by Nazi bombers in September 1940, the worst month of the Blitz. Once the dangers were realised, the Labour and Conservative parties worked together on Britain's pioneering clean air legislation of 1956.

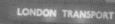

In November 1966, New York City was overwhelmed by a smog that more than doubled the sulphur dioxide content of the air at street level. This photograph by Neal Boenzi of the New York Times has been credited as a major impetus in the passing of America's Clean Air Act and the creation of the United States Environmental Protection Agency in 1970.

'Does the name Donora mean anything to you?'

As London's meteorologists struggled to understand the combination of factors that had generated the Great Smog of December 1952, they had a model to hand on the other side of the Atlantic – the small industrial town of Donora on a collar of the Monongahela River, just south of Pittsburgh, in Pennsylvania steel country. For four days at the end of October 1948 a layer of stagnant air over the town had trapped the poisonous exhaust fumes of the Donora Zinc Works, along with the pollutants from local steel mills, slag dumps and a sulphuric acid plant, to create a noxious fog that killed 800 animals, sickened 7,000 humans and killed at least 20 people, who died following agonising, asthma-like breathing difficulties. Moved by the tragedy, President Truman convened a national conference of scientists and weather experts who came up with a relatively straightforward diagnosis and remedy – the need for stringent smoke control regulations, some of which were embodied in America's first ever air pollution legislation, the Air Pollution Control Act of 1955.

This was followed by the Clean Air Act of 1963, which funded a federal programme to address air pollution reduction techniques, but, as in Britain, it took a major city disaster to stir up decisive action. At the end of November 1966, New York City's Thanksgiving celebrations were overwhelmed by a smog that more than doubled the sulphur dioxide content of the air at street level. The city's 11 municipal incinerators were shut down; landlords were asked to turn down apartment block thermostats to 60 degrees; Consolidated Edison and the Long Island Lighting Company limited their sulphur emissions by switching to natural gas from fuel oil; and state governor Nelson Rockefeller declared a 'first alert advisory' to cover the New York metropolitan area, Connecticut and New Jersey. By the time the alert was lifted three days later, 168 deaths had been reported from respiratory distress.

By comparison to Donora and London, New York got off comparatively lightly from its smog. But one striking photograph from the top of the Empire State Building by Neal Boenzi of the *New York Times* (see previous page) had a dramatic effect on national sentiment, helping to inspire the Clean Air Act of 1970 and the establishing of the United States Environmental Protection Agency by Richard Nixon in the same year. In Donora, meanwhile, where the Zinc Works closed in 1957 with the loss of 900 jobs, followed ten years later by the US Steel facility with the loss of 5,000 more, a group of activists opened the Donora Smog Museum to commemorate the 'folks [who] gave their lives so we could have clean air . . . We here in Donora say this episode was the beginning of the environmental movement.' On display inside the museum is one of the original oxygen tanks which firefighters carried round the darkened streets in 1948 to bring relief to gasping citizens, and outside is an orange sign that proudly proclaims, 'Clean Air Started Here'.

CLEAN AIR
STARTED
HERE

OCTOBER 1948
DONORA, PA

Rainbow One

Over Whitsun weekend towards the end of May 1953, Mike Parker, the Duke of Edinburgh's old naval comrade and now private secretary, found himself summoned to No. 10 Downing Street. There he was sent up to the prime minister's office, where Churchill kept him standing in front of his desk for no little time before he deigned to look up from his papers. 'Is it your intention,' he finally asked balefully, 'to wipe out the royal family in the shortest possible time?' The prime minister had been horrified to come across a newspaper report of the Queen's husband being transported to his pre-coronation engagements by helicopter, and wanted to know how such a risky method of travel had been adopted without the permission of Her Majesty's Government. It was only after much reassurance as to the sterling safety record of the Royal Navy Helicopter Squadron – and the offer of a naval helicopter for the PM's next trip outside London – that Churchill was even faintly mollified.

The prime minister had raised even more difficulties the previous October when confronted with the news that the Queen's husband wanted to learn to fly, and he had made it a matter for cabinet discussion. He was worried about Philip's own safety, but he was still more concerned that, once the young man had earned his wings, he might feel inclined to take his wife and family flying with him. Churchill's younger colleagues tried to argue Philip's case, pointing out that the late King himself had earned his wings as an RAF pilot – as had his brothers the Dukes of Windsor, Gloucester and Kent – and that flying 'was now widely regarded as a normal means of transport'. Skating tactfully around the prime minister's age (Churchill would be 78 the following month), they remarked how young men these days considered

On 4th May 1953, the Duke of Edinburgh was awarded his pilot's wings by the Chief of Air Staff at Buckingham Palace – in the approving presence of his wife, the Secretary of State for Air and the Captain of the Queen's Flight.

learning to fly 'little more hazardous than learning to drive a motor-car'. Perhaps their strongest argument, in view of the recent cabinet decisions that had gone against the Prince, was that it would be 'a great disappointment' if this young man's personal wishes were frustrated. Churchill said he would take up the matter with the Duke on his forthcoming visit to Balmoral, and two weeks later he was able to report back that he had secured the necessary assurances – and particularly that HRH 'had no intention of attempting to fly jet aircraft'. This had special resonance in the aftermath of the Farnborough Air Show disaster of the previous month, when a prototype DH110 jet had crashed into the crowds, killing 31 people. Most important of all, the Duke had undertaken not to pilot any plane in which the Queen was a passenger.

On reflection, the prime minister felt able to withdraw his objection to the Duke undergoing basic training as a pilot 'under the guidance of a Royal Air Force instructor', and the approval was duly minuted as Cabinet Conclusion 85 of 14th October 1952. Philip had always wanted to fly – 'like all small boys,' as he once put it, 'who want to drive railway engines.' As an adult, he came to see the exercise of piloting an aeroplane as 'an intellectual challenge', and, if he had had his way, he would have left school for a career in the Royal Air Force rather than in the Royal Navy. But Uncle Dickie had urged the cause of the navy as offering better family connections – and so it had proved, of course, in the most spectacular fashion.

One consequence of Elizabeth coming to the throne was that her husband was showered with high military ranks, among them Marshal of the Royal Air Force, and Philip decided that he could not morally accept that dignity without earning his wings as a pilot. *The Crown* shows Peter Townsend teaching Philip how to fly. In fact, the Duke's instructor was Flight Lieutenant Caryl Gordon of the RAF's Central Flying School, who took him up for his first proper lesson from White Waltham airfield near Maidenhead on 12th November 1952, and had him flying solo by Christmas. He rated his royal pupil as 'above average', though he admitted to being 'perturbed' when he watched the Duke's first solo spin 'by the number of turns he completed before recovering'. Windsocks were set up in Windsor Great Park to turn the polo field at Smith's Lawn into a landing strip, and Elizabeth brought Charles and Anne out to watch their father land his Chipmunk Trainer, then clamber up inside to inspect the cockpit – though not to fly off with him afterwards.

Philip had always wanted to fly.

By February 1953 Philip had graduated to a more advanced plane, the Harvard Trainer, and an RAF examining unit described his flying as 'thoughtful with a sense of safety and airmanship above average'. His navigation skills were outstanding, which was hardly surprising after his years of combat service in the navy, though Flight Lieutenant Gordon did have cause to lecture his charge on one occasion about the hazards of overconfidence – a lesson, he reported, that was received 'with humility'.

On 4th May 1953, a month before the coronation and a few weeks before his thirty-second birthday, the Duke of Edinburgh was duly awarded his pilot's wings by the Chief of Air Staff at Buckingham Palace in the presence of the Secretary of State for Air, the Captain of the Queen's Flight and a very broadly smiling Queen. The family were due to travel to Balmoral next day for a brief pre-coronation break, and, while Philip decided he would fly himself up to Aberdeen, his wife and his children travelled separately.

'I feel very strongly,' Philip later wrote, 'that flying isn't a sort of black art which can only be done by devotees or daredevils.' He loved flying, he said, because it was totally consuming – when you are piloting a plane, he explained, you cannot think of anything else. As the Duke gained experience, it became quite routine for him to

pilot all the aircraft of the Queen's Flight with a co-pilot beside him – his call sign was RAINBOW ONE – and in that fashion he did fly his wife and children for many hundreds of hours, as he had once assured the cabinet that he wouldn't. In 1956, he also took his first lessons in a helicopter and received his wings as a Royal Navy helicopter pilot. But by then Winston Churchill was no longer prime minister.

Two days later, the Duke celebrated his newly awarded wings by flying solo over Windsor Castle. He loved flying, he later said, because it was totally consuming – when you are piloting a plane, you cannot think of anything else.

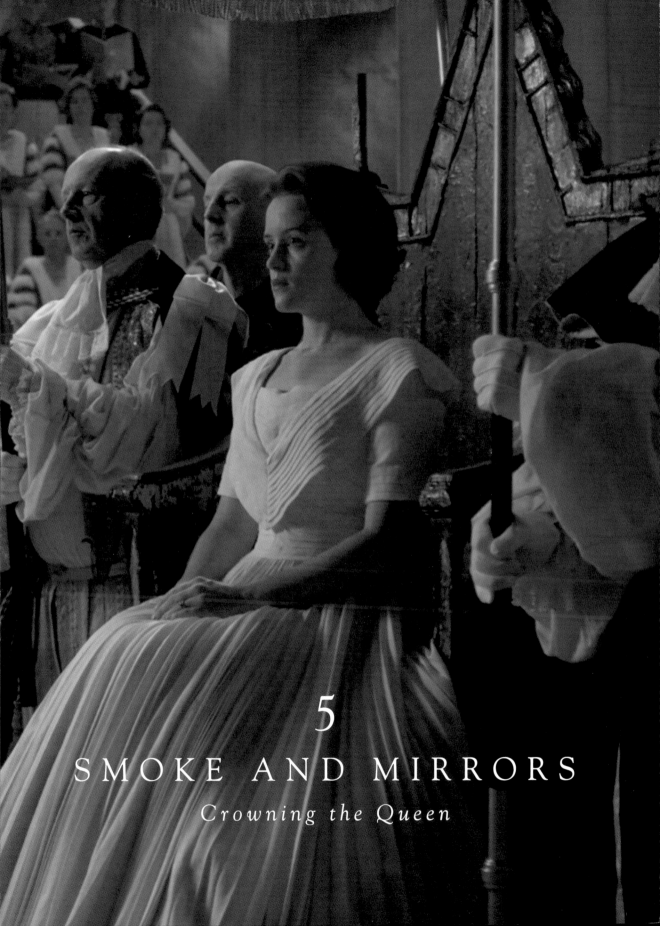

5
SMOKE AND MIRRORS
Crowning the Queen

5

'Be thy head anointed with holy oil, as kings, priests and prophets were anointed . . . As Solomon was anointed King by Zadok the Priest and Nathan the Prophet, so be thou anointed, blessed and consecrated Queen over the peoples whom the Lord Thy God has given thee to rule and govern.' The ancient ceremonial of Queen Elizabeth II's coronation provides the solemn climax to Episode 5 of *The Crown*, 'Smoke and Mirrors', with an ironic twist. Intercut with the ceremony in Westminster Abbey, we see the Duke and Duchess of Windsor viewing the coronation on television. On 2nd June 1953 the couple really did sit down to watch the BBC coverage of events in London live in France, thanks to a hook-up with a Paris television station – inspiring the show's creator Peter Morgan to imagine some poignant dialogue. The ex-King feels moved to explain the meaning of the ceremony's age-old rituals to a group of his American friends, thus giving us the perspective of the monarch who never wore the crown – and who also happened to have been the favourite uncle of the young woman at the centre of the ceremony.

On 2nd June, 1953, the Duke and Duchess of Windsor joined a group of American friends to watch the BBC's coverage of Elizabeth II's coronation celebrations that were transmitted live in Paris.

Princess Elizabeth, 'Lilibet', in 1933, aged seven, with her favourite uncle David, the Prince of Wales. He was about to embark on his love affair with Wallis Simpson that would lead to Elizabeth's eventual accession to the throne.

Princess Elizabeth was not yet five when her beloved Uncle David met Mrs Wallis Simpson in January 1931, and the little girl was oblivious to the significance of the meeting. What observer at the time, of any age, could have imagined the consequences that would flow from the encounter between the wilful Prince and the vivacious divorcee? Elizabeth only met Mrs Simpson once or twice in her childhood, then on a handful of strained occasions in later years. But Mrs Simpson was to make a most decisive impact on her life, for it was Wallis's passionate relationship with the future King Edward VIII that would transform the comparatively uncertain royal destiny of Elizabeth of York, daughter of a younger son. Edward's abdication of December 1936 placed his ten-year-old niece next in line of succession to the Crown, and, even more crucially, would provide the foundation myth for Elizabeth's subsequent reign. The complex passions of 1936 were to provide the awful example that overshadowed the Princess's adolescence, one that remains an ever-present challenge to the royal family to this day – how you should *not* behave when you are entrusted with the sacred covenant of monarchy.

The Prince of Wales was Princess Elizabeth's most exciting and naughtiest uncle, sharing that side of her childhood that indulgent uncles make their own. At the 1931 wedding of Queen Mary's niece, Lady May Cambridge, he was seen to catch the little girl's eye with a secret wink and to win her broad monkey grin in reply. A family home movie of the time shows Uncle David strutting round the garden rehearsing the young Elizabeth

Mrs Simpson was to make a most decisive impact on her life.

in spoof Nazi salutes. Her mother and father did not altogether approve. For her third birthday, the Prince of Wales had presented his niece with a baby Cairn terrier, the breed of which he was especially fond, even though her parents felt, according to one court-approved royal writer, 'that Princess Elizabeth was still too young for such exacting possessions as pets'.

At the time, however, no alarm bells rang. On the contrary, in the 1920s and early 1930s the Prince of Wales appeared to be blazing a promising new trail. A series of much-acclaimed foreign tours had made him a glittering international celebrity. He had successfully fought for the right to get close to the trenches in the Great War. He had been the first member of the royal family to speak on radio, the first to be photographed smoking a cigarette. He seemed to herald a more open and accessible approach to monarchy. When he spotted a group of Australian soldiers being refused entrance to the Carlton Grill, he went over to shake their hands and they were shown to a table. He had taps put on his shoes by Fred Astaire, and during his brief stay at Oxford (he spent two years at Magdalen College before war interrupted) he had sung 'The Red Flag' to his own banjo accompaniment. He inspired popular songwriters – 'I've danced with a man who's danced with a girl who danced with the Prince of Wales'.

The dancing partners were the problem. From the spring of 1918, the Prince of Wales had an on-off love affair with Freda Dudley Ward, the wife of a liberal MP, that lasted 16 years. Their relationship was played out in the semi-public ambiance of

David, the Prince of Wales, and his young brother Bertie, the Duke of York, were close from an early age. Those ties became even closer with the birth of Bertie's daughters Elizabeth and Margaret Rose, photographed here shortly before David's accession as King Edward VIII early in 1936.

Mayfair night clubs, where the Prince was also seen dancing with the likes of Tallulah Bankhead, the famously libertine American actress, and Florence Mills, the African American 'Queen of Happiness'. A longer lasting companion was Thelma, Lady Furness, who later described in her memoirs the experience of going on safari with the Prince: 'His arms about me were the only reality . . . Each night I felt more completely possessed by our love.' In 1929, the complications of the Prince's multiple and shifting liaisons prompted his assistant private secretary, Captain Tommy Lascelles, to resign in protest (he was later re-employed, in a significant gesture of sympathy, by the Prince's father, King George V). On one foreign tour, Lascelles had had to sort out the consequences of his master having bedded the wife of the Prince's official host, the local British governor.

It was Lady Furness who introduced her boyfriend to Wallis Simpson, born Bessie Wallis Warfield in Pennsylvania in 1896, a member of a once wealthy but now impoverished Baltimore family. Having divorced her first husband, Earl Winfield Spencer Jr, an Air Army officer in the United States Navy, Wallis had moved on to marry Ernest Simpson, a New Yorker whose father was English and who nursed ambitions of becoming a British subject. Simpson crossed the Atlantic, briefly joined the Coldstream Guards as a second lieutenant, then went to work in the London office of his father's international shipping firm. Proud of his family's British origins, and, strangely, more English than a typical Englishman, Ernest Simpson enjoyed introducing his wife into London's café society, which brought the couple into contact with Thelma Furness.

In January 1931, Lady Furness invited the Simpsons to make up the numbers at a weekend house party at which the Prince was a guest, and in the months that followed the Simpsons came to see more and more of him, usually in the company of Thelma Furness. But in January 1934, Lady Furness went to America, and Mrs Simpson moved in swiftly to replace her. Suddenly the diaries of the period are filled with references to the Prince and his new girlfriend, with Mrs Simpson 'glittering',

Wallis, the future Mrs. Simpson, born 1896, photographed in her mid-twenties during her marriage to her first husband, Earl Winfield Spencer Jr, an Air Army officer in the United States Navy.

according to Lady Diana Cooper, or 'dripping with emeralds . . . literally smothered in rubies', in the words of the diarist 'Chips' Channon. Many of the jewels were rumoured to be royal heirlooms, with the emeralds said to have come from the treasures that the Prince's grandmother, Queen Alexandra, had bequeathed to be worn by his future wife.

Society wags speculated that Mrs Simpson had some hold on the Prince that must be sexual. There was dark talk of Wallis having picked up exotic bedroom techniques – the 'Shanghai Squeeze' and the 'China Clinch' – during the 'lotus year' she spent in the Far East after separating from her first husband. But in June 1935 there arose gossip of a more serious kind.

The Prince of Wales nursed a not-so-secret admiration for Europe's rising Fascist dictators, and he used the occasion of the British Legion rally in London's Albert Hall to propose that the Legion should 'stretch forth the hand of friendship to the Germans'. German and American newspapers took this as an overt political endorsement of Hitler, and the cabinet asked that George V should convey their unhappiness to his son.

Taken in conjunction with the Prince's growing indifference to his ceremonial duties, it showed a sad ignorance of what the job of a British constitutional monarch entailed. George V spent long hours in the last September of his life at Balmoral in 1935 talking anxiously with the Archbishop of Canterbury, and both foresaw a gloomy future. 'After I am gone,' the King said, 'the boy will ruin himself in twelve months.' As Edward VIII

> *'After I am gone, the boy will ruin himself in twelve months.'*

succeeded his father in January 1936, the prime minister, Stanley Baldwin, voiced his doubts to Clement Attlee, the recently elected leader of the Labour Party, as to whether the new King would 'stay the course'.

Baldwin had rather hoped, he admitted to a colleague, 'to escape the responsibility of having to take charge of the Prince as King. But perhaps Providence has kept me here for that purpose.' Britain's newspaper proprietors had agreed between themselves not to mention the King's new friend, who was by now living apart from her husband.

But anxiety was growing behind the scenes, with insiders starting to speculate on what might come next. According to the Countess of Airlie, Queen Mary's friend and lady-in-waiting, George V had spoken quite frankly just a few months before his death: 'I pray to God that my eldest son will never marry and have children, and that nothing will come between Bertie and Lilibet and the throne.'

King Edward VIII had started his reign in a flurry of activity, energetically reading through all the official papers sent him by the government, initialling the documents enthusiastically and even scribbling comments of his own in the margin. This excess of zeal soon betrayed him, however, for after only a few months his initials and comments petered out, and confidential documents began to return obviously unread, occasionally marked with slopped cocktails and the rings of wet glass bottoms. Discreet enquiries revealed that red boxes containing crucial cabinet papers were going down

to Fort Belvedere, there to be left unguarded while an unsupervised selection of guests came and went. Stanley Baldwin, therefore, decided to restrict the documents available to the King, including papers requiring the royal signature – and Edward VIII's attention to his job was by now so scanty that he did not realise what was going on.

In October 1936 Mrs Simpson formally petitioned for divorce from her husband Ernest, and the King's private secretary, Alexander Hardinge, felt the time had come to pay a visit to the Duke of York at 145 Piccadilly, the Yorks' London home. The situation was now so grave, he warned Princess Elizabeth's father, that it could quite possibly end in the abdication of his elder brother. On the evening of 16th November, the King confirmed this when he went to dinner with the Queen Mary, speaking openly to her for the first time about his love for Wallis. He was surprised by his mother's sympathy for his

personal predicament – until he told her he was planning to bring the matter out into the open with a view to testing public support. 'To my mother,' Edward wrote later, 'the Monarchy was something sacred, and the sovereign a personage apart. The word "duty" fell between us.' This was the parting of ways, the first formal enunciation of the tragic difference of opinion that split the British royal family in 1936. What did duty mean? In Edward's eyes his duty lay to the woman he loved. His only doubt, he was to say, was not whether Wallis Simpson was acceptable, but whether he was worthy of her. When the King told his brothers next morning that he was prepared to abdicate if that was the price of marrying Wallis, their reaction was like their mother's. The Duke of York was especially overcome by what it meant for

3rd June 1937. The Duke of Windsor with his bride, the former Mrs Wallis Simpson, photographed by Cecil Beaton on their wedding day at the Château de Candé in the Loire valley in France.

KING EDWARD VIII

(Reigned 20th January–11th December 1936)
Officially Edward, Prince of Wales,
but known to his family as David.
Duke of Windsor 1936–72.

(1 8 9 4 – 1 9 7 2)

PLAYED BY ALEX JENNINGS

'The Prince of Wales, one feels, would not raise his finger to save his future sceptre,' wrote the diarist Henry 'Chips' Channon as early as 1925. 'In fact, many of his intimate friends think he would be only too happy to renounce it.' As the abdication crisis of 1936 drew ever closer, it is remarkable how many other observers talked of David seeking some pretext to shake off his royal destiny – as if the scenario of romance and renunciation was just a means to an end. If Wallis Simpson had not existed, we must ask ourselves, would the reluctant King have had to invent her? *The Crown* delivers an open verdict. The drama records how duty was observed and delivered by Edward VIII's successors George VI and Queen Elizabeth II. But there remains the challenge posed by the ex-King across the water. To what higher purpose should we dedicate ourselves if not to a loved one and to the eternal cause of love?

WALLIS WARFIELD SIMPSON

Duchess of Windsor

(1 8 9 6 – 1 9 8 6)

PLAYED BY LIA WILLIAMS

'A nice, quiet, well-bred mouse of a woman'

'Hark the herald angels sing, Mrs Simpson's pinched our King!' ran a doggerel Christmas carol in 1936. Whether people laughed about her or not, the popular verdict on Wallis Simpson was virtually unanimous: she was an evil temptress, a Lady Macbeth – and even worse, an *American*. But her fellow American 'Chips' Channon found Wallis quite the opposite when he met her in January 1935 – 'a nice, quiet, well-bred mouse of a woman,' he wrote, 'with large startled eyes and a huge mole [on her chin]'. 'No one,' wrote Winston Churchill, 'has been more victimised by gossip and scandal.' On 3rd December 1936, when Stanley Baldwin was still desperate for Edward VIII to keep the Crown, Wallis retired to France 'to remove myself from the King's life', offering 'to withdraw . . . and indeed to do anything to prevent the King from abdicating'. Cynics said she wanted David to take all the blame for what came next, and certainly the couple's life in exile proved far from idyllic. But is it possible the lady had really meant what she said?

his own life and that of his daughter Elizabeth. He was speechless.

National opinion was equally negative when the newspapers finally broke their silence. Early in December 1936, a speech by the Bishop of Bradford, who chose to make disapproving public comments on the irregularity of the King's church-going, provided the pretext the press needed to bring the royal relationship with Mrs Simpson into the open – and the tone of most comment was hostile. The prospect of Queen Wallis prompted horror. Mavericks like Winston Churchill might speak up for a so-called 'King's Party', but Edward VIII's cause was clearly doomed. The King must choose between love and duty, and he had already made his choice clear to his family.

'The Crown in this country . . . has been deprived of many of its prerogatives,' declared Stanley Baldwin in his speech to Parliament explaining why Edward VIII had decided to step down. 'But today, while that is true, it stands for more than it ever has done in its history. The importance of its integrity is, beyond all question, far greater than it has ever been.' Abdication, in other words, was Britain's vote for monarchy. Trying to take advantage of these events, socialist MP James Maxton put down a motion to replace the Crown with 'government of a republican kind' – to be defeated by 403 votes to 5. At 145 Piccadilly, it was impossible to hide from the children that something both very exciting and rather frightening was taking place. 'I am afraid there are going to be great changes in our lives, Crawfie,' the Duchess of York told the girls' governess, Marion

Crawford. 'We must take what is coming to us, and make the best of it.' Lady Cynthia Asquith, a friend of the new King and Queen, had been invited to tea on Friday 11th December 1936, the day abdication was formally ratified by Parliament, and she found the little princesses fully aware, in their own terms, of what was going on. Princess Elizabeth saw a letter on the hall table addressed to 'Her Majesty the Queen'. 'That's *Mummy* now, isn't it?' she said with awe. Princess Margaret Rose, six years old and just learning to write, was troubled by practical concerns. 'I had only just learned how to spell York – Y.O.R.K. – and now I am not to use it any more. I am to sign myself Margaret all alone.'

> '*We must take what is coming to us, and make the best of it.*'

Next day came the public proclamation of their father's new title from the balcony at St James's Palace. 'Lilibet and Margaret had run as usual to give their father a final hug as he went off,' remembered Crawfie, and when the King returned both his daughters bent their knees and swept him a graceful curtsey. 'Nothing that had occurred had brought the change in his condition to him as clearly as this did,' wrote the governess. 'He stood for a moment touched and taken aback. Then he stooped and kissed them both warmly.'

Eighteen months later the ex-King, now Duke of Windsor, wrote to his mother asking her to express her feelings about what had happened, and Queen Mary replied to him frankly: 'You will remember how miserable I was,' she wrote, 'when you informed me of your intended marriage and abdication and how I implored you not to do so for our sake and for the sake of the country.

You did not seem able to take in any point of view but your own . . . I do not think you have ever realised the shock which the attitude you took up caused your family and the whole nation. It seemed inconceivable to those who had made such sacrifices during the war that you, as their king, refused a lesser sacrifice . . . All my life I have put my Country before everything else, and I simply cannot change now.' Sacrifice and Duty, Crown and Country – these were the defining issues of the abdication, and when the moment came for Queen Mary's granddaughter to be crowned 17 years later, these were the guiding themes of her coronation.

'Pray for me on that day,' Elizabeth II had asked in December 1952 in her first Christmas broadcast. 'Pray that God will give me wisdom and strength to carry out the solemn promises I shall be making.' Deeply religious in childhood and throughout her life, the new Queen had been working with the Archbishop of Canterbury on a programme of daily readings and meditations, the better to understand every element in her crowning. Searching back for lessons and inspiration to her father's coronation in May 1937, she recalled the ceremony as a mystical experience. 'I thought that it was all very, very wonderful, and I expect the Abbey did too,' the 11-year-old Princess had written in her neat, rounded hand in a memoir she presented 'To Mummy and Papa, In Memory of Their Coronation, From Lilibet, By Herself'. 'The arches and beams at the top were covered with a sort of haze of wonder as Papa was crowned, at least I thought so.' The question for the 27-year-old Queen was how she could spread and share

'Pray for me on that day'

the haze of wonder on 2nd June 1953. Episode 5, 'Smoke and Mirrors', dramatically depicts the disagreements inside Buckingham Palace and Downing Street over whether television cameras should be allowed inside Westminster Abbey, with the modernising Duke of Edinburgh pitted against the reactionary forces led by Winston Churchill, the Archbishop of Canterbury and the Duke of Norfolk, the traditional organiser of coronation ceremonial. 'Britain today is not the Britain of past coronations . . .' argues Philip. 'We have a new sovereign, young and a woman. Let us give her a coronation that is befitting . . . modern and forward-looking at a moment in time where exciting technological developments are making things possible we never dreamt of.'

Elizabeth herself is depicted in the drama as cautiously supportive of her husband, using the dispute to advance her own cause – to get Philip to pay homage to her by kneeling. But that does not reflect the historical record. The Duke of Edinburgh was certainly an enthusiastic proponent of television (who did indeed kneel to his wife in the course of the coronation ceremony), but when the BBC first requested permission in June 1952 to situate cameras inside the abbey, it was Queen Elizabeth II herself who said no, and who led the opposition.

The records of the Coronation Joint Executive for 7th July 1952 make it quite clear. The Queen did not want cameras focused on her once the complicated and challenging ceremony had begun. She was worried that some personal gaffe might be transmitted live to the watching millions without the possibility of re-editing, and there

Television cameras filmed the crowning of Queen Elizabeth II in Westminster Abbey, but earlier they had looked away from the sacred moments of her anointing and taking Holy Communion. No close-ups of her face were broadcast at any time.

were the aspects of the ritual, like her taking of Holy Communion, and the anointing of the bared, upper part of her chest, which she felt were deeply private. More generally, she viewed the televised covering of sacred events as vulgar. The prevailing sentiment, recalled Mike Parker, who was processing the coronation documents for Philip, 'was that the television was just the same as the gutter press'.

As the Archbishop of Canterbury put it: 'Television is a mass-produced form of entertainment, which is potentially one of the greatest dangers of the world.' Confirmed by the cabinet on the grounds of 'avoiding unnecessary strain for Her Majesty', the decision not to televise was finally made public in October 1952 – and the outcry was immediate. It was a 'bad and

reactionary decision,' said the *Daily Express*. The *Daily Mirror* called it 'truly astonishing'. The ban was front-page news in every newspaper, condemned with remarkable unanimity. There was already disquiet that the elected members of the House of Commons were having to ballot for a limited number of places in the abbey, while every single member of the House of Lords, plus their wives, had a seat. Here was another example of the anachronistic, pre-war caste system, restricting participation to the privileged few. 'Beyond the precincts of Westminster,' wrote the *Daily Mirror*'s Cassandra, 'from the shores of Cornwall to the grey waters of the Clyde, from the warm sunlight of the Weald of Kent to the green-blue loveliness of the Lakes, at least fifteen million of Her Majesty's subjects will be abruptly shuttered

Periscopes improvised
from hand mirrors came
in useful for the spectators
who flocked into London
to watch the many hours
of coronation processions
through the streets of the
West End on 2nd June
1953. The inhabitants of
Britain and the Common-
wealth numbered nearly
650 million, and a fair
proportion of them seemed
to have congregated in the
centre of the capital.

off by what appears to be a monumental piece of misjudgment.' Philip's worst fears had been justified. MPs immediately laid down questions in Parliament, and when Churchill rose in an unusually crowded chamber to respond it was clear that the point had already been conceded. There was talk of consultations and the need for fresh lighting tests, but the real issue was working out a compromise that was personally acceptable to the apprehensive Queen.

In the end, it was agreed that the cameras would look away from the sacred moments of her anointing and her taking of Communion, and there would be no close-ups of her face at any time. But television would present live, on-the-spot coverage of virtually everything else. The overruling of the television ban was loyally presented as having come personally from the Queen, as if she had been offended at the attempt to stop her people from joining in her sacred moment and had hastened to put things right. But what Elizabeth really felt about 'the telly' had been made clear by her rejection of the BBC's request that her first Christmas Broadcast should be televised. On 25th December 1952, television licence holders had to be content with hearing the speech as it was broadcast on the radio, with just a still, flickering photograph of the Queen and her radio microphone to occupy their screens. It would take some time to overcome Elizabeth's camera shyness – though one of the events that gave her more confidence turned out to be the tel-evising of her own coronation, which would turn out to be a remarkable international success.

Coronation Day, 2nd June 1953, dawned dark and damp. It had been chosen from Met

The bells rang out and shouts of 'God Save The Queen' re-echoed inside the Abbey. Meanwhile four-year-old Prince Charles patiently watched his mother's crowning, flanked by his grandmother and aunt.

Office statistics as a date likely to be blessed with sunshine, but the weather broke several days before and the vast crowds camping out overnight along the route were soaked. Sheltering beneath umbrellas and makeshift shelters, the people remained defiantly upbeat. In 1953 the inhabitants of Britain and the Commonwealth numbered nearly 650 million, and a fair proportion of them seemed to have congregated in London. The hotels and boarding houses were full. The Ministry of Works had turned central London into a ceremonial theme park, adorned with processional arches and long, covered stands that gave the Mall and

Whitehall the appearance of a race track. All seats in the stands had been reserved as soon as booking opened, and tickets on the black market were selling for £40 or £50 each – some £950 in 2017 values. Balconies overlooking the route cost even more, and in cities, towns and villages outside the capital many improvised street committees organised the distribution of neighbours around the recently available television sets – which, after all the fuss and bother, turned out to be the best coronation souvenir of all. The Cold War was in full swing, and western reports from Russia ridiculed the cult of personality surrounding

Stalin, but that was nothing compared to Britain's home-grown profusion of posters and souvenirs, from tin pots to tea towels, emblazoned with the solemn, dark-eyed likeness of the young Elizabeth.

Through the course of her coronation day, Queen Elizabeth II wore no fewer than three crowns – starting with Queen Victoria's diadem that she wore on her way to the abbey. This low diamond circlet, originally made for George IV, featured the Cross of St George and the emblems of the other component parts of the United Kingdom. It had been Elizabeth's headdress in the postage stamps issued prior to her actual crowning, and has remained the coronet favoured by stamp designers on most issues ever since. In the abbey the solemn ceremony of consecration involved St Edward's Crown, made in 1661 for Charles II to replace the regalia of St Edward the Confessor, destroyed by Oliver Cromwell and the Parliamentarians after the Civil War. This huge and heavy, solid gold crown, gaudily set with pearls and precious stones, is most easily identified by its generously bowed arches.

Then, on leaving the abbey, modern sovereigns since Queen Victoria have exchanged this massive weight – over 5lbs – for the Imperial Crown of State, with less dramatically bowed arches and weighing in comparatively lighter – at 'only' 3lbs. This was what Elizabeth wore throughout her coronation processions and is accordingly the crown in which she was most frequently photographed on 2nd June 1953. As the 'working' crown that she would wear most frequently during her reign, it was remodelled to fit her head more

'Sirs, I here present unto you Queen Elizabeth, your undoubted Queen.'

precisely soon after her accession, fitting on top and around a rich velvet Cap of Maintenance whose thick ermine fringe rolls out and up around the metal base of the framework. At eleven o'clock Queen Elizabeth II arrived at Westminster Abbey with her husband in the gilded State Coach. Extravagantly decorated with gamboling cherubs and tritons, the coach had been built in 1761 for George III and was attended by scarlet-and-gold-coated beefeaters and postilions. 'I was glad when they said unto me, we will go to the House of the Lord,' rang out the notes of the opening anthem, and Elizabeth II stepped out on her progress down the aisle.

'Sirs, I here present unto you Queen Elizabeth, your undoubted Queen,' called out the Archbishop of Canterbury, as he offered her to the four corners of the abbey – east, south, west, and then north, where the foreign newspaper correspondents were seated. This 'Recognition' was intended only for the Queen's subjects in the abbey, but already the atmosphere was so charged that the foreign pressmen joined in the shouts of 'God Save Queen Elizabeth'. As Handel's setting of 'Zadok the Priest and Nathan the Prophet' carried through the church, the text which had been recited at every crowning in England from the coronation of King Edgar in 973 AD, the Queen's jewellery and robes were lifted off her piece by piece by her maids of honour. Her ceremonial train made a rich crimson pile overflowing the extended arms of the Groom of the Robes, and Elizabeth II stood divested of all her finery, ready for her consecration. These were the moments that were not televised, as the archbishop anointed Elizabeth's forehead and upper chest with oil.

Viewers at home received atmospheric shots of the abbey, along with commentary explaining how, according to the first Book of Kings in the Old Testament, the oldest known description of a religious coronation, Zadok and Nathan had anointed King Solomon in this very fashion. But the cameras came on again as Elizabeth began to receive the tokens of responsibility with which she was being invested: the Orb – 'remember,' the archbishop enunciated to her, 'that the whole world is subject to the power and empire of Christ'; the Sceptre with the Cross, 'ensign of kingly power and justice'; the Rod of Mercy; and also the Royal Ring with a sapphire and ruby cross – the so-called 'Wedding Ring of England'. Then came the moment of the crowning itself as the

archbishop raised St Edward's Crown glittering high in the air. Elizabeth II bowed her head and as the crown descended upon her, reported Dermot Morrah, one of the officials who was standing near the throne, 'the sense of spiritual exultation that radiated from her was almost tangible'.

Until this point the peers in their groups around the centre of the abbey had been bareheaded. Now they all simultaneously donned their caps and coronets – with the duchesses, thought 'Chips' Channon from his niche in the gallery, looking like so many swans as they swept up their arms above their heads. 'God Save The Queen' came the shouts from all sides, and the entire congregation continued in this vein as trumpets blared, church

The Queen's Maids of
Honour after the ceremony,
photographed by Cecil Beaton
in the Green Drawing Room
at Buckingham Palace:
(left to right)
Lady Moyra Hamilton,
Lady Anne Coke,
Lady Jane Stewart,
Lady Mary Baillie-Hamilton,
Lady Jane Heathcote-
Drummond-Willoughby,
and Lady Rosemary
Spencer-Churchill.

bells rang and cannon fired salutes all over London. Inside the abbey the cacophony joined the echoes of ancient centuries in the rafters – little Princess Elizabeth's 'haze of wonder'. Led by Prince Philip, who knelt in front of his wife, the senior peers of each degree – dukes, marquesses, earls, viscounts and barons – came forward to do homage while the choir sang. And then, after taking Communion (with the cameras once again focused elsewhere) the Queen went out of the abbey to meet her people. When it was all over two sociologists tried to explain what had happened. In the *Sociological Review* for December 1953, Professor Edward Shils and Michael Young, the former American and a University of Chicago academic, the latter a Labour Party member and a confessed sceptic so far as monarchy was concerned, weighed up the data of the coronation year, including statistics showing that, despite the enormous numbers on the streets, there had been fewer cases of pickpocketing on 2nd June than on a normal day in London, along with significantly fewer housebreakings. 'There can be no society,' they declared, quoting Emile Durkheim, the French father of sociology, 'which does not feel the need of upholding and reaffirming at regular intervals the collective sentiments and the collective ideas which make its unity and personality.' The coronation of 1953, they decided, was 'exactly this kind of ceremonial in which the society reaffirms the moral values which constitute it as a society.'

The educated classes might sneer because of 'an aversion towards all sentiments and practices associated with religion' – and also, perhaps, because they were reluctant to acknowledge 'the existence of these somewhat alarming sentiments within themselves'. But the fact remained that 'the Coronation provided at one time, and for practically the entire society, such an intensive

contact with the sacred that we believe we are justified in interpreting it as a great act of national communion.'

'Oil and oaths. Orbs, sceptres, symbol upon symbol!' declares the Duke of Windsor at the end of 'Smoke and Mirrors' in Peter Morgan's version of this anthropological discussion. '[It's an] unfathomable web of arcane mystery and liturgy, blurring so many lines, no clergyman, historian or lawyer could ever untangle any of it.' 'It's crazy,' agrees one of his American friends who has been watching the televised service – to be politely contradicted by his host. 'On the contrary,' says the Duke. 'It's perfectly sane. Who wants transparency when you can have magic? Who wants prose when you can have poetry? Pull away the veil, and what are you left with? An ordinary young woman of modest ability and little imagination. But wrap her up like this, anoint her with oil, and hey presto, what do you have? A goddess!'

His friend reflects pensively: 'And to think you turned all that down. The chance to be a god!' Once again, the Duke contradicts him. 'I turned it down,' he says, 'for something greater still', turning fondly to look at his wife. 'For LOVE,' smiles the former Mrs Simpson.

It makes for a powerful conclusion, with the Duke of Windsor shrewdly skewering the complex and deceptive myth of what adds up to 'royalness'. Equally complex and deceptive, of course, is the myth of what adds up to 'love'.

THE MOST REVEREND GEOFFREY FISHER

Archbishop of Canterbury

(1887–1972)

PLAYED BY RONALD PICKUP

*C*antuar (from the Latin for 'Canterbury') is a title by which the Archbishop of Canterbury signs his name, and it inspired a sneering poem after one of Geoffrey Fisher's predecessors, Cosmo Gordon Lang, had declared that King Edward VIII and his social circle should 'stand rebuked by the judgement of the nation': 'My Lord Archbishop, what a scold you are! And when your man is down, how bold you are! Of charity how oddly scant you are! Old Lang swine, how full of Cantuar!' In Episode 5 of *The Crown*, Peter Morgan gives the Duke of Windsor the chance to spit these lines back in the face of Geoffrey Fisher, the *Cantuar* of the day, who presided over Elizabeth II's coronation with dignity, but shared his predecessor's gift for insensitive pronouncements. Asked if he was worried about the recently developed H-bomb, Fisher replied: 'The very worst the Bomb can do is to sweep a vast number of people from this world into the next, into which they must all go anyway.'

'My Lord Archbishop, what a scold you are!'

Cecil Beaton

PHOTOGRAPHER AND DIARIST

If, in the coronation summer of 1937, you had asked which photographer might possibly be selected to shoot the official royal portraits at the *next* coronation, the camp and often waspish Cecil Beaton would have been the very last name on the list. At the time, Beaton was notorious in royal circles for his flattering photographs and sketches of his friend Mrs Ernest Simpson – he called them his 'Wallis' Collection – culminating in his alluring set of pictures of the new Duke and Duchess of Windsor to mark their wedding at the Château de Candé in June 1937 (see p. 143). The social-climbing snapper was the visual propagandist for the King's Party, and ultimately for the scandal of the Abdication.

But in the summer of 1939, on the eve of war, George VI's wife Queen Elizabeth (one of Wallis Simpson's fiercest foes) imaginatively set enmity aside. She summoned the great glamoriser to work his magic on her, and the resulting sequence of images caused a sensation. 'I wanted so much,' Beaton wrote in his diary, 'that these should be different from the formal, somewhat anonymous-looking photographs . . . that had until then been taken of the Royal Family' – and his misty, drifting images of the hitherto mousy Queen Elizabeth beside the windows of Buckingham Palace succeeded magnificently.

'These pictures will be treasured in hundreds of thousands of homes throughout Britain and the Empire,' enthused the *Daily Sketch*. 'How often have you "taken" mother standing by the back door of her drawing-room,' asked the *Daily Mirror*, 'to send to members of the family in distant lands?'

Below: Cecil Beaton's portrait of himself c.1930. Right: 'Yes, the crown does get rather heavy,' the Queen told Beaton during the shoot.

Throughout the war years, Cecil Beaton was the photographer of choice when it came to royal images that mingled splendour with humanity. He shot some arch, Gainsborough-style poses of the young Princesses Elizabeth and Margaret Rose against the elaborate painted stage-set backdrops that he was making his trademark, along with a gritty and anything-but-sentimental portfolio of the King and Queen among the debris of the numerous German bombing raids on Buckingham Palace. Beaton himself had a good war.

In 1940, in the 'darkest hour', he signed up with the War Artists' Advisory Committee (WAAC) and served for four years, travelling over 100,000 miles and producing more than 30,000 war images – one of which, his moving portrait of Eileen Dunne, a wounded three-year-old 'Blitz' baby nursing her teddy bear in hospital, helped swing American opinion behind the British war effort. Designing haute couture and stage sets, Beaton was much more than 'just' a photographer – in later life his sparkling costume designs for *Gigi* and *My Fair Lady* would win him a host of awards, including two Academy Awards. His successful stage and movie day jobs gave his photography a memorable theatricality, so when, in 1953, royal thoughts turned to who should photograph the June coronation, he had come to seem the obvious man for the job.

But there was a complication. As he approached the age of 50, Beaton seemed to have fallen out of favour with the new regime. The young Queen and her husband had commissioned Philip's friend and lunchtime companion, the raffish Sterling

Left: A strip of Cecil Beaton's contact prints.
Right: Beaton even coaxed Elizabeth II
into one of her elusive full-face 'monkey'
smiles, with her astonishing array of teeth.

Just when the session was flagging, Cecil Beaton snapped this un-posed shot of the three-year-old Princess Anne as she paced out the long ermine run of her grandmother, the Queen Mother's Coronation train. 'All at once . . . I was enjoying my work. Prince Charles and Princess Anne were buzzing about in the wildest excitement, and would not keep still for a moment,' he recorded in his diary.

Henry Nahum, known professionally as 'Baron', to photograph their wedding and the christenings of their children, Prince Charles and Princess Anne. 'Have been wondering,' Beaton confided disconsolately to his diary in May 1953, 'if my day as photographer at the Palace is over. Baron, a most unexpected friend of Prince Philip's, has been taking all the recent pictures.'

Baron's informal style of photography chimed with the modern approach that Philip was championing for the coronation. But the new Queen Mother was firmly in the traditional camp. She disapproved of Baron and, even more, of her spikey and opinionated son-in-law – about whom, according to some of Philip's friends, she retained reservations until the very end of her life. Queen Elizabeth had helped outflank Philip over the question of the family name, and now she went into action on behalf of her beloved Cecil, who had been courting her assiduously. 'I stopped at my favourite florist,' he recorded in his diary early in the coronation year. 'For once I would be as extravagant as I wished. I took enormous care to choose a bouquet of all the first spring flowers to be sent to that adorable human being living in that cold, bleak Palace!'

The gesture was not wasted. The Queen Mother felt strongly that Beaton's history-steeped approach was right for the thousand-year heritage of the coronation, and her daughter agreed. Philip had got his way over television cameras in the abbey, but tradition would triumph when it came to the end-of-the-day photographs for posterity that would be taken inside Buckingham Palace. 'An enormous relief,' wrote Beaton when he received the news with just weeks to go – and that very evening, by coincidence, he was invited to a ball at the American Embassy where the Queen was guest of honour. 'No, I'm very glad you're going to take them,' Elizabeth told the delighted photographer, 'but, by the time we get through to the photographs, we'll have circles down to here (she pointed half way down her cheeks), then the Crown comes down to here (to the eye), then the court train comes bundling up here, and I'm out to here (stomach sticks out). There are layers upon layers: skirt and mantles and trains.'

The high point of his evening came when he bumped into the Queen Mother and took the opportunity to thank her 'for what I am sure must have been her help in bringing about this "coup" for me'. The older Queen said nothing, but 'laughed knowingly', he recorded, launching 'one finger high in the air' in a gesture of triumph. Reflecting on the Queen's anxiety that she would have bags under her eyes after her long morning in the abbey, followed by an afternoon bumping round the streets of central London in the bone-shaking discomfort of the Gold State Coach, Beaton started planning immediately. He wanted to make his photo session as smooth as possible for his all-important sitter, and his first order of business was the production of the two towering backdrops – Beaton called them 'backgrounds' – that would evoke Westminster Abbey inside Buckingham Palace in a realistic, but also faintly dream-like way.

The first tableau depicted the spectacular ceiling of fan-vaulted arches inside the abbey's Lady Chapel (Elizabeth's 'haze of wonder' again); the second derived from a Victorian engraving of the towers of the abbey as seen from the river. The plan was for the light-framed canvases to be slid and shifted in front of each other to create different tableaus without disturbing the sitter, with the entire stage set framed by opulently patterned

Cecil Beaton at work inside Buckingham Palace with his lighting and camera assistants. His painted 'blow-up' backdrop to re-create Westminster Abbey's fan-vaulted Lady Chapel was reserved for his shots of Queen Elizabeth II.

curtains in the corner of the Palace's Green Drawing Room. On 1st June, the day before the ceremony, Beaton headed for the Green Drawing Room to set up his studio with his friend Patrick Matthews, the director of Vogue Studios, and his team of technicians and electricians. There were tripods and stepladders, mini-mountains of spare fuses, film and light bulbs, and cables snaking all over the floor: it was as if, he wrote, 'one might be organising a vast crowd scene for an early Cecil B. de Mille moving picture'. Beaton had brought flowers – roses, gladioli and clematis – from his home in Wiltshire to decorate his sets, along with his sister Baba. Her job would be to 'straighten the trains' – especially the lengthy train of the Queen herself, so long and heavy it would require the attentions of six fit young maids of honour selected from some of the country's grandest aristocratic families – Leicesters, Londonderrys and Marlboroughs among them.

Feeling himself superfluous as the technicians carried out their work, Beaton sneaked off down the labyrinth of Palace corridors to discover a luncheon in progress for the visiting Commonwealth prime ministers and their wives, whose fur stoles and handbags he encountered lying on gilt chairs in the passage. Peering through a crack in the door the photographer spied Churchill 'standing and glowering with his legs apart', beside Princess Margaret with her 'Hanover-turquoise eyes' and cigarette smoke exhaling from her nostrils.

As he gawked shamelessly at the high and mighty, Beaton felt like a ragamuffin 'Bisto kid', he wrote in his diary, citing the popular advertising campaign of the time. What struck him most were the high spirits of the young Queen, giggling and 'quite obviously elated at being the delightful, gay and attractive cynosure [centre of attention] of all. She wore a pale, dove-fawn coloured dress, with handbag to match . . . The excitement, nourished by the newspapers, mounting every day, has obviously affected her spirits, and she seemed to be in an exultant mood with a blush of triumph in her cheeks.' The royal temper augured well for the morrow. Next morning the photographer woke at 5am to get dressed in his morning suit, filling his grey top hat with his sketching implements, sandwiches and a packet of barley sugars to keep up his strength – as

'No time to lose! Please turn this way, now that; a certain shape was formed, a picture came to life.'

one of the 8,000 guests in the Abbey bidden to be in their places soon after dawn. Beaton had been allotted an observation post high in the rafters near the pipes of the great organ, so chilly on that cold June morning that he imagined himself climbing Everest alongside the Commonwealth climbers (whose achievement in reaching the summit was the talk of the morning papers).

'One has seen many woodcuts, and pictures of all sorts,' he wrote, looking down on the scene in stage designer mode, 'of the earliest Kings and Queens being crowned . . . In all periods, painters have had a shot at recording the ceremony . . . Yet this spectacle today transcended all preconceived notions.' The one-time propagandist for abdication had become a sentimental royalist, and his coronation diary for June 1953 is a fascinating period piece, in which he writes as both a dazzled spectator and a knowing participant in the process. 'The ceremonial,' he wrote, 'seemed to be as fresh and inspiring as some great play or musical event that was being enacted upon a spontaneous impulse of genius. Perhaps it was the background of lofty vaulted stone – like a silver forest – that made everything seem so particularly surprising.'

The array of colours, 'red, gold and smoke-blue', beguiled the photographer. 'The brilliant gold carpet was the perfect floor covering for the slippered feet of the pages, the trainbearers, and the scarlet, blue and gold-clad heralds . . . A mote of light caught a gold sequin fallen on the carpet, on a jewel in a bishop's ring . . . It was all living and new: it was history, but of today and of the future. It was something that is pulsating and vital to us, and an essential part of the life we believe in.' Looking down on the parade of visiting royalties, Beaton caught sight of the deaf and eccentric Princess Alice of Battenberg, 'the mother of the Duke of Edinburgh, a contrast to the grandeur, in the ash-grey draperies of a nun'. But 'most dramatic and spectacular,' he recorded, 'at the head of her retinue of white, lily-like ladies, [walked] the Queen.

'Her cheeks are sugar pink: her hair tightly curled around the Victorian diadem of precious stones perched straight on her brow. Her pink hands are folded meekly on the elaborate grandeur of her encrusted skirt; she is still a young girl with a demeanour of simplicity and humility . . . As she walks she allows her heavy skirt to swing backwards and forwards in a beautiful rhythmic effect. This girlish figure has enormous dignity: she belongs in this scene of almost Byzantine magnificence.' The photographer had the master image he needed – the picture of Elizabeth at her crowning moment that his studio photographs would have to capture later at the Palace.

When the abbey service ended just before 2pm, Beaton hurried back to his London base, his mother's home in Chelsea, to find Etty Beaton in place beside the wireless, listening to the BBC's commentary on the long procession of coaches around London that was just beginning. Grabbing a handful of aspirins, he managed to snatch an hour's sleep before dashing off, refreshed, to the Palace. Inside the Green Drawing Room the backdrops, lights and technicians were all in place by the time the Gold State Coach came bowling home through the central arch into the courtyard around half past four. 'The Queen looked back over her shoulder and appeared somewhat dazed and exhausted,' he noticed with anxiety. Cups of tea and fish paste sandwiches seemed to work wonders. 'Not long after, girlish voices were heard at the end of the Picture Gallery. "Oh hullo! Did you watch it? When did you get home?" From the mirror-doors of the Green Drawing Room I spied the Queen with her ladies, her excited children; the family asking questions, jokes, smiles and laughter, the high-pitched voices of the Queen and Princess Margaret heard above the others.' The Queen and the maids were heading for the Throne Room for the urgent press photographs to be taken and wired out around the world that very evening by *The Times*. Meanwhile, following the schedule drawn up by the Palace's stern press secretary, Commander Richard Colville, Beaton began taking photographs of the other members of the family, starting with the Queen Mother 'dimpled and chuckling, with her eyes as bright as any of her jewels' and Princess Margaret, in whose eyes the photographer detected a saucy 'sex twinkle of understanding'.

'No time to lose! Please turn this way, now that; a certain shape was formed, a picture came to life. Quick! Quick!' Beaton began to feel flustered. People were popping their heads in and out of the doors of the Green Drawing Room – Prince Bernhard of the Netherlands, then the Duke of Edinburgh. Prince Charles and Princess Anne seemed to be running amok, climbing up and around and under their Aunt Margaret's purple velvet train. Only the Queen Mother exuded calm – 'the great mother figure and nanny to us all', wrapping everyone, Beaton felt, in a warm counterpane of reassurance. 'Suddenly I had this wonderful accomplice – someone who would help me through everything. All at once, and because of her, I was enjoying my work.' As the session

A production still from Episode 1 depicts Cecil Beaton at work with his shifting backdrops at the wedding of Elizabeth and Philip in 1947. In fact, it was the Duke of Edinburgh's friend Baron Nahum who took the photographs on that occasion – without any backdrops.

got under way, Prince Charles and Princess Anne were still buzzing about 'with the wildest excitement'. Their nannies were nowhere to be seen and they would not keep still, until 'the Queen Mother anchored them in her arms, put her head down to kiss Prince Charles's hair, and made a terrific picture'. In just a few flashes Beaton had snapped a set of informal and human images of the royal children he had never expected, plus a unique shot of the three-year-old Princess Anne, pacing out the long ermine run of her grandmother's train. 'Then, ashen-faced and like the wicked uncle in a pantomime, Richard Colville, who deals so sternly with all of us who are in any way connected with the Press, appeared prematurely and, as if to sound my death-knell, informed me: "The Queen has already been kept waiting. You must take the Queen now!"'

The crucial moment had arrived. 'In came the Queen with her ladies, cool, smiling, sovereign of the situation', and Beaton asked his subject to start by posing alone in front of his 'blow-up' backdrop of the abbey fan vaulting which, he had decided, would be reserved for his pictures of the Queen alone in her grandeur, holding orb and sceptre. 'The lighting was not at all as I would have wished, but no time for readjustments: every second of importance.'

He was working with an old-fashioned upright plate camera on a tripod, along with a Rolleiflex twin lens reflex camera which he kept hanging from a strap around his neck. As film needed replacing, Beaton reached behind him for a freshly charged camera from one of his assistants. 'I was banging away and getting pictures at a great rate,' he wrote, 'but I had only the foggiest notion of whether I was taking black and white, or colour, or giving the right exposures.' He also worried that

his subject 'looked extremely minute under her robes and Crown, her nose and hands chilled, and her eyes tired.' 'Yes,' she told him in reply to his question, 'the Crown does get rather heavy.' In the context of an entire reign, that was a quote for the history books, but for the moment photography took precedence. Somehow, getting the Queen to pivot forward, then look up at him as he photographed her from above, Beaton coaxed her into one of her rare and dazzling full-face 'monkey' smiles, with her astonishing array of teeth on display – a smiling Lilibet in black and white to partner the solemn and dignified sovereign he had shot in colour a few minutes earlier: no bags under the eyes, two photographs for the ages!

Now to photograph the heroine's husband, who, in Beaton's view, 'was definitely adopting a rather ragging attitude towards the proceedings'. The photographer felt on the back foot when it came to the Duke of Edinburgh, intimidated by his wry jokes and 'his lips pursed in a smile that put the fear of God into me. I believe he doesn't like or approve of me . . . Perhaps he was disappointed that his friend, Baron, was not doing this job today . . .' Lady Anne Coke, one of the maids of honour who knew about the rivalry with Baron, saw Beaton getting irritated by the way in which the Duke was obviously trying to take control, or perhaps even sabotage the proceedings, 'making suggestions about who should sit here and there', and she rather admired the courtesy with which the photographer finally snapped. 'Cecil just stopped very politely and firmly,' she recalled, 'and asked, "Would *you* like to take them, Sir?" There was no more trouble from the Duke.' Keeping the situation light, Beaton worked especially hard on a set of shots of Philip on his own, proudly recording in his diary that he had been able to make the Duke look 'extremely handsome'

'I tried,' wrote Beaton, 'in the few seconds at my disposal (like a vaudeville comedian establishing contact with his audience) to keep the situation light', and was rewarded with photographs that made the Duke of Edinburgh look 'extremely handsome'.

in his naval uniform. 'What shall we do now?' asked the Queen. 'Will you go into the corner?' replied Beaton in a quick and cursory manner that he instantly regretted. 'Go into the corner?' responded Elizabeth, her eyes wide open with surprise at his tone, but showing no offence. It was time for the final session of photographs of the six Maids of Honour grouped around their mistress, for which Patrick Matthews and the *Vogue* team had set up a sofa and lights in another corner of room. 'You must be tired, Ma'am,' Beaton asked. 'Yes,' she replied, 'but this is the last thing we have to do' – and with that she was off down the passage with Philip, the children, the maids and the rest of the family in her wake, all heading for the Palace balcony again to watch the RAF 'fly past'. Left alone in the suddenly deserted Green Drawing Room, Cecil and his sister Baba located a glass of champagne from which the Queen had been drinking, and drained its contents together in a loyal toast – but with a sense of anticlimax.

'I felt somewhat dissatisfied . . .' confessed the diarist. 'For better or worse, I'd had my chance . . . The sensation of achievement had escaped me all day long. Now I wondered if I had got any worthwhile pictures. Except with the Queen Mother and her grandchildren, I felt I'd never become airborne. The bulk of my pictures had been a smash and grab affair; I couldn't imagine they would be successful.' Baba and Cecil went home together through the rain feeling 'utterly whacked' – with a series of articles and interviews to complete for Australia and Canada on Cecil's impressions of the day. But at three in the morning, after some restorative food and drink at a French Embassy party, Beaton rang his studio to discover that they were delighted with the colour pictures of the Queen – the main object of the exercise – and when he went in early that morning to see

for himself, he was 'surprised that so many of the pictures were excellent'. Posterity has endorsed that judgement. The surreal, almost Hollywood nature of Beaton's confected abbey backdrops and studio lighting could have appeared artificial and even effete – as the Duke of Edinburgh and the Baron school of realism doubtless expected. But as the final pictures turned out, with the solid figure of the robed Queen with her regalia in the foreground, and the conviction on her features, both solemn and smiling, there was a transcendental glow to the images – Elizabeth's childhood 'haze of wonder' – or, as another critic has described it, 'the strangely transfiguring radiance that encircles those who occupy a throne'. Snapped in seconds, Cecil Beaton's 'smash and grab' portraits of June 1953 stand comparison with weighty coronation paintings from past centuries that eminent artists laboured for months to compose.

All that remained was to rush the prints and contact sheets to the Palace to have a selection approved for publication, then to get the chosen shots out to the world. 'The rest of the week was a complicated nightmare,' wrote Beaton, 'trying to supply to the Press the requisite number of pictures. Messengers were waiting in the various rooms of my mother's house for another messenger who never arrived. I talked myself hoarse on the phone.' Only by a fraction of a second did the exhausted photographer finally catch his train from Waterloo Station that Friday night to make his escape to the country, and, as he settled back in his seat at the end of his busy week of achievement, there he saw it – publication for the first time! 'One of my pictures of the Queen was planted across the front page of the *Evening News*!'

6

GELIGNITE

The Princess and the pilot

6

The magic of Elizabeth II's coronation was shattered with a speed that no one could have imagined – within minutes, in fact, of the new Queen being crowned. As the royal entourage moved out of Westminster Abbey at the end of the historic ceremony of 2nd June 1953, Princess Margaret reached out playfully to brush a piece of fluff from the uniform of the handsome Comptroller of her mother's recently formed household, RAF Group Captain Peter Townsend, DSO, DFC. The Princess ran her white-gloved hand along the medals above the war hero's breast pocket with a flirtatiousness that caught the eye of a watching journalist, and, with that gesture, the story of the new reign took a turn in a darker and more complicated direction. 'It didn't mean a thing to us at the time,' Peter Townsend was to tell the journalist Jean Rook many years later. 'It must have been a bit of fur coat I picked up from some dowager in the abbey. I never thought a thing about it.' But the press thought about it hard, and they drew their own conclusions.

In 1953, Princess Margaret's romance with a divorced man provoked the same conflicts of religion, politics, and changing social attitudes that shook the monarchy during the abdication crisis of 1936.

'Picking fluff off a man's jacket – that's a gesture as intimate as a kiss,' remarks Bill Mattheson, the sardonic muck-raking reporter devised by series creator Peter Morgan to ignite the 'Gelignite' of royal scandal in Episode 6 of *The Crown*. '[It's] *more* intimate, since it suggests the kiss has already happened.'

Princess Margaret first met Peter Townsend in February 1944 when she was 13 and wearing ankle socks, the very same age at which her elder sister had met and fallen in love with Philip. But whereas Lilibet's love affair with Philip developed over the years into a marriage that would provide a solid underpinning to the Crown, Margaret's romance with a divorced man led in record time to the same controversy and scandal that had produced the unforgettable crisis of 1936. 'Historically, when this lot brush up against divorce,' says Bill Mattheson to his editor, 'you end up with either Reformation or Abdication.'

In 1944, the two teenage princesses had been lying in wait to catch a glimpse of an exciting new recruit to the royal household – and Palace lore relates the 18-year-old Elizabeth's all-too-prophetic reaction: 'Bad luck, he's married!' Group Captain Townsend, 29 in February 1944, was arriving at the Palace as a new sort of equerry, a battle hero who would serve and stand beside the King. An equerry was the male equivalent of a lady-in-waiting, and it had been George VI's idea, in time of war, to replace the conventionally upper-crust holder of the job with an 'Equerry of

1950. Peter Townsend in the cockpit of the plane sponsored by Princess Margaret for his air races. The Group Captain was awarded the Distinguished Service Order and the Distinguished Flying Cross and bar for his service in the Second World War.

1946. Princess Margaret (aged 16), King George VI, Queen Elizabeth, Peter Townsend (aged 32) . . . and Princess Elizabeth (aged 20) attend a theatre performance in London's West End. At the time, Townsend was the King's equerry.

Honour', who had won the place by sheer valour – and who, frankly, deserved the cushiness of living for a spell in the company of the monarch.

Townsend was a Battle of Britain fighter ace. He had led crack squadrons of Hurricanes and Spitfires in a brave and sparkling career that included downing 11 enemy planes, being shot down twice and a brief period of mental strain and collapse – a 'nervous breakdown' in the language of the time. He had the good looks of a film star, and could deploy his delicate, slightly nervous charm in super-abundance. 'He was like Jean-Louis Barrault,' recalled the future Master of the Queen's Pictures, Sir Oliver Millar, referring to the dashing French actor of the time. 'You expected him at any moment to leap up lightly

onto the nearest chandelier.'

Townsend came from an honourable, empire-building background. Haileybury, his public school, had been founded to educate the sons of employees of the East India Company. In the 1940s the school's most famous alumnus was Clement Attlee, the Labour Party leader who had acquired his social conscience when working in the progressive Haileybury Mission that the school funded and ran in the East End of London.

Townsend's grandfather was a general in the Indian Army and his father was Deputy High Commissioner of Burma. Brought up among tiger skins and brass gongs, young Peter grew up with a strong sense of social service, with a tweaking

1953: Peter Townsend aged 38. His tour of duty at the Palace was originally supposed to be for three months. But he stayed for nearly 10 years.

of Eastern musings and mysticism. His decision to join the socially undistinguished RAF in the 1930s was a form of rebellion. 'At the time,' he remembered, 'it was not at all the right place for a nice young man to go.'

Townsend's tour of duty at the Palace was originally supposed to be for just three months, but he stayed for nearly 10 years. King George VI, who shared both a stammer and a love for the RAF with his calm and capable young assistant, found Townsend's sensitivity a balm as he grew increasingly unwell. He treated 'Peter', as he soon became to all the family, as the son he never had, and the King's wife also came to lean on the new equerry. 'Peter had a rather "lost" quality that was both vague and glamorous,' remembered Oliver Millar. 'It somehow fitted well with the Indian

summer character of those last years of George VI. He was not quite connected to reality – and when that was linked with his extreme good looks and genuine friendliness it turned out to make the situation, unintentionally, very dangerous indeed.'

The price of royal favour turned out to be the fighter ace's romantically hasty wartime marriage. His wife, Rosemary, became rapidly disenchanted with being left alone with two small children while her husband played cards and went to the opera with his grand adoptive family. After Princess Elizabeth married, Townsend was effectively co-opted as the elder sibling's replacement in the old Windsor family unit of 'Us Four', which now became Father, Mother, Margaret and Peter. 'There was a sense in which the King and Queen rather encouraged the closeness,' remembered Philip's friend Mike Parker.

To retain Townsend's services and congenial company, George VI eventually promoted the group captain from equerry to Deputy Master of the Household, a uniquely demanding post. The job not only required supervision of the chauffeurs, valets, cooks and cleaners who started work in the Palace at dawn, but Townsend was also expected to travel as a full-time Mr Fixit with the family, going everywhere, including Windsor, Sandringham and Balmoral, eating every meal at the royal table, and helping to organise the clan's beloved al fresco picnics. One modern holder of the post has calculated that these so-called 'holiday duties' alone kept him away from his wife for 90 days and nights a year – this particular Deputy Master resigned after five years.

In the old days, courtiers married women who took such separation for granted: royal service was seen as a type of military posting. But neither Peter nor Rosemary Townsend rose to the challenge. One courtier remembers a birthday party for one of Townsend's sons at Adelaide Cottage, the Townsend's grace and favour residence at Windsor, once the country retreat of Queen Adelaide, the wife of King William IV.

The telephone rang to ask if Peter would go riding with Princess Margaret, and, though he was not on duty, he jumped to the call. Rosemary, for her part, looked for solace outside the marriage. When the couple divorced, she took the legal role of the 'guilty party', not contesting her own adultery with John de Laszlo, son of Philip de Laszlo, the society portrait painter, whom she married in a matter of months (her second of three marriages). The divorce came through shortly after the death of George VI, leaving Townsend needy and available precisely at the moment when Princess Margaret was also in personal distress.

'After the king's death, there was an awful sense of being in a black hole,' the normally polished Princess frankly confessed to the royal historian Ben Pimlott 40 years later.

Often snootier than her elder sister, Margaret could also be more openly vulnerable, and it was in shared loss and pain that the Princess and the war hero came together. The romance might have started as early as 1947, according to several sources, when Townsend and Margaret went riding together on the royal tour of South Africa, and it grew secretly from there. But it was not until

the beginning of 1953, according to Townsend, a few months before the coronation, that matters came to a head, when the couple found themselves alone at Windsor Castle one day with the rest of the family up in London. 'She listened, without uttering a word,' recalled Townsend in his memoir, *Time and Chance*, 'as I told her, very quietly, of my feelings. Then she simply said: "That is exactly how I feel, too".'

Margaret told her sister almost immediately, and

1952: Princess Margaret heads out of Clarence House on royal duties with the Comptroller of her mother's household, Peter Townsend. The romance between the Princess and the Group Captain may have started as early as 1947 when they went riding together during the royal tour of South Africa.

the new Queen's response was faintly encouraging – and certainly sisterly. 'A few days later,' remembered Townsend in his memoir, 'at Buckingham Palace, Her Majesty invited us both to spend the evening with her and Prince Philip.' There was a friendly equality about the two young couples, each sister with her dashing and handsome military partner, and Townsend later recalled an atmosphere of informal supportiveness. No one was minimising the problems that lay ahead, with Philip making it his job to bring them up with the pointed banter that was becoming his trademark. Elizabeth herself was more opaque, and Townsend was impressed by her 'movingly simple and sympathetic acceptance of the disturbing fact of her sister's love for me'. But as he sat with his feet under the royal table, 'the thought occurred to me that the Queen, behind all her warm goodwill, must have harboured not a little anxiety'.

In 'Gelignite', Peter Morgan imagines the conversation that the Queen and her husband might have had that night as they prepared for bed – Elizabeth trying hard to support her sister, with Philip pointing out the difficulties, starting with the parallels to Edward VIII: 'Has everyone forgotten the catastrophe that was your uncle already?' 'The situation's different,' replies Elizabeth defensively. 'One party divorced?' retorts Philip. 'The other royal? Sounds pretty similar to me' – while he also brushes aside Elizabeth's protest that Peter had been the 'blameless' party in the divorce: 'There is no such thing as a blameless party in a divorce' is his riposte. Elizabeth's final argument tries to boost Townsend's comparative maturity, arguing that the elder man is 'a good influence' on Margaret. 'Is he?' replies Philip grimly. 'If he were really a good influence, he'd patch things up with his wife and leave Margaret well alone.'

In real life, Tommy Lascelles dished out the same grim medicine – to Peter Townsend's face. 'You must be either mad or bad,' declared the private secretary darkly, making no attempt to feign sympathy when Townsend went to the veteran courtier for help. The group captain should be removed at once, Lascelles advised the Queen – and as far away as possible to some remote overseas posting.

But, as Margaret's only sister and her closest confidante, Elizabeth declined to be so hardhearted. She agreed it was impossible for Townsend to stay in Clarence House, yet ignoring several back-room offices to which she could have dispatched him, she chose the post that brought him most visibly and frequently into contact with her. She made Townsend one of her own equerries. It was a sisterly and supportive gesture to Margaret – though with the coronation, at this point, just a few months away, it did not seem unreasonable for Elizabeth to ask the couple to keep everything private for the time being, and to wait to see how things might be worked out.

Margaret's careless gesture on Coronation Day was a poor repayment for her elder sister's understanding, for it disastrously sabotaged the key element of the agreement – that the romance should, for the moment, remain a secret. There was a lot of fixing to accomplish behind the scenes, particularly with Downing Street, before there could be any prospect of the marriage Margaret longed for, and publicity would hurt people on all sides. Subconsciously or otherwise, Margaret's public act of possessiveness was the ultimate upstaging by the younger sister, who, as Elizabeth once complained to Crawfie, 'always wants what I have'. Elizabeth II had got her crown on 2nd June 1953, but Princess Margaret had got her man, and as she left the scene of her sister's great triumph she could not resist showing off her own talisman.

A curious interlude ensued. American newspapers reported what came to be known as the 'tender hand' incident next day, in line with the speculation they had been printing about the couple for some months. Following the pattern of the abdication crisis, the British press kept silent.

But the self-restraint lasted less than two weeks, and when the dam broke on 14th June it was with typical Fleet Street self-righteousness, with newspapers repeating the foreign rumours of Margaret's love for a divorced man – 'It is high time for the British public to be made aware etc. etc.' – while suggesting that the rumours could not possibly be true. 'It is quite unthinkable,' pronounced the *People*, 'that a Royal Princess, third in line to the throne, should even contemplate a marriage with a man who has been through the divorce courts. Group Captain Townsend was the innocent party . . . But his innocence cannot alter the fact that a marriage between Princess Margaret and himself would fly in the face of Royal and Christian tradition.'

Down at Chartwell, his Kent country home, Winston Churchill's initial reaction was surprisingly favourable. The course of true love 'must always be allowed to run smooth', declaimed the Prime Minister benevolently when Tommy Lascelles arrived for a council of war. Why shouldn't the beautiful young Princess marry her handsome war hero? It took Clementine Churchill to remind her sentimental husband that he had made the very same mistake back in 1936, when his support for

'It is high time for the British public to be made aware'

Edward VIII and Mrs Simpson had proved so unpopular and politically damaging – and abdication parallels lay at the heart of the matter. For what purpose had the Duke of Windsor been made to suffer, if his niece was now allowed to marry a divorced man?

As in 1936, exile was the solution – though this time on a temporary basis. It was decided that Townsend would be dispatched as air attaché to the British Embassy in Brussels to work as a mixture of spy and salesman, reporting back to London on Belgian aviation developments and sniffing out commercial opportunities for the British aircraft industry. Margaret, for her part, would have to delay her marriage decision until after August 1955, when she would become 25. She would then be outside the scope of the Royal Marriages Act of 1772, which required the assent of the Queen – in other words, of the Prime Minister and cabinet, since this matter of public interest and debate was ultimately a political matter.

Public opinion, at least as measured in the newspapers, seemed wholeheartedly in favour of the couple being allowed to marry. On 13th July 1953, the *Daily Mirror* cheekily printed a 'Princess Poll' voting form on its front page that put the question in these terms: 'Group-Captain Peter Townsend, 38 years old Battle of Britain pilot, was the innocent party in a divorce. He was given custody of his two children, and his former wife has recently remarried. If Princess Margaret, now 22, so desires, should she be allowed to marry him?' No fewer than 70,000 readers took the trouble to fill in the form and post a reply (at the expense of a penny-halfpenny per letter) – a world record for a newspaper poll, according to the *Mirror* – with 67,907 voting in favour and only 2,235 against. The Press Council, the recently founded and voluntary body set up to organise the self-regulation of British journalism, promptly reprimanded the newspaper for its impertinence.

There is some reason to doubt whether the self-selected 67,907 'yes' voters of the *Daily Mirror* were representative of a country that, in 1953, was still socially conservative and quite heavily influenced by traditional religious values. A newspaper poll that had enquired two years earlier whether young people should have sex before they married came up with a 52 per cent vote for chastity for men, and 63 per cent for women. The reasons against pre-marital sex ranged from 'Marriage should be a new experience' to 'People wouldn't marry if they could get it without doing so'. Church attendances were falling, but people still expected public figures, and especially the royal family, to 'set a good example'. 'Life, especially for those in high places, is not for self-satisfaction,' wrote S. M. M. of Clapham Common to the *Daily Mirror* on 20th July 1953. 'Renunciation by Princess Margaret would be a wonderful example and proof of the faith she professes in the Church of England.' 'The laws of the Church of England on divorce are quite definite,' agreed P. F. Hall of Gerrards Cross in the same correspondence column. 'To suggest that a Christian should be allowed to break those laws to achieve her heart's desire is tantamount to suggesting that one may steal something just because one wants it.'

Daily Mirror

FRI JULY 17 1953

1½d **FORWARD WITH THE PEOPLE**
No. 15,450 ✦ ✦ ✦

Should Princess Margaret be allowed to marry Peter Townsend?

70,142 VOTE AND THE VERDICT IS: YES

THE "Daily Mirror's" call for the people's views on the problem of Princess Margaret and her friend Group-Captain Peter Townsend has resulted in the greatest poll in newspaper history.

The votes totalled 70,142 and more than 1,000 people wrote letters.

This is what the "Mirror's" voting form said:

● Group-Captain Peter Townsend, thirty-eight-year-old Battle of Britain pilot was the innocent party in a divorce. He was given the custody of his two children and his former wife has recently remarried.

● If Princess Margaret, now twenty-two, so desires, should she be allowed to marry him?

The result of the voting was:

Yes: 67,907
No: 2,235

The percentages were:

Yes .... 96.81 per cent.
No .... 3.19 per cent.

The "Daily Mirror" launched the poll in the belief that the views and feelings of the British people on the problem confronting a beloved Princess should be given expression. The amazing response of our readers indicates their deep interest in the subject, and more than justifies the holding of the poll.

Today Princess Margaret returns from Rhodesia to a Britain which knows that she and Group-Captain Townsend would like to marry.

She will have to wait while Church and State dignitaries discuss what, in their opinion, she may do or may not do.

The "Daily Mirror" poll gives a clear guide to the feelings of the PEOPLE of Britain.

☆

● THE GREAT DEBATE.—Points from the letters the "Mirror" has received will be published on Monday.

Rhodesia
Princess Margaret smiles and waves to officials as she boards the Comet in which she and the Queen Mother left for home yesterday, after their tour of Southern Rhodesia. They were due at London Airport at 8 a.m. today. And to welcome them—the Queen and the Duke of Edinburgh. The Comet had four scheduled stops on the way home, leaving Rome for the last "leg" of the flight at 4.15 this morning.

Brussels
Group-Captain Peter Townsend, former royal equerry, driving his car yesterday in Brussels where he has just taken up his appointment as Air Attache at the British Embassy.

●

He took up his duties at 10 a.m. in a 15ft. square office by signing the "handing-over chit" which put him in temporary possession of a small desk and three chairs in the office. He lunched with the Military Attache, Lieutenant-Colonel Drummond Wolff.

COLONEL CLEARED —'WITH HONOUR'

LIEUTENANT-COLONEL Alfred Gleave, 46, commanding officer of Moston Hall Military Hospital, Chester, was "honourably" acquitted by court-martial yesterday of charges arising out of the Dying Soldier case.

Findings of Not Guilty were returned at his trial at Saighton Camp, Chester.

The court took thirty-four minutes to consider their findings.

There was a burst of clapping in the small court-room when the verdict was read to Colonel Gleave.

Friends stepped forward to shake hands with the colonel and congratulate him.

Hearing is reported on Centre Pages.

July 1953: Tabloid newspaper debate over the issues raised by the romance between Princess Margaret and Peter Townsend demolished the previous barriers of reticence in press coverage of the royal family.

PRINCESS MARGARET

(1930–2002)

*Formerly Princess Margaret Rose,
later Countess of Snowdon*

PLAYED BY VANESSA KIRBY

'Already she is a public character,' mused Chips Channon after observing the polished yet oddly subversive Princess Margaret, aged 18, parading in her fashionable best during Ascot week in 1949, 'and I wonder what will happen to her? There is already a Marie Antoinette aroma about her.' When told of the comment, the Princess appeared not to understand. 'I wonder what he meant by that?' she asked – disingenuously, surely, since every royal knows the cautionary tale of the wilful French Queen who played at being a shepherdess and ended up a victim of the guillotine. It was not difficult to see the parallel in the pleasure-loving Princess and her 'Princess Margaret set' who haunted London's dance floors to the small hours of the morning in the 1940s and 1950s, while she privately set her heart on a marriage to a divorcee that flouted the canons of the established Church. 'I am terrified of being bored' was Marie Antoinette's motto, and Margaret certainly seemed to practise that.

GROUP CAPTAIN
PETER TOWNSEND
(1 9 1 4 – 9 5)

PLAYED BY BEN MILES

In February 1940, fighter pilot Peter Townsend shot down a German bomber – the first to fall on British soil since the First World War. Twenty months of heady and heedless combat later, he retired from active service with the Distinguished Service Order, the Distinguished Flying Cross and bar – and the shredded nerves of a man haunted by perpetual fear. 'The fight had gone out of me,' he wrote. 'I had flown myself to a standstill.' The heady and heedless adventures that marked the rest of his life left him similarly scarred. From the ruins of a hasty wartime marriage sprang his ill-fated romance with Princess Margaret and a series of dogfights he could never win with British courtiers, politicians and, most merciless of all, the British press. In every scrap, Townsend displayed the naïve bravery, honesty and unfailing courtesy that had won him the trust of George VI, never an easy king to please. But was 'dear Peter' guilty of betraying that trust when he took the King's daughter on their adventure to the heavens from which neither could hope to return to earth unscathed?

Winston Churchill knew how many of his Tory MPs would nod sagely at such opinions and decided, on reflection, there was no chance he could persuade his cabinet to give approval to a Margaret–Townsend marriage in 1953, even though there were divorcees among his ministers, starting with his number two Anthony Eden, who had recently remarried (this time to Churchill's own niece, Clarissa). Margaret would have to delay her gratification for another two years – and that posed something of a challenge to a young woman who was accustomed to getting her own way.

'I am unique,' Princess Margaret was given to pronouncing over dinner, à propos of nothing in particular. 'I am the daughter of a King and the sister of a Queen.' The derivative nature of this conversation stopper summed up the unhappiness of the Queen's younger sister, who spent her life struggling to establish a satisfying identity of her own. A birthright of incredible privilege that could have been a platform for constructive endeavour was never quite fulfilled, leaving the Princess with the perpetual grievance of the also-ran – to which a succession of backstairs anecdotes bore witness.

In 1937, for example, while trying on their robes for their father's coronation, the six-year-old Margaret was said to have thrown a fit when she discovered that the purple velvet train edged with ermine behind her ceremonial outfit was cut slightly shorter than that of her elder sister. It wasn't fair, she complained, and she flung herself to the floor in a tantrum. Only when it

1943: Princess Margaret Rose, 13, watches while her sister Elizabeth, 17, broadcasts to the children of the Empire during the Second World War. At this stage of their lives, Margaret was next in the line of royal succession.

was explained to her that the two sisters' trains had been designed in direct proportion to their height – and that Lilibet was nearly four inches taller – was the Princess placated, and then only grudgingly so. 'What a good thing,' courtiers would murmur, 'that Margaret is the *younger* one.'

In adult life, according to Lord Snowdon's biographer Anne de Courcy, Margaret's inferiority complex showed itself in her lack of consideration towards the staff that she shared with her mother in Clarence House. If there was a Christmas party 'down the road' at Buckingham Palace to which the staff of Clarence House were invited, the Queen Mother would arrange to dine out that evening, or eat something light so that her servants could get to the party – while Princess Margaret, to the contrary, would make a point of arranging

a full-scale dinner party for that very night. Such perversity, suggested de Courcy, 'could perhaps be explained by the fact that, unlike the Queen Mother and the Queen, who had successively been the first lady in the land, Princess Margaret, always number two, was determined to insist on her royal status'. Kenneth Rose, the royal confidant and biographer of King George V, used to attempt a brave defence of the Princess's sometimes contrary behaviour. 'We show no lack of sympathy,' he once declared, 'for those who are denied an inspiring education for social reasons like poverty or colour. But there are shortcomings at both ends of the social scale.

The two princesses Elizabeth and Margaret Rose were not educated in a rigorous or testing fashion. They never experienced the challenge of going

27 June, 1953

PICTURE
POST

THE PRINCESS
Leader
of fashion

Colour pages inside

4ᴰ | THE STORY OF THE WOMEN'S INSTITUTE | 3-D NIGHT CLUB IN A | 3-D SPECTACLES FREE

27 JUNE 1953   HULTON'S NATIONAL WEEKLY   VOL 59 · NO 13

27th June 1953: Fashion was the excuse for putting the Princess on this magazine cover when US newspapers were discussing her romance, but British newspapers were ignoring the story. The news broke in London on 3rd July.

to school – and that certainly left an unsatisfied appetite in the younger of the two sisters.' From private conversations with the Princess, Rose learned how bitterly she resented not being allowed to accompany her elder sister, or even to follow her at a later age, when Elizabeth was sent for constitutional history lessons at Eton College with the vice-provost Henry Marten in the early 1940s. At that stage in their lives, after all, Margaret was next in the line of succession.

Her grandmother Queen Mary also worried about the deficiencies of both girls' home-schooling. 'Queen Mary tried to beef up the princess's lessons,' recalled Rose, 'but Queen Elizabeth didn't think education [for women] necessary.' Rose related how the former Princess May of Teck, herself extremely cultured and well versed in the fine arts, took up the matter with her daughter-in-law Queen Elizabeth – only for her plea to fall on stony ground. 'I don't know what she's complaining about,' the home-schooled Queen Elizabeth later said to her friends. 'My sisters and I were all educated at home by a governess and we all married very well. In fact, you might say that one of us married very well indeed!'

To Margaret's credit, she did make valiant efforts to educate herself, particularly in the artistic subjects that fired her imagination – history, art, architecture, dance, music and theatre. She seems to have been the origin of the famous wartime Windsor pantomimes that grew out of a modest nativity play that the Princesses performed with child evacuees during the second Christmas of the war, in December 1940. Margaret sang 'Gentle Jesus, meek and mild' so affectingly in the nativity play that her father was moved to tears. 'I wept through most of it,' wrote the King in his diary, and when Marion Crawford suggested that the

girls might attempt something more ambitious the following year, the younger Margaret leapt at the idea. 'From that moment,' the governess later wrote, 'I had no peace. Margaret was after me incessantly. "Crawfie, you did say . . ." she would begin a dozen times a week.'

The 10-year-old was so keen she started designing costumes and sets, pushing her father until he gave permission for the ambitious series of pantomime productions that became the highlight of Windsor Christmases during the war. She also worked seriously at her own mastery of music, and of the piano in particular. Princess Margaret Rose (she dropped the 'Rose' soon after she became a teenager) made a point of growing up more rapidly than her elder sister, delightedly abandoning the velvet-collared coats (and ankle socks) of childhood. She was not yet 14 when she made her first public speech in July 1944, visiting the Princess Margaret Royal Free School in Windsor, named in her honour. Accompanied by her mother, she felt 'dreadfully sick' with nerves and did not enjoy the experience. But she fared better two years later, on her first solo engagement, when she opened the Hopscotch Inn, a children's play centre in Camden, north London. 'One has to remember that she was only fifteen at the time,' recalled Audrey Russell, sent by the BBC to cover the event in March 1946, 'but I was first struck by her marvellous poise. I think she was trying very hard to follow her mother's example, talking to everybody and asking questions all the time, which she did very professionally.'

By the time she was 16, Princess Margaret had that poise in abundance, stylishly dressing in tailored suits, designer hats, silk stockings and high-heels, with long dresses of silk, satin or chiffon for evenings. Her father had organised her

own coat of arms, to be followed by a specially created cipher for her personal use – a classically styled 'M' beneath a coronet embossed in red on her private stationery. 'Let us pray . . . for Princess Margaret,' pronounced the chaplain at Crathie Church, Balmoral, when she celebrated her eighteenth birthday in August 1948, 'that God may bless and prosper her in such purposes as she has in her heart.' With Elizabeth's love and marriage an old story, the press now turned their attentions towards the sophisticated younger sister, her complexion 'smooth as a peach', her curvaceous figure and 18-inch waist, with her vivid blue eyes – 'the only thing about me worth looking at', she once said. Reporters suggestively described her lips as both 'generous' and 'sensitive', for while it was not done to say as much in so many words, sex appeal was the fresh ingredient that Princess Margaret brought to the royal package. She was talked of as 'one of the beauties of her generation'. She did prefer her friends to curtsey and to call her 'Ma'am', but after a few gin and tonics she was the life and soul of every party.

Noël Coward was impressed when he encountered her in November 1949 at a private dinner party at the American Embassy. 'Princess Margaret obliged with songs at the piano,' noted 'The Master' in his diary. 'Surprisingly good. She has an impeccable ear, her piano playing is simple but has perfect rhythm, and her method of singing is really very funny.' Invited to entertain a Scottish

April, 1953. Two months before the coronation, Peter Townsend (standing left) was at the heart of the royal family on their favourite Easter outing to the Badminton Horse Trials in Gloucestershire with the Queen (front right) and Princess Margaret (with cigarette holder).

cleric who came to tea with her parents, Margaret launched into a spirited rendering of 'I'm Just a Girl Who Can't Say No' from the Rodgers and Hammerstein hit musical *Oklahoma!* – to the horror of her mother and the delight of her father, whose roar of regal laughter made it clear to the minister that he was expected to laugh as well. 'Espiègle' – 'roguish' – was Queen Mary's word for her granddaughter's sense of mischief, a corruption of the French name for Till Eulenspiegel, the peasant prankster of German folklore. 'She is so outrageously amusing,' remarked the Queen, 'that one can't help encouraging her.' 'Elizabeth is my pride,' said George VI on one telling occasion, 'and Margaret is my joy.' The King had egged on his irreverent younger daughter, a natural mimic, to indulge her cheekiness from an early age, and in this glow of parental approval Margaret had developed a more extrovert personality than Elizabeth: less solemn, less conscientious – and altogether less well mannered.

This was the nub of the problem: Princess Margaret was, quite simply, spoilt. Her elders indulged her because she was amusing, but also because they felt she was owed something – some correction or compensation for her junior role in the royal set-up, with Princess Elizabeth feeling most guilty of all. A cook from the Yorks' home at 145 Piccadilly in the mid-1930s recalled how the elder sister would go out of her way to spare Margaret the more arduous duties of the girls' compulsory housework by taking them on herself.

Conscious of her own seniority and advantages, the elder sibling seems to have bent over backwards to 'be nice to Margaret' in the family

'Let us pray . . . for Princess Margaret'

'That's when I really fell in love with him.'

tradition – when it might actually have benefited Margaret to have a nasty elder sister who put her in her place from time to time. 'We are only young once, Crawfie,' her mother told Marion Crawford when the governess, still on the family payroll in the late 1940s, expressed her concerns that Margaret was 'all over the place' after a succession of late nights out. 'We want her to have a good time. With Lilibet gone, it is lonely for her here.'

So Margaret took to lolling in bed of a morning – 10 or 10.30 came to be her routine breakfast time for the rest of her life – after long nights out with a group of young people that the newspapers took to calling 'the Princess Margaret Set', all of them high-spirited and of independent means, with none of them needing to start their day early: Old Etonian Billy Wallace; Colin Tennant, the future Lord Glenconner; 'Sonny' Blandford, the future Duke of Marlborough; and American Sharman Douglas, the ebullient daughter of Lewis Douglas, Harry Truman's ambassador to The Court of St James. 'Princess Margaret High Kicks It!' ran the headline over one description of a ball at the American Embassy where the Princess and Jennifer Bevan, her first lady-in-waiting, danced a well-rehearsed can-can with Sharman Douglas and three other girlfriends, all dressed in authentic frilly petticoats, black fishnet stockings and feathered bonnets. 'Princess Margaret is great news value . . .' wrote Cecil Beaton in his diary

when he took the photographs for her twenty-first birthday in 1951. 'She is grown-up – an independent character showing more signs of interest in unconventional life than any member of the royal family since Edward Prince of Wales.' A few years earlier, Duff Cooper, the former British Ambassador to Paris, had put it even more directly after a Buckingham Palace luncheon party at which Margaret had shone in 1948 – 'lovely skin, lovely eyes, lovely mouth, very sure of herself and full of humour . . . She might get into trouble before she's finished.'

Neither Beaton nor Cooper knew about Peter Townsend when they made their prophetic diary entries, but by at least one account Princess Margaret had made up her mind about him the previous year, during the February–April 1947 royal tour of South Africa. 'We rode together every morning in that wonderful country, in marvellous weather,' the Princess told a confidante. 'That's when I really fell in love with him.' It was also, presumably, when she fell out of love with being royal, since renunciation was the only possible price of the man she had come to desire. Did Princess Margaret really want to be a princess? Once the gallant group captain went off to Brussels in July 1953, she had just over two years to make up her mind.

'*Princess Margaret is great news value*' *wrote Cecil Beaton in his diary when he took this photograph of the princess wearing a Christian Dior ball gown in Buckingham Palace on the occasion of her twenty-first birthday in the summer of 1951. 'She likes dressing up, flirtations, going to nightclubs until all hours. Her "press" is rather scandalous. The American papers [are] most anxious for any snippets they can get of her . . .'*

Defender of
the Faith

Every modern British coin carries the face of Queen Elizabeth II. Along with all the trillions of bank notes and postage stamps bearing her effigy that have been issued since 1952, it makes the Queen's face the most multiplied and duplicated set of features in human history. The letters around the rim of the coins also indicate the religious nature of her authority – 'D G', standing for *Dei Gratia* ('By the Grace of God'), alongside 'F D' or sometimes 'FID DEF', both abbreviations for the Queen's Latin title *Fidei Defensor*, 'Defender of the Faith'.

This historic and religious title, first won and proudly borne by her Tudor predecessor King Henry VIII, indicates that Elizabeth II is not merely an earthly monarch. 'Elizabeth the Second, by the Grace of God,' runs her full official designation, 'of the United Kingdom of Great Britain and Northern Ireland and of Her Other Realms and Territories Queen, Head of the Commonwealth, Defender of the Faith.' So, the Queen's special role in the protection and governance of the Churches of both England and Scotland gives her links to the divine – or to divine law, at least. That was why Elizabeth II encountered such trouble in 1953 when her sister wanted to marry a man who was divorced.

Fidei Defensor is a curious title in several respects. Henry VIII did not earn it personally – it was the reward from a grateful Pope Leo X in 1521 for a ghost-written pamphlet composed for Henry by his future Lord Chancellor Thomas More (executed by Henry in 1535). Even more curious, the

King Henry VIII (1509-47) with his third wife, Jane Seymour, and his only son, the future King Edward VI. Henry was proud to have won and passed on to Edward and all succeeding English monarchs, the title 'Defender of the Faith'.

pamphlet was a stoutly anti-Protestant broadside, the *Defence of the Seven* [Catholic] *Sacraments*, aimed against Martin Luther, the inspirer of the European Reformation – and the Pope indignantly revoked the title after Henry reversed himself and followed Luther's example to break away from Rome.

It was Henry VIII's urgent and increasingly angry desire to divorce Catherine of Aragon, and the Pope's refusal to grant him his wish, that led to the English Reformation and the creation of the Anglican Church in 1534. But that did not prevent the now-Protestant English Parliament from reviving the popish title and bestowing it

upon Henry in 1544 – and FID DEF has been sported proudly by British monarchs and coins ever since. When a two-shilling piece (or 'florin') was inadvertently issued in 1849 bearing Queen Victoria's head without the magic letters, there was national outrage and the 'godless florin' was withdrawn from circulation. Henry VIII's other religious title was 'Head of the Church of England', also bestowed on him by Parliament through the Act of Supremacy of 1534. Renouncing Rome and

Henry's younger daughter Queen Elizabeth I (1588–1603) modified her father's title as 'Head' of the Church of England to become 'Supreme Governor' – on the grounds that only God Himself could rule as the head of the Church.

Queen Elizabeth II shown on the face of a 1953 sixpence, with her Latin title: 'ELIZABETH II DEI GRATIA REGINA' — 'Elizabeth II, by the Grace of God, Queen'.

declaring the King to be 'the only supreme head in earth of the Church of England', the act effectively gave Henry the eminence of an English pope – or more precisely, perhaps, the quasi-spiritual authority of the Holy Roman emperors who had claimed lordship over Europe since the days of the Emperor Charlemagne.

Henry's Catholic daughter Mary renounced the headship during her brief reign from 1553 to 1558, but her sister Queen Elizabeth I restored the dignity to herself in modified form as 'Supreme Governor' – on the grounds that only God could rule as the head of a Church.

In 1563, the thirty-seventh of the Church of England's 39 Articles set out the powers of the Supreme Governor as they have lasted to the present day: 'The King's Majesty hath the chief power in this realm of England, and other his Dominions, unto whom the chief Government of all Estates of this Realm, whether they be Ecclesiastical or Civil, in all causes doth appertain.'

Meeting at Canterbury in 1563, the convocation of Anglican archbishops, bishops,

deans, archdeacons and proctors made very clear that 'we give not to our Princes the ministering of God's Word, or of the sacraments'. It was not for the Supreme Governor, in other words, to preach sermons or to lay down theology – so, jumping to 1953, the question of divorce was not a matter on which Elizabeth II was supposed to have any doctrinal opinion or personal authority. But as the Church's earthly protector and manager, it was her job to defend the reputation and authority of the Church's canons or doctrinal laws, 'which we see,' continued Article 37, 'to have been given always to all godly Princes in Holy Scriptures by God himself'. At her coronation in June 1953 – even as she was pondering over the quandary that her sister and Peter Townsend had just laid in front of her – Elizabeth solemnly swore to 'maintain and preserve inviolably the settlement of the Church of England, and the doctrine, worship, discipline, and government thereof, as by law established in England'. So, since the Church had its face set against divorce, Elizabeth had no choice but to follow that direction. The Crown's Church responsibilities doubled in 1603, when the death of Queen Elizabeth I brought King James VI and I (James VI of Scotland and James I of England)

On the obverse is an abbreviation of the Latin title 'FID DEF', 'Defender of the Faith' with the national flowers of England (rose), Scotland (thistle), Wales (leek) and Ireland (shamrock).

down to London from Edinburgh. The Church of Scotland recognised only Jesus Christ as 'King and Head of the Church', so there was no question of any title of Supreme Governor north of the border. But from 1603 it became the duty of the Kings of England, in their capacity as Kings of Scotland, to swear to 'preserve the settlement of the true Protestant religion as established by the laws made in Scotland' – and this was formalised in the 1707 Act of Union between England and Scotland.

To this day, new British monarchs make no mention of the Church of England when they accede to the throne – that is dealt with later when they swear their oaths at their coronation. But the first item of business at their Accession Council, usually held on the day following the death of their predecessor, is to swear to defend and uphold the Scottish Presbyterian Church. Elizabeth II made such a pledge at the first Privy Council meeting of her reign, following her return from Africa in February 1952.

'I was just wondering,' says Elizabeth on the telephone to her sister Margaret in Episode 6 of *The Crown*, 'if you and Peter [had] considered

Scotland . . . Marriage isn't regarded as a sacrament in the Church of Scotland. It's not as binding in the same way as here.' Margaret jumps at this idea in the dialogue imagined by Peter Morgan. 'Meaning,' she asks, 'we could even get married in a church?' 'I'd have to check,' replies Elizabeth. 'But I think so . . . It would make my life a lot easier, too.' In the event, the Scottish option did not provide an easy way for Elizabeth and Margaret to sidestep their dilemma. Divorce and the taboos attached to it in 1953 were no minor matter. Ongoing convocations of the Church of England – effectively the parliament of the Church – had consistently pronounced against the remarriage of divorced persons, and Elizabeth had no choice but to comply with what those convocations said. That was the reason, after all, why she was now occupying the throne. The historical irony, of course, was that the Church of England had been created, and Elizabeth was bound by its rulings, because Henry VIII had himself wanted a divorce.

7

SCIENTIA POTENTIA EST

Knowledge is power

7

Inkwells and exercise books – with the occasional croak from a bright-eyed pet raven. We join Episode 7 of *The Crown* in a dimly lit schoolmaster's study, where a glossy black-plumaged bird hops among the piles of volumes scattered in cheerful chaos across the floor. The raven cocks her head knowingly from side to side, then flies up on to the shoulder of the venerable tutor to give his ear a friendly peck. No, we have not ventured into the fictitious world of Harry Potter. We have stumbled upon the historic den of Henry Marten, the eccentric and raven-owning Vice-Provost of Eton College, Windsor, as re-created for *The Crown* from the memories of his students in the 1940s – one of whom was the future Queen Elizabeth II. 'There are two elements of the Constitution . . .' we hear Henry Marten explaining to the young Elizabeth as Episode 7 begins, 'the "efficient" and the "dignified". Which is the monarch?' His pupil appears distracted by the raven, which has now perched on the back of the Vice-Provost's chair. 'Your Royal Highness?' he prompts her.

Royal apprenticeship. In April 1942, 10 days before her sixteenth birthday, George VI prepares his daughter Elizabeth for one of her future duties as Queen – to peruse the government documents sent for her daily inspection in their red leather-bound dispatch cases – 'The Boxes'.

'The dignified,' comes her belated response. 'Very good,' says Marten approvingly. 'The "efficient" has the power to make and execute policy and is answerable to the electorate. "What touches all should be approved by all".' With Elizabeth remaining transfixed by the antics of the raven, the vice-provost moves towards the climax of his exposition: 'The two institutions – Crown and government – the dignified and the efficient – only work when they support each other. When they *trust* each other. You can underline that.' And the young Elizabeth duly underlines the word 'trust' in her exercise book. 'Trust' becomes a highly significant word in the episode that follows . . .

Princess Elizabeth was just 13 when Henry Marten was assigned the task of teaching her the complexities of the British Constitution – in the summer of 1939, with Germany poised to invade Poland, the trigger for the Second World War. The 66-year-old tutor came cycling up from Eton to Windsor Castle, sometimes forgetting to remove his bicycle clips as he embarked on his lessons.

The Princess rather enjoyed his forget-fulness, along with the way in which the vice-provost started each session with the salutation he used to his Eton pupils, 'Gen'lemen!' The lessons turned into a correspondence course when the family went away – for both holidays and reasons of safety – to Balmoral and Sandringham. But as Elizabeth grew older, with the royal family firmly based in Windsor, she would make the journey to Marten on foot and accompanied by only her governess, Marion Crawford – as we see on screen at the start of Episode 7. Out of the Henry VIII Gateway and down the hill the young Princess would walk, across the bridge over the Thames and along Eton High Street through the medieval, pillared gates of the college past the tail-coated students – their black gowns flapping on a windy day rather like ravens themselves – to end up in the wizard's den.

On 12th March 1945, after nearly six years of lessons, George VI came down to Eton to bestow a knighthood on the much-loved tutor in recognition of his work with Princess Elizabeth. The dubbing ceremony took place on the steps of the college chapel in front of the Queen, the two princesses and several hundred cheering pupils, and the new Sir Henry served out the rest of his life as Provost of the College, bequeathing his library to Eton when he died, including the volumes from which he had instructed the young Princess.

From the outside, they look like any other set of dry and faded old schoolbooks that you might find at a jumble sale – Sir William Anson's *The Law and Custom of the Constitution* in three volumes. But they are kept under lock and key in the Marten Library, for when you open volume I (*Parliament*,

SIR HENRY MARTEN

(1872–1948)

Vice-Provost of Eton College
Constitutional History Tutor to Elizabeth II

PLAYED BY MICHAEL COCHRANE

Dispensing sugar lumps from his pocket to feed his pet raven, the avuncular Henry Marten had the knack of maintaining the interest of his pupils at Eton. 'Now, gen'lemen,' he would say, as he embarked on one of his stories from British history that would vividly bring the past to life. 'He was the first of my teachers,' said Lord Home, who later became one of Elizabeth II's prime ministers, 'to make me realise that the characters of history had once been human beings like us.' The vice-provost evidently communicated the same enthusiasm to his young royal pupil. When Queen Victoria's granddaughter, Princess Marie Louise (1872–1956), who was proud to have lived through six reigns (from Victoria to Elizabeth II), once apologised to the future Queen for talking so much about what had happened in the past, Princess Elizabeth looked surprised. 'But cousin Louise,' she replied without hesitating, 'it's history, and therefore so thrilling!'

'It's history, and therefore so thrilling!'

The Princesses Elizabeth, 13, and Margaret Rose, 8, visit the headquarters of the YWCA (Young Women's Christian Association) in Great Russell Street, London, in May 1939 as one of their excursions to get to know the outside world, organised by their governess Marion Crawford (right, holding the hand of Princess Margaret). Their mother's lady-in-waiting, Lady Helen Graham (left), leads the way to another real world experience – a trip home on the 'Tube'.

fifth edition) you discover a rare signature inside – 'Elizabeth, 1944' – followed by neat, pencilled comments in a round and still childlike hand: the notes of the 18-year-old Princess on how to be a queen.

In choosing Henry Marten, Elizabeth's parents had done their best to ensure that a dry subject should be taught in a stimulating fashion. The vice-provost was an outsized and whimsical character with a gift for storytelling – 'a dramatic, racy, enthusiastic teacher', according to Old Etonian Sir Alec Douglas-Home, Elizabeth's fourth prime minister – well known for sucking on his handkerchief, almost as a comforter, when explaining some especially complicated passage from history. 'Books cascaded from the shelves, surging over tables and chairs in apparent disorder,' recalled one of his pupils. Elizabeth's hours in this wizard's cave, where the piles of books on the floor grew 'like sta- lagmites' according to Crawfie, was the closest that the future Queen ever came to 'going to school', and some years later her Merlin made a revealing disclosure.

Whenever Sir Henry had posed a question to the 13-year-old, he noticed that she did not reply directly. In the early years of her lessons, at least, the Princess was so unused to being quizzed that her first instinct was to turn away from her teacher and 'look for confidence and support to her beloved governess, Miss Crawford'. The answer when she did make it was 'almost invariably correct', and it was not as if Princess Elizabeth lacked social con- fidence in a public forum. By the age of 13 she was already starting to make short speeches – as

when the President of France came to London on a state visit in the spring of 1939. The teenage Princess, who was so shy that she could not give a direct answer to the kindly Dr Marten, was able to welcome President Lebrun with a fluent speech in well-rehearsed French. Her social skills might not measure up to those of an 'ordinary', run- around-the-playground child of her age – but they were exactly what she would need for her future job. Not blurting out a quick, personal response, but turning to others for advice – the cautious, sideways style of the figurehead monarch.

From the carefully marked volumes of Anson's *The Law and Custom of the Constitution* we can reconstruct the principles that Henry Marten stressed to his pupil, for here was a job description of monarchy that went far beyond unveiling plaques and waving graciously to the crowds. Anson picturesquely introduced the British Constitution as 'a somewhat rambling structure . . . like a house which many successive owners have altered'.

> '*You might as well adopt a father as make a monarchy.*'

This was a clue to its essential char- acteristic, explained a passage that attracted one of the Princess's first pencil markings, carefully underlined where appropriate: 'the more complex a constitution, the more guarantees of liberty it offered'. The Chinese Empire was held up to the student as an example of crude autocracy, while the US Constitution with all its amendments over the years was presented as an example of the complications that liberty requires to flourish. Alongside his British constitutional tutoring of Elizabeth, Henry Marten threw in an extra course on American history.

There were relatively few notes in the margin on the prerogatives of the Crown, and some passing glances at constitutional development. The Anglo-Saxon monarchy was described as 'a consultative' and 'tentative absolutism' – here the Princess underlined the words 'consultative' and 'tentative' – with the Witenagemot, the 'meeting of wise men', the royal council of great landowners and bishops known as the Witan for short, being portrayed as an early form of Parliament. 'If the King had a strong will,' wrote Anson, 'and a good capacity for business, he ruled the witan; if not, the witan was the prevailing power in the State.' (Princess Elizabeth's emphasis again.)

To teach the Princess about the powers that she would wield as Queen, Marten supplemented Anson with the thoughts of Walter Bagehot, the Victorian founder of the *National Review* and editor-in-chief of *The Economist*, who first articulated the distinction between the 'dignified' and 'efficient' functions of government in his book *The English Constitution*, published in 1867. Whereas Anson, a cerebral classicist, lawyer and Member of Parliament with an interest in education, would solemnly set out the historical and legal precedents for the nation's evolving methods of government, Bagehot revelled in the philosophical and even irrational aspects of the Crown, rather savouring its emotional appeal. 'The mystic reverence, the religious allegiance, which are essential to a true monarchy,' he wrote, 'are imaginative sentiments that no legislature can manufacture in any people. You might as well adopt a father as make a monarchy.' Kings emerged favourably from the pages of both Anson and Bagehot, depicted as generally benign and protective figures, with an instinct for the common weal. But the principal focus of the 13-year-old's pencilled attention was on the power of Parliament

– the voice and instrument of the people. This was where she set to annotating seriously. She marked the basic principle that 'what touches all should be approved by all', noting that Parliament had the power to effect any change it wished, to such an extent that no Parliament could bind its successors irrevocably. Reflecting different circumstances and the will of the people, a new Parliament could always undo the work of those who went before.

Pupil and teacher clearly worked hard at mastering the abstruse technicalities of legislation, leading up to the royal assent at the end of the parliamentary process, which formally turned bills into law. The Princess's notes traced the procedures for the passing of finance or money bills, and the observation that, when it came to practical transactions, 'every change of recent times has tended to enhance the power of the Cabinet.' The longest passage of all, a full page of pencilled notes where Sir Henry had evidently abandoned Anson's text to deliver one of his famous 'great tales' from British history, related the day-by-day events of James II's ignominious flight from his throne in 1688. It was a well-told story, culminating in the King throwing the Great Seal of the Realm, the ultimate expression of his royal authority, into the River Thames – the 17th-century parallel to the 20th-century abdication.

The message of Anson, Bagehot and Henry Marten was clear: the monarch of the day might wear the crown, but in the age of mass democracy the true king was Parliament, and no modern sovereign should forget it. The era when monarchs called or dissolved Parliaments without the advice of elected ministers was dismissed as 'the days before responsible government', with Elizabeth noting the differences between dissolving, proroguing and adjourning Parliament.

Her notes traced the procedural minutiae that might fill the head of the ultimate civil servant and, in one sense, that is what this little girl was to become – the most civil of national servants.

In these painstaking preparations for her future life and work, we can find the roots of the modern Elizabeth II, diligent mistress of the red boxes full of government documents sent to her every day of her reign – even, on occasion, at Christmas. No sovereign in history would read and mark more sheets of paper more dutifully. 'Do you teach this to your other pupils?' asks the young Elizabeth in the dialogue imagined by series creator Peter Morgan. 'No,' Marten replies, 'just you' – reaching for a sheaf of algebra, trigonometry and English comprehension papers for her to leaf through. 'This is what I teach them.' 'Shouldn't I know all of this too?' Elizabeth asks wide-eyed as she reviews the range and detail of the different subjects. 'No, Ma'am,' answers Marten, his reply punctuated by the raven's squawk. 'All very undignified . . .'

The developing theme of the episode is how Elizabeth came to feel dissatisfied with the limited focus of her education, denying her the power (*potentia*) that comes with knowledge (*scientia*). But when it came to the first major constitutional crisis of her reign, it turned out that Anson, Bagehot and Henry Marten had really served her quite solidly. The crisis stemmed from her 79-year-old prime minister Winston Churchill and his failing health. There had already been the scare of February 1952, diagnosed by his doctor, Charles Moran, as an arterial 'spasm', when Churchill had temporarily lost his powers of speech (see

Chapter 4, p. 116). Now, on the evening of 24th June 1953, only three weeks after the coronation, the prime minister had just finished a sparkling after-dinner speech in Downing Street in honour of his visiting Italian counterpart – Churchill's remarks had centred humorously on how much the ancient Britons had benefited from the Roman conquest – when he slumped backwards in his chair, the lower left corner of his mouth drooping slackly.

He managed to say goodbye to his guests without rising, but his son-in-law Christopher Soames and Jock Colville, his private secretary, had to help him to his bedroom. Next day, Moran diagnosed another 'spasm' in a small artery of the brain, and said the prime minister could not possibly attend the forthcoming cabinet meeting.

Churchill ignored his doctor's advice. At cabinet on 25th June, R. A. Butler, the chancellor of the exchequer, noticed how the prime minister seemed uncharacteristically reluctant to speak, reticently delegating different parts of the agenda to the appropriate ministers with a wave of his hand. But no one suspected anything was wrong, and that afternoon Churchill was driven down to Chartwell. Next morning, Friday 26th June 1953, Colville was working in the library at Chartwell when Dr Moran came in. The prime minister, he said, might well not live through the next four days and seemed destined for long-term incapacity at the best. His paralysis was getting worse, so that one whole side was now out of action. 'I think it is quite likely,' said the doctor, 'that he will die during the weekend.'

The news was even worse than it seemed. The prospect of Churchill's death was bad enough, but that very day Anthony Eden, Churchill's heir apparent since the early 1940s, was in America at the Lahey Clinic in Boston, undergoing a bile duct operation from which he would take several months to recover. The 56-year-old foreign secretary was not in good health, often in pain from a duodenal ulcer and turning increasingly to the black tin box of pain

'I think it is quite likely that he will die'

Anthony Eden and Winston Churchill tried hard to look friends when they posed on the steps of Downing Street in May 1954. But behind the scenes, Eden, 56, was plotting to force the 79-year-old prime minister to step down. Churchill, for his part, had no intention of retiring before he was 80.

relief drugs that travelled with him everywhere. The drugs ranged from aspirin to full-scale morphine injections which, from 1951 onwards, had started to serve as his solace.

We do not know if Anthony Eden was caught snoring in the presence of US President Eisenhower, as depicted in this episode, but he had certainly become dependent on regular opiate injections. If Churchill had died over the weekend of 27th/ 28th June 1953, or had remained as seriously incapacitated as his doctor had predicted, Elizabeth II would have been faced with an unprecedented constitutional dilemma, since Anthony Eden could not possibly have accepted her commission to form a government. 'Do you mean to tell me,' asks the horrified Clementine Churchill as she discovers the full extent of the crisis in Episode 7, 'that, at the moment, this country is without a fit leader or a deputy leader?' 'Sshh . . . sshh,' responds her husband tetchily.

'Not so loud.' In their textbooks, both Anson and Bagehot made clear that, when a constitutional monarch was required to choose a prime minister, it was their job to pick out the political figure who could command a working majority in Parliament. The support of the House of Commons was the guiding principle, and Eden was undoubtedly the man whom the Conservatives, as the majority party, wanted as Churchill's successor. But if Eden was sick and out of the country, there was no constitutional process whereby a caretaker prime minister could be appointed – and how would that work, in any case? What red-blooded politician would consent to step up and run the country for three or four months, then step aside meekly when Anthony Eden's convalescence allowed him to return from America?

'The only thing the Queen could do,' Colville remembers reasoning at the time, 'would be to send for somebody she knew very well and could trust implicitly to resign immediately [when] Eden was well.' Robert 'Bobbety' Salisbury, the long-standing ally of Eden who had been fighting for nearly 10 years to secure the succession for his friend Anthony (see chapter 4, p.116), was the obvious candidate for this role. As Colville conferred urgently with Churchill, via Soames, they fixed on Bobbety, with his heritage of family service and his strong religious principles, as the best bet for doing the decent thing – and so it proved. When the 'caretaker' proposal was put to him, the fifth marquess duly agreed to play that role, if necessary. So, the plan was hatched over that weekend of 27th/28th June, involving Colville, Salisbury, Dr Moran and Churchill, working through Christopher Soames, who, as well as being the PM's trusted son-in-law, was also his parliamentary private secretary. Other senior Conservatives were consulted, notably R. A. Butler, the effective number three in the Tory power structure whose consent was crucial. Once Butler said yes (rather nobly, since he might plausibly have tried for the top job himself), Churchill felt able, via Lascelles over the telephone, to recommend the 'caretaker' arrangement to the Queen in the event of illness enforcing his resignation. But, crucially, the prime minister did *not* make clear just how ill he was. 'My dear Prime Minister', Elizabeth had written sympathetically at the first news of Churchill's 'temporary inconvenience', 'I am sorry to hear from Tommy Lascelles that you have not been feeling too well these last few days. I do hope it is not serious . . .'

Temporary inconvenience? In Episode 7, the polite yet clearly unalarmed tenor of the Queen's letter alerts Clementine Churchill to her husband's lack of candour: 'How much does she know exactly?' she asks suspiciously. 'Because from the tone of this . . .' 'She thinks it's a cold,' her husband confesses sheepishly. 'If she knew the truth, she would bid me step down.' The historical record shows clearly that Churchill had decided to 'pig it' – his favoured expression in a crisis for resorting to any tactic, however grubby, to get his way. The prime minister made sure that talk of the word 'stroke' did not go further than the walls of Chartwell that June; the phrase 'disturbance of the cerebral circulation' was cut from the official medical bulletin; and he swore Soames and Colville to secrecy in their dealings with the Palace. 'He told the Queen', according to Dr Moran, 'that he was not without hope that he might soon be about and able to discharge his duties.'

This is the act of wilful deception on which Peter Morgan fixes to bring Episode 7 of *The Crown* to a dramatic conclusion. As events unfolded in late June and July 1953, Churchill managed quite a remarkable recovery from his stroke and he lasted another 20 months in Downing Street. By the time Elizabeth II discovered the truth about his seizure, her prime minister was back in action, conferring with US President Eisenhower on the threat posed by Soviet Russia's detonation of the H-bomb, speaking in the House of Commons, and even rallying the Conservative Party conference at Margate in October with a fighting speech. It was not in the nature of Elizabeth II, nor would it have been productive, for her to revisit the events of that post-coronation summer. So, we conclude Episode 7 with an enjoyable exercise in what might have been.

'It is not my job to govern,' Elizabeth tells the contrite Marquess of Salisbury, whom she has summoned to the Palace. 'But it *is* my job to ensure proper governance . . . How can I do that if my ministers lie and plot and hide the truth from me? You have prevented me from doing my duty.

SIR JOHN RUPERT 'JOCK' COLVILLE

(1915–87)

Private Secretary to Princess Elizabeth (1947–49)
and to Winston Churchill (1951–55)

PLAYED BY NICHOLAS ROWE

When Winston Churchill returned to Downing Street in 1951 he declared the private secretary's office to be 'drenched in Socialism' left over from Clement Attlee, and sent for Jock Colville, who had served him as assistant private secretary through much of the war. Thus, Colville's shrewd and amusing diaries are a principal source for Churchill's political manoeuvrings and misadventures in his final prime ministerial years. As private secretary to Princess Elizabeth, Colville also got the measure of the future Queen when he casually accepted a Labour government proposal to send her wedding dress on a trade tour of North America. 'I can think of five very good reasons against it,' said Her Royal Highness, instantly reeling off the objections, which Colville passed on to the chancellor of the exchequer. A few days later the chancellor sent a handwritten apology admitting he had signed the original proposal without giving it any thought. He accepted every one of the Princess's points, and the wedding dress was spared commercial exposure.

'I can think of five very good reasons against it'

You have hampered and bamboozled the proper functioning of the Crown!'

To Churchill, Morgan imagines the sovereign being even more severe. 'I am just a young woman, starting out in public service,' says Elizabeth, 'and I would never presume to give a man, so much my senior, and who has given this country so much, a lecture. However, you were at my coronation. And you therefore heard for yourself as I took the solemn oath to govern the people of my realms according to their respective laws and customs. Now, one of those customs is that their elected prime minister should be of reasonably sound body and mind . . . Not an outrageous expectation, one would've thought.'

'No,' agrees the downcast prime minister, hanging his head while his sovereign continues: 'But it seems to me that you have *not* been of sound body and mind these past weeks. And that you chose to withhold that information from me . . . a decision which feels like a betrayal, not just of the covenant of trust between us and the institutions that we both represent, but of our personal relationship.'

At this point in the action, Elizabeth walks over to a drawer to retrieve her ancient, much-scribbled-in exercise book and opens it to reveal her childish handwriting. 'In 1867,' she reads to her contrite prime minister, 'Walter Bagehot wrote: "*There are two elements of the Constitution: the efficient and the dignified.*" The monarch is the dignified and the government is the efficient. These two institutions only work when they support each other – when they *trust* one another . . . Your breaking of that trust was irresponsible, and it might have had serious ramifications for the security of this country.' The Queen pauses to let the message

sink in, then asks her prime minister to assure her that he is now 'better . . . Sufficiently better? Fit for office better?' – forcing Churchill to concede 'that the time is fast approaching for me to step down'. This is where dramatic invention falls back in step with history, since one positive outcome of the June 1953 crisis was Churchill's eventual willingness to acknowledge that his faculties were waning and that he must surrender his hold on Downing Street.

At the beginning of August 1953, the prime minister travelled to Windsor, according to Colville's memoirs, to inform the Queen that he would step down if he was not able to face Parliament or the party conference that autumn. While he teased Eden cruelly about his intentions, he told his sovereign the truth. Later he managed to utter the dreaded 'stroke' word, first to President Eisenhower and later to Parliament, when describing the nature of his summer indisposition. Most practically, he agreed secret arrangements with the Palace to transfer power to Anthony Eden in the event of his illness or death during the six months of the Queen's post-coronation tour of the Commonwealth, which was due to commence that November.

In the event, these precautions proved unnecessary. Winston Churchill soldiered on in office with no more untoward health scares, finally retiring in April 1955 at the age of 80. But the unthinkable had been thought, the worst had been discussed – and, more importantly, trust had been restored between the dignified and the efficient branches of government. Did anyone hear the approving croak of a raven?

Educating Elizabeth

'This *is* a surprise!' exclaims the Queen Mother warmly, as her eldest daughter pays her an unexpected late-night visit at Clarence House towards the end of June 1953. 'To what do I owe the pleasure?' 'I came,' replies Elizabeth, whom we have just seen embroiled in the problems caused by her ailing prime minister, 'because I wanted to ask you a question about my education.' 'What about it?' responds her 52-year-old mother, whose attention is distracted by a cheesy variety show on the television. 'The fact that I didn't receive one!' asks Elizabeth sharply. 'You *did*,' retorts the elder Queen – to which Elizabeth responds angrily: 'Sewing, needlework and saying poems with Crawfie? That is *not* an education!'

So here is the question posed by Episode 7 – should Britain's longest-serving Queen have received better schooling? Peter Morgan's Latin title for the episode, '*Scientia Potentia Est*' – 'Knowledge is power' – is inspired by the apologetic comments that Queen Elizabeth II has let drop from time to time about her lack of formal education: 'You and I would never have got into university,' she once said to her sister Margaret in the presence of the Labour politician Barbara Castle, prompting Mrs Castle to reassure the sisters that university 'wasn't as formidable as it seemed'.

A thoughtful Princess Elizabeth with a book in June 1940. By the age of 14 she was reading Jane Austen and Charles Dickens. 'I read quite quickly now,' she told the author J. K. Rowling in 2001. 'I have to read a lot.'

The Queen's self-deprecating remarks are a device she has regularly deployed to put nervous guests at their ease. But their theme clearly represents some sort of personal concern – is grievance too strong a word? – and in Episode 7 the Queen Mother presents the case for the defence. She points out robustly to her recently crowned daughter, 27 years old at this stage of the action, that she has spent no less than six years with the Vice-Provost of Eton studying the intricacies of the Constitution – and this on top of 'an entirely appropriate education' for a woman of her background. 'We taught you to be a lady . . .' says the elder Queen Elizabeth. 'No one wants a bluestocking or college lecturer as sovereign. They want a Queen.'

The older Queen Elizabeth could have made a stronger case. It was certainly true that her daughter had no experience of the communal classroom. In 1936, a tentative plan for the 10-year-old Elizabeth to be sent away to boarding school was said to have been vetoed by her uncle, the new King Edward VIII, on the grounds it would break with the traditions laid down by George V. But there was a further argument to be made, that dispatching royal children to a posh country house with a pack of other privileged, upper-class brats did not, in fact, prepare them so well for royal or even regular life as the strategy of the future George VI and his wife did – to hand over their children to the care of working-class servants inside the Palace. '[The Queen] was brought up by strict nannies,' recalled a friend, describing to the biographer Sally Bedell Smith how the young Elizabeth once came to tea and put her elbows on the table cloth. 'Take them off!' snapped the Princess's first nursery nanny, Mrs Clara Knight,

Life tutors could teach better lessons than school tutors.

without ceremony, and the elbows came shooting off the table. Life tutors could teach better lessons than school tutors.

Clara Knight was a solidly built Hertfordshire farmer's daughter who had raised several members of the Queen Mother's prolific Scottish family, including the Queen Mother herself and her favourite brother, David Bowes Lyon. The nanny's young charges often had difficulty getting their tongues around 'Clara', so she was usually referred to as 'Alla'. With her square jaw, ample bosom and her round black hat pulled down to her ears, Alla Knight resembled no one so much, to the modern eye, as Mrs Doubtfire, the movie governess creation of the comedian Robin Williams. Alla was a spinster, but, following the nursery etiquette of the day, she was accorded the courtesy title of 'Mrs'.

Old-fashioned and firm, Alla ran her nursery floor as a 'state within a state' over which she presided as a benign dictator, installing discipline and regularity into her charges in everything from mealtimes to bowel movements. In later years, Princess Elizabeth was reported to be a remarkably neat and tidy child, going to great trouble to line up both her shoes and her array of toy horses with military precision. 'I don't think any child could be more sensibly brought up,' noted her grandmother Queen Mary with approval, '. . . and she's always punished when she's naughty.' The old Queen had the chance to monitor Alla's nursery regime at close quarters at the beginning of 1927 when Elizabeth's parents were dispatched on a visit to Australia and New Zealand for nearly six months, leaving their newborn baby behind, in line with upper-class parental practice at the time, to be cared for by her nannies under the supervision of her two sets of grandparents, Bowes Lyon and Windsor, between whose homes she was shuttled.

Between the ages of nine months and her first birthday, the little Princess was a lodger on the upper floors of Buckingham Palace, where she was spruced up by Alla and her staff every afternoon to be brought downstairs for tea in the presence of the King and Queen. Contemporary accounts make much of the informality of the gathering. 'Here comes the Bambino!' the normally staid Queen Mary was said to have exclaimed with delight at her granddaughter's arrival – though a modern mind might wonder at the impact on the 11-month-old child of the daily cleansing, changing, hair-brushing and ritualistic dressing-up, then to be borne reverentially down long corridors into the holy of holies by servants who were tingling with awe and homage.

When her parents eventually returned from the other end of the earth at the close of June 1927, they were strangers who can scarcely have recognised the smell and texture of the child they had left any more than she recognised them. Revealing more than she realised, the Duchess of York's authorised biographer, Lady Cynthia Asquith, reported that the little girl was 'almost as pleased' to see her mother as if the duchess had been 'quite a large

Princess Elizabeth, two, with her nanny, Clara 'Alla' Knight, the no-nonsense daughter of a Hertfordshire farmer, outside the London home of the Duke and Duchess of York at 145 Piccadilly.

crowd' – to whom she held out her arms with a smile, copying the gesture she had learned to make when onlookers gathered round her pram during her excursions with Alla in Hyde Park. 'She is a character,' reported Winston Churchill when he met the two-and-a-half-year-old Princess the following year at Balmoral. 'She had an air of authority and reflectiveness astonishing in an infant.' With the birth of Princess Margaret in 1930, Alla's nursery priorities switched to the care of the new arrival, with supervision of the four-year-old Elizabeth being transferred to the nanny's senior assistant, Margaret 'Bobo' MacDonald, the daughter of a Highland railway signalman, who

A photograph identified in Queen Mary's own handwriting. The Queen looked after her nine-month-old granddaughter early in 1927 while Elizabeth's parents were touring New Zealand and Australia.

had grown up in a tied cottage beside the Aberdeen to Inverness line. This forthright, red-haired young Scotswoman would sleep in the Princess's bedroom through most of her childhood and would, in adult life, become her most intimate female companion and confidante – looking after the royal wardrobe as her dresser and being generally credited as the source of her mistress's famous frugality. The railwayman's daughter trained the Princess to open each of her Christmas and birthday presents carefully, then smooth out and save the wrapping paper and ribbon, preserving them in a special drawer for future use, a practice the Queen is said to have continued throughout her life.

We know the details of this thriftiness thanks to the Princess's governess Marion Crawford, another feisty young Scottish woman, who joined the York household just before Elizabeth's sixth birthday and later published an internationally bestselling book, *The Little Princesses*, about her life behind Palace doors. 'Crawfie' came to Windsor in the spring of 1932 for a month's trial as governess, was dubbed with an affectionate nickname to match those of Alla and Bobo, and stayed for 17 years. Prepared with the help of a ghostwriter, *The Little Princesses* reads today as a kindly and wholly positive account of the future Queen's upbringing; everyone emerges from the pages with great credit. But no such intimate, day-to-day revelations had appeared on such a scale before, and the royal family – who tried to stop the governess publishing – came to regard the book, first published in November 1950, as a gross act of betrayal. 'Crawfie snaked,' Princess Margaret used to hiss with disdain.

Until she embarked on her career of royal revelation, however, Miss Crawford was cherished as an inspiring and creative teacher – singled out

by *The Times*, no less, on Elizabeth's 18th birthday in April 1942, for having 'upheld through the years of tutelage the standards of simple living and honest thinking that Scotland peculiarly respects'. Of lower-middle-class Presbyterian stock, Crawfie had come to the attention of the Duke and Duchess of York in the early 1930s as tutor to a number of their aristocratic friends who lived in the hills around Dunfermline, between whose homes the governess would hike several dozen miles a week, in all weathers. Prince Bertie admired the young woman's energy, and both parents felt that her carefree, spirited style, very much in the mould of child-centred, progressive nursery teaching at that time, was exactly what their daughters needed. So, in September 1932 the governess took over full-time responsibility for the daytime activities of Princess Elizabeth, and she found she was given a surprisingly free hand.

'No one ever had employers who interfered so little [she later wrote]. I had often the feeling that the Duke and Duchess, most happy in their own married life, were not over-concerned with the higher education of their daughters. They wanted most for them a really happy childhood, with lots of pleasant memories stored up against the days that might come and, later, happy marriages.' Their grandfather King George V wanted a little more. 'For goodness' sake,' he boomed at Miss Crawford when he met her, 'teach Margaret and Lilibet to write a decent hand, that's all I ask of you. None of my children could write properly. They all do it exactly the same way. I like a hand with some character in it.'

Miss Crawford discovered that Princess Elizabeth could read already. She had been taught by her mother. The Duchess of York told Lady Cynthia Asquith that she had read Bible stories aloud to

Elizabeth on Sunday mornings from an early age, and had selected some of the most cherished books from her own childhood to read in this manner on winter evenings.

The family would sing songs round the piano after tea, reported the duchess, then start digging into 'fairy stories, Alice, *Black Beauty, At the Back of the North Wind, Peter Pan,* anything we can find about horses and dogs, and gay poetry like "Come Unto These Yellow Sands"'. Over the years Miss Crawford would extend this list to include Robert Louis Stevenson, Jane Austen, Rudyard Kipling, the Brontës, Sir Walter Scott, Charles Dickens and Anthony Trollope – all consumed in periods of 'silent reading', which stood the future monarch 'in good stead', as Her Majesty would later explain to J. K. Rowling, when the author of the Harry Potter series came to the Palace for an investiture. 'I read quite quickly now,' the Queen explained. 'I have to read a lot.'

The silent reading sessions were part of a carefully tabulated, six-day-per-week curriculum drawn up by Miss Crawford, the mornings filled with half-hour lessons, the afternoons devoted to less academic accomplishments – singing, drawing, music or dancing. The governess sent a draft version of the timetable to Queen Mary and was told the Queen considered too little time had been allocated to history, geography and Bible readings: 'Her Majesty felt that genealogies, historical and dynastic, were very interesting to children and, for these children, really important.' Detailed knowledge of the physical geography of the Dominions and India would also be valuable, thought their grandmoth-

'I like a hand with some character in it.'

er, along with regular learning of poetry by heart – 'wonderful memory training'.

Working with the governess, the old Queen helped organise regular Monday excursions to historic venues such as Hampton Court or the Tower of London, with private tours of the capital's finest libraries and museums. Thus, the young Elizabeth got to touch the blood-stained shirt worn by her predecessor Charles I on the day he was beheaded, and the lead shot extracted from the body of Admiral Nelson at Trafalgar – 'instructive amusements', in the opinion of her grandmother. 'It would have been impossible for anyone so devoted to the monarchy as Queen Mary,' wrote her friend Lady Airlie, 'to lose sight of the future Queen in this favourite grandchild.' In this spirit, Crawfie conferred with the curators of the incomparable Royal Collection to select a 'painting of the week' – a Vermeer or Canaletto, or even a Rubens or a Titian – to sit in the Palace schoolroom on an easel.

To reduce the dangers of elitism that went with such privileges, the governess tried to ensure that her charges' Monday excursions should not be by chauffeur-driven car but by public transport on the London Underground – the 'Tube'. Queen Mary thoroughly approved. On one famous occasion the old Queen had noticed her granddaughter wriggling impatiently during a concert and asked if she would not prefer to go home. 'Oh no, Granny,' came the

As war threatened, Marion Crawford started a subscription for Elizabeth to the Children's Newspaper – 'The Story of the World Today for the Men and Women of Tomorrow.'

C N CALLING
We sailed wherever
ships could sail,
We founded many a
mighty State,
Pray God our great-
ness may not fail
Through craven
fears of being great
Tennyson

CHILDREN'S NEWSPAPER

EDITED BY ARTHUR MEE

To die is a little
thing: it is a great
thing to live in
freedom and honour

Number 1020   **OCTOBER 8, 1938**

Thursday, 2d   Postage Anywhere One Halfpenny

Children of the Flag, I Want to Talk to You

As this goes to press the clouds are lifting and a ray of light comes through. It is as if the world's prayer has been answered.

A GREAT shadow has come over the world. Perhaps it may pass away and all be well again in this happy land. Perhaps the sun may go on shining and Peace may come.

It may be that an enemy will come in the night and take away our peace and freedom, that a cruel war will burst upon us, and that for some time (perhaps a little time, perhaps a long time) life will not be the same. Perhaps we may have to leave our homes in towns and go into the country. Perhaps our fathers and brothers may have to fight for their lives and for ours. Perhaps men may come with bombs and poison gas to try to break the spirit of this ancient little land.

Be Prepared

If this should be, our country expects that every man and woman, and every boy and girl, will do their duty and be brave. We must be prepared, like the Guides and Scouts. Do you remember the story of the Scouts who were on a sinking ship and scorned to be saved when the cry went forth, Women and Children First? A Scout is a little man, a Guide is a little woman, ready for danger when it comes.

It is better for us all in times of danger that we should not be crowded together in great cities, but should spread ourselves about our lovely countryside, where life can be made more happy for us and we can all be safer. Let us go calmly if we are asked to go. Let us do quietly whatever we are asked to do. Let there be no question of our willingness, our patience, our courage. We make it easier for those we love, and easier for the country that we love, by being instantly ready to do anything.

That is all that matters now. We must give our life, our strength, our heart, our soul, for the sake of our country, threatened by hate and cruelty and war.

If war should come it will be because our country could do no other. Our Prime Minister has been a hero of peace. He has done all that a man could do, and the nation has done all that a nation could do, to save this cruel stroke of fate. Now for the second time in our generation the loathsome god of war has flung a sword into the midst of Europe and threatens the lives of hundreds of millions of people. We should lose our freedom and our honour, our happiness and all we have worth living for, if we let this spirit rule the world.

Many times Old England has gone out into the Valley of the Shadow to save its good name and to bring the world freedom and peace. The clouds are gathering round us once again, but nothing can defeat us. We have to lift our heads high and be unafraid, whatever comes. We are all one family now, one great brotherhood of young and old, living our lives for the country that has made us free and given us all our opportunities.

The Everlasting Arms

Let us give it our good courage now, our patience, our strength, and our powers of endurance. We must be willing to put up with things and do our best to bother nobody, for everyone will have enough to do. If we can help, let us help; if we cannot help, let us get out of the way and suffer what comes as calmly as we may.

It is for a little time, and for the country and the Flag, and it is to banish from the world the horror and the cruelty of evil men.

We shall know when these words appear whether it is Peace or War. If it be Peace, let us lift up our hearts and thank God; if it be War, let us be brave and remember that the spirit of Old England is in us, and that she will keep us free. God is our Refuge and Strength, and underneath us are the Everlasting Arms.   **Arthur Mee**

The Greatest Peace Man Since the World Began

American view of Mr Chamberlain

world were all at the same moment some day to broadcast thoughts of peace? It is not possible that this could be done without dramatic effect.

We have to think of ourselves as the real creators of events, the inspirers and the makers of history. We are the people responsible for everything that happens. We, all the common people of the world, can have what we want if we want it enough. We are more than machines and more than all the inventions. If machines are the great business of life all the teachers of men have been on the wrong road, for they have taught that man's business is not with things outside him, but with his own soul. If machines are the business of man what a lot of time we have wasted! But look ahead. Imagine the world

in the year 2000. Picture a human race which need not exert a muscle of the body to get anything it needs. Toil is abolished. Everyone is healthy and well-housed, with machines for everything. Everything is perfect. Everyone is satisfied? No; not satisfied. A man comes along who says:

We are like children playing with toys. These machines are the clumsiest things that were ever thought of. The human race has been wasting time. With infinite trouble it has been making clumsy machines, and all the time it has overlooked the fact that the brain which can make machines is itself the most marvellous machine in existence.

Break your inventions to pieces! I reveal to you a new and greater mystery; I put you on the road to a discovery

Continued on page 4

LET US BROADCAST PEACE

WHATEVER is happening when these words appear, one thing is certain—the hearts of common people everywhere will be longing for peace.

It is the most hopeful fact of our time that, in spite of all the bitterness that has grown up since the Great War, the yearning for peace has been universal among men. It is impossible that a yearning so deeply planted in the human heart should be frustrated for ever, and it is not to be doubted

that the prayer of the common people of the world will be fulfilled.

What would happen, we wonder, if every human being who longs for peace knelt down to pray for it as if it were the deepest longing in his heart? What would happen if we all thought of ourselves as broadcasting stations, broadcasting the thought of peace into the world, if every brain were its own wireless station and the two thousand million people in the

1st May 1939. Ten days after her thirteenth birthday and 10 weeks before she met Prince Philip at Dartmouth Naval College, Princess Elizabeth (standing in ankle socks) visited London's docks, sailing along the River Thames aboard the steamer St. Katharine. This was one of her regular educational excursions to get a taste of the world outside the Palace that were organised by her grandmother, Queen Mary (seated second from left, with her back to the camera), and her Scottish nanny Marion Crawford (far right in the fur stole and black hat).

reply, 'we can't leave before the end. Think of all the people who'll be waiting to see us outside!' – whereupon Granny immediately had the little girl escorted out of the back way by a lady-in-waiting and taken home in a taxi.

To keep in touch with the outside world in another fashion, Miss Crawford started a subscription for Princess Elizabeth to the *Children's Newspaper*, a tabloid weekly that presented current affairs and samples of adult literature adapted for young readers, with all references to alcohol changed to soft beverages – orange squash for wine, and fizzy pop for beer – reflecting the temperance principles of its editor, Arthur Mee, a crusader for self-education. Subtitled *The Story of the World Today for the Men and Women of Tomorrow*, the paper reflected the editor's Baptist faith and loyalty to the British Empire, with the aim of keeping young people up to date with the latest in world news and science. 'What would happen, we wonder,' Mee asked his young readers at the time of the Munich crisis of 1938, 'if every human being who longs for peace knelt down to pray for it as if it were the deepest longing in his heart? What would happen if we all thought of ourselves as broadcasting stations, broadcasting the thought of peace into the world?'

Elizabeth became an avid reader of the *Children's Newspaper*, discussing its articles with her father, who pitched in with cartoons and humorous articles from his own favourite magazine, *Punch* – the *Private Eye* of the day. The King would also draw his daughter's attention to grown-up newspaper articles he thought she should read – usually in the royal edition of *The Times*, then specially printed on rag paper for Buckingham Palace, the British Museum and the Copyright libraries.

Working with Elizabeth's parents and grandmother, the governess whom Ben Pimlott would later compare to Muriel Spark's inspirational Miss Jean Brodie, seems to have delivered rather more to her young charges than just sewing, needlework and poetry. It was Miss Crawford who pushed for the creation of special Girl Guide and Brownie 'packs' inside the Palace so the Princesses could have contact with girls from the outside world. Keen on sport and physical exercise – Elizabeth had had weekend riding lessons at Windsor from an early age – Crawfie organised swimming and life-saving lessons at the Bath Club in Mayfair, and also in the Buckingham Palace pool. Then there were the French literature and language lessons with Toni de Bellaigue, a Belgian tutor who insisted that the sisters spoke nothing but French with her at mealtimes. In 1972, President Pompidou was so impressed with the Queen's command of French on her state visit to Paris that he stopped the car as they left the airport and told his translator to find his own way back to the office. He had no further need of his services.

Elizabeth II's unhappiness about her education is embodied in Episode 7 by Professor Hodge, a fictitious character who comes into the Palace, at her invitation, to help the Queen plug the gaps in her learning – only to conclude there are no significant gaps to plug. The professor discovers that Her Majesty is a walking encyclopaedia on her specialist subjects, horse breeding and horse racing, and as for disciplining devious politicians: 'Ma'am, you say you don't have what it takes to do battle with these people. You do. You were drilled for years in the finer points of our Constitution; you know it better than me. Better than all of us. You have the only education that matters . . . Summon them and give them a good dressing down like children . . . They're English, male and

Learning the finer points of knot-tying at a Girl Guides meeting in Frogmore, Windsor, gave the sixteen-year-old Princess Elizabeth a rare chance to mix and mingle with girls of her own age.

upper class. A good dressing down from Nanny is what they want most in life.'

And so it proves. 'Something's different,' muses Philip when he encounters his wife at the end of the episode, after she has finished chastising Winston Churchill and Lord Salisbury with a verbal spanking. 'You seem . . . taller, somehow. Or is it just that I've shrunk?' In her notorious book, Crawfie relates a tale with a similar moral about a Girl Guide and Brownie game that the nanny-educated Princesses used to play with school-educated girls from outside the Palace. It involved everyone taking off their shoes, throwing them

into a pile, then finding them again, putting them back on and racing back to the starting line. 'This never went very well,' Crawfie wrote, 'as quite half the children did not know their own shoes! Lilibet and Margaret told me this with scorn. There was never any nonsense of that kind in *their* nursery.'

The tragedy of Marion Crawford

Early in 1949, Bruce and Beatrice Gould, the ambitious publishers of *Ladies' Home Journal*, America's leading women's magazine, approached Buckingham Palace with a project to instruct and entertain their 4.7 million readers – a series of articles on the education of the future Queen and her sister. The Palace eventually agreed, on the condition that the articles would be written by Dermot Morrah, a pro-monarchist who was trusted by the family, and whom they connected with the obvious source, the Princesses' beloved governess Marion Crawford. With Elizabeth married and Margaret having passed her eighteenth birthday, Crawfie had recently retired, at the age of 38, to marry her long-term sweetheart George Buthlay, an employee of Drummonds Bank.

Morrah and the Goulds found Crawfie strangely uncooperative, however, and quickly identified the root of the problem. The pushy Buthlay had already tried to persuade the royal family, through his wife, to switch their accounts from Coutts to Drummonds – without success. Now it became clear he felt that his wife's 17

years of devoted service deserved more than her royal pension of £300 a year (about £10,000 in 2017 values), with the lifetime use of the grace and favour Nottingham Cottage in the grounds of Kensington Palace, and the letters CVO (Commander of the Victorian Order) after her name. Sensing Crawfie's reluctance to hand her story to another writer for nothing, the Americans

Near right, Marion Crawford, 'Crawfie', the beloved governess of Elizabeth and Margaret, on her retirement in 1949 after 17 years of loyal service. Far right, the book that made her a traitor.

The Little Princesses

The intimate story of H.R.H. Princess Elizabeth and H.R.H. Princess Margaret by their governess

MARION CRAWFORD

*Princess Elizabeth, aged 10 in 1936, walking her dog in Hyde Park with her governess, Marion Crawford.
'I do feel . . .' Elizabeth's mother would later write to Crawfie, 'that you should not write and sign articles
about the children, as people in positions of confidence with us must be utterly oyster.'*

promptly flew to London and offered her a deal. 'Her awe of the royal family almost paralysed her,' recalled Bruce Gould. 'Even in her own sanctuary, close as it was to Kensington Palace, she would hardly speak . . . above a whisper.' The governess took the Goulds' proposal to her former employer, and received a firmly negative response. 'I do feel most definitely,' wrote Queen Elizabeth on 4th April 1949, 'that you should not write and sign articles about the children, as people in positions of confidence with us must be utterly oyster.'

This appealing use of a family catchphrase was part of a long and carefully phrased letter that deployed charm and threats in equal measure. 'You would lose all your friends,' warned the Queen, 'because such a thing has never been done or even contemplated amongst the people who serve us so loyally . . . I do feel most strongly that you must resist the allure of American money & persistent editors, & say No No No to offers of dollars about something as private & as precious as our family.'

The weakness in the Queen's argument was that she herself had helped create this profitable genre that was so attractive to persistent editors. As Duchess of York in the 1920s and 1930s, the young Princesses' mother had given her blessing to numerous sugary magazine articles and several 'authorised' books about her daughters in a style that was scarcely different from what the Goulds were now proposing. The sticking point was the maintaining of royal control of the disclosure process, along with opening the floodgates to other employees. As the Queen put it to Crawfie, 'we should never feel confidence in anyone again'.

The Queen finished her letter by inviting the governess 'to come & see me again about a job . . . I feel sure that you could do some teaching,

'Dear Crawfie, Poor Bobo's father died yesterday morning and we are all feeling very sad except Margaret who laughs and is naughty and enjoys herself just as much . . . With lots of love from Lilibet (in mourning).'

which after all is your "forte", and I would be so glad to help in any way I can.' Her Majesty even said she was happy for Crawfie to help Dermot Morrah with his articles (which the Palace, of course, would be able to control) 'and get paid from America . . . as long as your name did not come into it'.

But nothing could match the tempting offer of the Goulds for Crawfie's unrestricted personal story: a lump sum of $80,000 ($801,000 or £614,000 in 2017 values) – and for this fortune Crawfie did not even have to do any writing. She surrendered to the now-familiar newspaper process of being confined to a hotel room for days on end

'Sewing, needlework and saying poems with Crawfie. That is not an education.'

with a journalist, who 'pumped' her mercilessly to extract her story. To satisfy the ex-governess's continuing fear of the Palace, the Goulds flew over an American shorthand typist 'recommended for discretion in recording wartime secret conferences', and they moved into the Dorchester themselves to oversee the process. When the first of eight instalments ran in January 1950, *Ladies' Home Journal* sold out.

Thousands took out subscriptions to make sure they would not miss the next instalment, and in Britain, *Woman's Own*, which bought British rights in the series, increased its normal print run by 500,000. Similar serialisations in Canada, Australia, New Zealand and South Africa made the fortunes of the magazines which ran them — and then came the book. *The Little Princesses* went hardcover in lavishly illustrated editions that were bestsellers around the world.

Crawfie shared in this bonanza for a time, putting her name to further ghostwritten books and to a weekly syndicated column in *Women's Own* purporting to describe royal events from the

inside. 'Ascot this season had an excitement about it never seen there before,' reported 'Crawfie's Column' of 16th June 1955, going on to praise 'the bearing and dignity of the Queen' at the annual Trooping the Colour ceremony as causing great 'admiration among the spectators'. Unfortunately for Crawfie, both Ascot and the Colour ceremony were cancelled that year because of a rail strike, so her column created a sensation she did not intend. She concluded her career as a writer more rapidly than as a governess. Nor did her private life prove much happier. George Buthlay — the inspiration for her betrayal in the opinion of those who knew him — proved a bullying and controlling husband. When he predeceased her in 1977, his will went to the trouble of excluding his widow from the ceremony of disposing of his ashes. The couple had chosen to retire to a mansion in Aberdeen, just 200 yards from the road taken by royal car cavalcades on their way to and from Balmoral – on the forlorn fantasy, it would seem, that a cavalcade might one day choose to stop. 'I can't bear those I love to pass me by on the road,' wrote the mournful governess in a note that accompanied a failed suicide attempt in the 1980s. There were no royal wreaths or flowers at Crawfie's funeral in February 1988. But her name does live on inside Buckingham Palace, since there have been a few others – very few, it must be said – who have followed the governess's path of unauthorised disclosure. Their treachery is always described in the same terms: 'doing a Crawfie'.

8
PRIDE AND JOY

100 dresses, 36 hats, 50 pairs of shoes

8

Episode 8 of *The Crown* opens with the depression and mourning of the widowed Queen Mother. 'Loss has followed loss,' she confides sadly to her friends Commander Clare and Lady Doris 'Fasty' Vyner, on whose Caithness estate in the north-eastern corner of Scotland she has taken refuge in the autumn of 1953. 'I don't want to sound self-piteous, but . . . the loss of a husband, then the loss of a home. Having to leave the Palace . . .' Her voice tails off. 'Imagine, 17 years' experience as Queen and being head of the family. Bertie was a wonderful husband and father, but he needed a great deal of help as King . . .' The Oscar-winning film *The King's Speech* rightly gives credit to Lionel Logue, the Australian speech therapist who helped George VI overcome the worst of his stutter. But the real secret of the King's success – the person who continuously gave Bertie the love and strength to persist in his battle – was his wife Elizabeth, first as Duchess of York, then as Queen. Long before Peter Townsend entered the service of George VI, or had any idea that

King George VI and Queen Elizabeth celebrate their Silver Wedding on 13th September 1948. The nervous and stammering king had been made by the steely resolve and love of his wife – but it took him at least three proposals to win her hand.

he would one day serve as the King's equerry, he was one of an audience of Haileybury schoolboys gathered to witness the then Duke of York open the school's new dining hall in 1932. Scarcely had the Duke started speaking than he froze, unable to say another word, and the whole assemblage froze with him, tensing with embarrassment. But the Duchess kept smiling as if nothing had happened. She seemed to whisper to her husband, recalled Townsend, 'willing him over the wall of silence and into the next sentence. Her sense of partnership was sublime.'

A dozen years later, now working in the Palace at the side of the King, Townsend was to witness the technique at first hand, and he learned to imitate the shrewd good humour with which the Queen could sense the squalls of ill temper blowing up and defuse them with a smile or change of subject. Elizabeth knew how to divert her husband, heading him off from confrontation, and when he did explode she was quite unflustered. 'Oh Bertie,' she would say, feeling for his pulse and pretending to count like a clock – 'tick, tick, tick'. The anger would just drain away.

Bertie's fits of bad temper were known as his 'gnashes', and his prickly temperament was one of the reasons why Elizabeth Bowes Lyon turned down his suits when Prince Albert, Duke of York, first came courting her in the early 1920s. It was new ground for Bertie, the first occasion in modern times that a senior member of the royal family had gone out into the domestic market-place in search of a bride. Until 1914, the British royal family had negotiated its matches with foreign royalties privately, via family channels – Queen Victoria had been a maestro in the marital game of thrones. But the Great War had left few royal families standing in Europe, and George V decided that the next generation of the recently minted House of Windsor should find nice young British folk with whom to bond and marry.

They hardly came nicer than Lady Elizabeth Bowes Lyon, the ninth child and fourth daughter of the Earl and Countess of Strathmore, born 4th August 1900 and one of the most eligible catches in London. In the capital's frantic lifestyle of the post-war years, there was something vulnerable and old-fashioned about her. She was pretty and sensual in a wistful way, with big round eyes and her dark hair pulled back into the bun she wore for the rest of her life. She was not stuffy. The Lady Elizabeth was rather good fun, in fact – flirtatious even. But you would not dream of presuming on the invitation. 'Holding hands in a boat, that was her idea of courting' were the famous words of her friend in those days, Lady Helen Cecil. Lord Strathmore's playful daughter was different from the close-cropped and brittle young ladies of the 'flapper' generation. She was the sort of partner you could visualise as a soothing companion and home-maker, a marvellous mother – exactly the qualities that appealed to the shy and stuttering Prince Albert.

The couple had met as children at a tea party, when the five-year-old Elizabeth was said to have given the 10-year-old Prince the cherry off her cake. They met again casually in their teens

They hardly came nicer than Lady Elizabeth Bowes Lyon

Lady Elizabeth Bowes Lyon as portrayed in 1923, aged 23, by the society photographer Vandyk. She had a softness that set her apart from the flappers of the jazz and cocktail age. 'Holding hands in a boat,' said one of her friends. 'That was her idea of courting.'

A triptych by Samuel Warburton of Elizabeth Bowes Lyon set against the heather on the hills surrounding the home of her parents, the Earl and Countess of Strathmore at Glamis Castle in Scotland.

at Spencer House, but it was not until the Royal Air Force Ball at the Ritz in July 1920 that they made an impression on each other. 'I danced with Prince Albert who I hadn't known before,' wrote Elizabeth to Beryl Poignand, her former governess and friend, 'he is quite a nice youth.' For his part, the besotted Prince Albert later said that he fell in love with Elizabeth that evening.

The young Prince was just recovering from a liaison that had earned the disapproval of his parents – a flirtation with Sheila, Lady Loughborough, née Chisholm, the famously attractive Australian said to have been the origin of the expression 'a good-looking Sheila'. Later a lover of Rudolph Valentino and of at least two Russian princes, Sheila had been unhappily

married for some years to the alcoholic Lord Loughborough and was a close friend of Freda Dudley Ward, the mistress of the Prince of Wales. The sight of the two princes dancing openly at balls with their married lady friends had been the scandal of London in the winter season of 1919, and the following April George V confronted his second son sternly. 'He is going to make me Duke of York on his birthday provided he hears nothing more about Sheila & me!!!!' wrote Bertie to his elder brother, then touring New Zealand and Australia, adding passionately to David that Sheila was 'the one & only person in this world who means anything to me'.

On reflection – and unlike his elder brother – Bertie decided to yield to his father's wishes, explaining the situation to the understanding Sheila, and accepting the royal terms. 'I can tell you that I fulfilled your conditions to the letter,' he wrote to his father on 6th June 1920, 'and that nothing more will come of it' – provoking a rare letter of approval from the normally gruff King: 'Dearest Bertie, I was delighted to get your letter this morning . . . I know that you behaved very well, in a difficult situation for a young man . . . I feel that this splendid old title will be safe in your hands.' So it was as Duke of York that Bertie invited himself over from Balmoral in the autumn of 1920 to Glamis Castle, the historic home of the Strathmores, 12 miles north of Dundee. 'P.S. Prince Albert is coming to stay here on Saturday,' wrote Elizabeth to Beryl on 20th September 1920. 'Ghastly!' The P.S. was written across the top of a letter discussing the news of the second proposal of marriage that Elizabeth had recently received in a matter of months. 'People were rather inclined to propose to you in those days,' the Queen Mother recalled many years later.

Already sensing the possibility of a royal proposal, perhaps, Elizabeth asked her closest friends to rally round – Helen Cecil, Diamond Hardinge and Lady Doris Gordon-Lennox, nicknamed 'Fasty' – and together they cooked up a weekend of boisterous entertainment for the Prince and his younger sister, Princess Mary. Under the jovial aegis of the Strathmore clan, Glamis Castle was anything but the sinister site where Shakespeare wrongly had Macbeth murder King Duncan (the real Macbeth killed Duncan in open battle near Elgin in 1040, and never lived at Glamis). The Bowes Lyon house parties featured charades and parlour games and eightsome reels,

'Elizabeth was the girl whom he must marry'

to which Elizabeth and her friend 'Fasty' added raucous sing-songs and apple-pie beds. 'Elizabeth is playing "Oh Hell" on the piano on purpose for me . . .' wrote Helen Cecil as they waited for the Prince and his sister to arrive. 'We are to have reels & all sorts of strange wild things tonight.' Elizabeth showed the royals round the castle '& terrified them with ghost stories,' she wrote to Beryl. 'We also played ridiculous games of hide & seek, they really are babies!' Bertie and Mary were enchanted by the Strathmores' boisterous teasing, so much more relaxed than the formality of Balmoral, where cocktails were banned and the guest list was heavy on bishops. When the Glamis party went out for a walk, 'Elizabeth & Prince A. were allowed to go on miles ahead,' remembered Helen Cecil, 'which agitated the former rather.' Behind their backs the other guests played hide and seek in the bushes, the men pelting the girls with mud to get revenge for their apple-pie beds. Elizabeth had to retire to her own bed 'utterly exhausted' once her royal guests had left, writing to Beryl that Prince Albert had 'kept us pretty busy! He was very nice, tho', & very much improved in every way.'

Prince Albert, for his part, now had no doubt that Elizabeth was the girl whom he must marry, and he set about courting her in earnest when the winter season resumed in London. 'Our Bert stayed till 7, talking 100 to 20, or even 200 to the dozen,' wrote Elizabeth to Beryl after one unexpected visit. The couple met at balls and parties and exchanged letters, and at the end of February 1921, after five months of courtship, the Prince screwed up his courage to make his proposal after Sunday lunch at St Paul's Walden Bury, the

26th April 1923. 'There's
not a man in England
today who doesn't envy him.
The clubs are in gloom.' The
young Duke of York rides
out of Buckingham Palace
in triumph with his bride,
the new Duchess of York, on
their wedding day.

Strathmore's country home near Welwyn, north-west of London – only for the lady to reject him. 'Dear Prince Bertie, I must write one line to say how <u>dreadfully</u> sorry I am about yesterday,' wrote Elizabeth on Monday, 28th February 1921. 'It makes me miserable to think of it – you have been so <u>very</u> nice about it all – please do forgive me . . . I do understand so well what you feel, and sympathize so much, & I hate to think that I am the cause of it. I honestly can't explain to you how terribly sorry I am – it worries me <u>so</u> much to think that you may be unhappy – I do hope you won't be.' Having said that she would only write one line, the 20-year-old Elizabeth went on to write nearly a dozen. '<u>Anyway</u>,' she continued, liberally cluttering her text with underlinings, 'we can be good friends, can't we? Please do look on me as one. I shall <u>never</u> say anything about our talks I promise you – and nobody need ever know. I thought I must just write this short letter to try and tell you <u>how </u>sorry I am. Very sincerely yours, Elizabeth.' In this letter of apparent rejection, Elizabeth signed off with her Christian name alone for the very first time.

We owe sight of this intimate missive, and dozens more like it, to William Shawcross's magisterial biography of the Queen Mother published in 2009, with its companion volume of personal letters, *Counting One's Blessings*, published in 2012. Seldom can a courtship have been so intimately logged. The correspondence ebbs to and fro for more than two and a half years, concluding with Elizabeth resorting to 'back-slang' or 'mirror-writing' in her diary to conceal – or maybe was it to emphasise? – her deepest thoughts: 'I ma tsom

The newly married Bertie and Elizabeth, the Duke and Duchess of York, in April 1923 on their honeymoon at Polesden Lacey in Surrey.

dexelprep,' she wrote backwards in her diary on 4th January 1923 ('*I am most perplexed*'), following that up the next morning with 'Ma gnikniht oot hcum. I hsiw I wenk' (*Am thinking too much. I wish I knew.*')

Prince Bertie had just made his third proposal of marriage since February 1921 – though with his technique of multiple beseechings it could easily have counted as his thirty-third – and after nearly two years of prevaricating, Elizabeth knew that she could not delay much longer. 'I ma yrev deirrow oot,' she noted on 11th January ('*I am very worried too.*') The following weekend she motored down to St Paul's Walden with Bertie for an afternoon with her eccentric father whose hobby was sawing wood. 'Prince Bertie sawed <u>hard</u>,' she noted. 'Talked after tea for hours – dediced ot tiaw a elttil – epoh I ma ton gnivaheb yldab. ('*Decided to wait a little – hope I am not behaving badly.*')

The wood-sawing may have done the trick. Lord Strathmore had an aristocratic disdain for the middle-class monarchy – he had strictly warned his sons away from equerry-like positions at court – and his wife shared his suspicions: 'As far as I can see,' Lady Strathmore once remarked, 'some people have to be fed royalty like sea-lions fish.' An endless round of royal chores and ceaseless public scrutiny seemed a cruel life sentence for their charming daughter, who had the pick of any duke in the country, with all the comfort and freedom that entailed. According to Mabell Airlie, a confidante of both Lady Strathmore and Queen Mary, 'She was frankly doubtful, uncertain of her feelings, and afraid of the public life which would lie ahead of her as the King's daughter-in-law.'

But Elizabeth had come to love and admire her persistent suitor. Her supportive letters to him about his speech handicap show she was fully signed up for the Bertie project – she had encouraged his attempts at therapy from the start – and on that weekend early in 1923, the young Prince pulled out all the stops. 'He came down to St. P.W. suddenly on Friday, & proposed continuously until Sunday night, when she said Yes at 11.30!' wrote an excited Lady Strathmore. 'My head is completely bewildered, as all these days E was hesitating & miserable, but now she is absolutely happy – & he is radiant.' 'There's not a man in England today who doesn't envy him,' recorded 'Chips' Channon in his diary for 16th January 1923, the day the engagement was announced. 'The clubs are in gloom.' The House of Windsor loved her. Elizabeth had such a capacity for smiling, bringing out the spritely side of Queen Mary – and not even the King's passion for timekeeping was proof against his future daughter-in-law. All her life Elizabeth was an unpunctual person, but when she arrived late at the royal dinner table, she was invariably forgiven. 'You are not late, my dear,' the King would declare. 'We must have sat down two minutes too early.'

She believed in him

Her children, born in 1926 and 1930, made her even more beloved. Motherliness became a component of her appeal from quite an early date. Until the arrival of the Princesses Elizabeth and Margaret Rose, the royal family had been comparatively childless – a gap in their own lives and also in their public persona, and the young Duchess presided ably over the cult of the little princesses, welcoming carefully vetted journalists and authors into the Yorks' family home, a town house facing Buckingham Palace across Green Park at 145 Piccadilly. Readers were taken upstairs to the nursery floor, saw the rocking horse on the landing, could almost touch the little scarlet brushes and dustpans 'with which every morning the little princesses sweep the thick pile carpet', and heard the screams and splashes through the bathroom door where the Duke, a man, was actually bathing his daughters.

Here at 145 Piccadilly, just a few yards away from a bus stop, was the first small, royal, nuclear family unit, a model of dreamlike domesticity – for all the world, as the biographer John Pearson has remarked, like the characters in an Ovaltine advertisement.

These cleverly supervised revelations displayed another side to the smiling Duchess – her shrewd grasp of public relations. Nothing quite so graphic and intimate had ever been published about living members of the royal family with royal approval – which was why, 20 years later, Queen Elizabeth would come to feel so wounded by the non-approved disclosures of the governess, Marion Crawford. As his reign approached its close, George V voiced his praise of the cosy, domestic example that Bertie and his wife had been able to create – 'so different,' as the old King wrote, 'to dear David' – and the confidence with which government and nation looked to the Yorks after the crisis of abdication that ended the brief reign of Edward VIII owed much to the evident solidity of the Duchess.

September 1940. Queen Elizabeth and her husband inspect the crater of a bomb which damaged much of the North Wing of Buckingham Palace. The palace was bombed 16 times in World War II. 'I'm glad we've been bombed,' the Queen declared. 'It makes me feel I can look the East End in the face.'

The new Queen Elizabeth took to her new job like a duck to water – in particular in support of her husband as he faced up to the challenge of becoming King George VI. According to Dermot Morrah, the constitutional expert who was in the royal couple's confidence in these years, the new Queen made a deliberate decision, knowing the power of her own theatricality, never to upstage the King. She saw something in Bertie that so many other people did not, and, in seeing it, she helped make it come true. Elizabeth Bowes Lyon, wooed three times and finally won, had been George VI's first great triumph in a life not greatly noted for its successes. She believed in him, and under the warming influence of her faith, a delicate and rather fine persona found better ways than 'gnashes' to assert itself. She transferred her strength to him in quite an old-fashioned, sacrificial sort of way, and he repaid her with softness and devotion – a total, almost slavish adoration. Their partnership flourished most strongly during the war.

One day in the summer of 1940, when the Battle of Britain was at its height, the diarist Harold Nicolson, then working at the Ministry of Information, lunched at Buckingham Palace. The year had seen a succession of catastrophes – the surrender of Belgium, the fall of France, the seemingly inexorable advance of the German armies that now stood on the other side of the Channel. Nicolson felt demoralised and under strain. The terrible emergency was keeping him up in town, night after night, away from his beloved Kent retreat at Sissinghurst, and he confided to the Queen how he sometimes felt homesick. 'But that is right,' she said. 'That is personal patriotism. That is what keeps us going. I should die if I had to leave.' She told Nicolson that she was taking revolver lessons for self-defence every morning.

'I shall not go down like the others,' she said – the others being the assorted European royal relatives who had pitched up in London with their suitcases, turning Buckingham Palace into something of a rooming house. 'I cannot tell you how superb she was,' wrote Nicolson that night to his wife, Vita Sackville-West. Nicolson was also impressed by the transformation that kingship and a creative wife had wrought in George VI, whom he had once thought of as 'rather a foolish loutish boy'. The King had, somehow, taken on some of the lightness and charm of his elder brother, the Duke of Windsor – and Nicolson walked out of the Palace feeling elated. 'He was so gay and she was so calm,' he told his wife. 'They did me all the good in the world . . . WE SHALL WIN. I know that. I have no doubts at all.'

'They will not leave me. I will not leave the King – and the King will never leave.' These famous words of Queen Elizabeth in response to the suggestion, in the darkest days of the war, that she might send her daughters out of the country for safekeeping, have often been repeated. Their fortitude went with her revolver practice on the Palace lawn. It was like her response to the bombing of Buckingham Palace in September 1940: 'I'm glad we've been bombed,' she said. 'It makes me feel I can look the East End in the face.'

The firm little figure picking her way through the rubble in a Norman Hartnell suit – 'very sweet and soignée,' as Mrs Winston Churchill put it, 'like a plump turtle dove' – became one of the vignettes that encapsulated people's wartime experience. 'The Queen nips out into the snow and goes straight into the middle of the crowd and starts talking to them,' said Lord Harlech, who accompanied her on one of her visits, this one to Sheffield in 1941. 'For a moment or two they just

NORMAN HARTNELL

(1901–79)

Royal Fashion Designer and Couturier

PLAYED BY RICHARD CLIFFORD

Never noted as a fashion plate, the shy and stocky Elizabeth Bowes Lyon was transformed into shimmering elegance by the dresses that Norman Hartnell designed for her state visit to France in 1938. Inspired (at the suggestion of her loving husband) by the gauzy crinolines depicted in the countless paintings by Franz Xaver Winterhalter (1805–73) lining the corridors of Buckingham Palace, the Bruton Street frock-maker created a vision of gleaming lace cobwebs that helped raise national morale in the tense pre-war years. When in a July 1939 photo session the photographer Cecil Beaton, with his nose for glamour to match Hartnell's, etched the modern Winterhalter Queen into the soft greys of his silver nitrate plates, he completed the process that made her a national emblem. A few months later, Hartnell went back to the drawing board to sketch the everyday coats and hats appropriate for his patron's bombsite appearances, coming up with a second successful formula that Elizabeth wore for the rest of her life – part Women's Institute, part Pearly Queen.

He completed the process that made her a national emblem

gaze and gape in astonishment. But then they all start talking at once.'

'She really does manage to convey to each individual in the crowd that he or she has had a personal greeting,' wrote Harold Nicolson on another of her personal appearances that left him with a lump in his throat. 'It is due, I think, to the brilliance of her eyes . . . She is in truth one of the most amazing Queens since Cleopatra.'

The death of her husband a mere seven years after victory was a cruel and early deprivation – too early in so many respects. They had celebrated their Silver Wedding only a few years before he died, they were just about grandparents. But they had never really had a proper run at anything – pitchforked into Buckingham Palace, rushing through the tensions of the pre-war period and then coping with all the dangers and challenges of the conflict. In the tense years since the war, it had been one sickness and worry after another. 'I was sent a message that his servant couldn't wake him,' wrote Queen Elizabeth to her mother-in-law Queen Mary, on 6th February 1952. 'I flew to his room, & thought that he was in a deep sleep, he looked so peaceful – and then I realised what had happened . . . Last night he was in wonderful form & looking so well.' Suddenly there was so much to attend to – the new Queen and her husband to be welcomed back home, the funeral to think of, telegrams to send, new living

The Queen Mother and her corgi Honey at the Castle of Mey on the north-east tip of Scotland, 'this romantic looking castle down by the sea' which she decided to purchase and restore in the summer of 1952.

ELIZABETH BOWES LYON

(1900–2002)

Duchess of York (1923–36)

Queen Elizabeth (1936–52)

Queen Elizabeth the Queen Mother

(1952–2002)

PLAYED BY VICTORIA HAMILTON

Queen Elizabeth the Queen Mother was sustained through her half-century of widowhood by the knowledge – of this she had no doubt – that she would be reunited with her beloved Bertie in heaven. Hers was a deep and literal faith stemming from daily worship as a child in the Glamis chapel where her mother played the harmonium and all the women prayed in white lace caps. She experienced the Second World War as a battle against godlessness – Fascism showed what could happen when a nation abandoned the teachings of Christ – and after the war she welcomed Billy Graham, the American evangelist, when he brought his crusades to Britain, switching to tomato juice when she met him instead of her favoured gin and Dubonnet. 'As I walked in . . .' wrote Rev. Graham, recalling one of his visits to preach at Windsor, 'she deliberately caught my eye and gestured slightly to me to let me know she was supporting me and praying for me.' As a child, Elizabeth was taught by her mother to kneel at her bedside every night to say her prayers, and she continued this devotion for the rest of her life. So far as is known, her daughter Queen Elizabeth II does the same to this day.

arrangements to be made. 'Poor lady,' said Kemp, one of her pages, remembering all the bustle of those days. 'She never had time to cry.' A few days after her husband's funeral, she announced that she wished in future to be known as 'Queen Elizabeth the Queen Mother', though she made clear to friends and family that she disliked the title intensely – 'horrible name,' she sniffed more than once: 'Queen Mum' was definitely for the newspapers. Taking their cue from this, her staff were at pains to refer to her simply as 'Queen Elizabeth' for the rest of her life. 'He loved you all, every one of you, most truly,' she declared on 18th February in a tribute to her husband that she prepared with the help of Tommy Lascelles '. . . My only wish now is that I may be allowed to continue the work we sought to do together.' A month or so after the funeral, old Princess Marie Louise, Queen Victoria's granddaughter, complimented her on the fortitude with which she was bearing her loss – putting such a very brave face on things. 'Not in private,' the widow quietly replied. She went back to the woods at St Paul's Walden Bury where Bertie had proposed to her while sawing wood. She kept a little sitting room at Glamis Castle as a sort of shrine, its photographs and mementoes all dating from their long-drawn courtship and the first, simple years of their marriage. 'One cannot yet believe that it has all happened,' she wrote in one letter. 'One feels rather dazed.' A beautiful day, she wrote to Lascelles, 'is almost unbearable, & seems to make everything a thousand times worse. I suppose it will get better someday.'

There are several theories as to what coaxed her out of the darkness. Winston Churchill went for a long, serious talk with her at Balmoral, speaking of duty and joy, it is thought. Then there was the abandoned home she found in the very north-east tip of Scotland, the Castle of Mey, which

she resolved to bring back to life, as a parable for the rebuilding she now had to do for herself. In the summer of 1952, she went up to Scotland to stay with her old friends Clare and Doris Vyner – 'Fasty', who had organised the apple-pie beds the first time that Bertie had come to stay at Glamis – and went out with them on an excursion towards John O'Groats. Looking out between the road and the waves, as she later described it, she caught sight of 'this romantic looking castle down by the sea'. They drove down the track, to find it was deserted. 'And then the next day we discovered it was going to be pulled down and I thought this would be a terrible pity. One had seen so much destruction in one's life.'

When he heard of the royal interest, the owner, Captain Frederic Bouhier Imbert-Terry, wanted to make Queen Elizabeth a present of the ruin.

He was embarrassed by its run-down state. Commandeered for military accommodation during the war, Barrogill, as it was then known, had been devastated by a violent storm that spring, and the only sniff of a purchase had been from scrap-metal merchants who wanted the lead from the demolished roof. The captain was delighted when Queen Elizabeth accepted his suggestion of £100 as a nominal price, and when she also decided to restore not only the building, but its original and evocative title, the Castle of Mey. 'It is near the sea,' wrote the Queen Mother to Queen Mary, 'with lovely views, & might be nice for a change sometimes, and perhaps one could lend it to tired people for a rest.'

The revival had begun. Going private had always been one option for her widowhood – Queen Victoria did it quite spectacularly, Queen Alexandra to a lesser degree. But for Queen Elizabeth the Queen Mother that was never a possibility. 'That is no age to give up your job,' sniffed Queen Mary on hearing that Queen Wilhelmina of the Netherlands, then 68, was planning to retire, and the older Queen Elizabeth had always been of the same mind. Royalty, in her opinion, was a job for life, a pleasure and a duty to be continued to the very end. There was a suggestion, in the early years following the death of her husband, that she might be dispatched for two or three years on a tour of duty to one of the dominions – Canada, perhaps, or Australia – as a governor-general or some form of semi-permanent royal ambassador. But Queen Elizabeth II would not hear of that. 'Oh no,' she said, 'we could not possibly do without Mummy.'

Miss World

O ne hundred dresses, 36 hats, 50 pairs of shoes . . . 'Couldn't we try to economise?' asks Elizabeth II at the start of Episode 8, 'Pride and Joy', as Norman Hartnell, one of her two principal dressmakers, reels off the huge collection of clothes to be designed, cut and sewn from scratch for her forthcoming tour of the Commonwealth through the winter of 1953–54. 'Isn't this all a bit much?'

'It is,' agrees Hartnell, clearly himself daunted by the scale of the task as his mannequins parade their costumes in front of the Queen and 'Bobo' MacDonald, the nursery-nurse-turned-dresser who is now in charge of the royal wardrobe. But, as Hartnell explains, the request for a top-notch array of touring costumes 'was a directive from the government itself, from the very top of the government. To put our best foot forward . . . our very best foot.'

It does not seem likely that Winston Churchill himself ('the very top of the government') spoke directly to Norman Hartnell about how to dress the Queen on her great post-coronation Commonwealth tour. But it was certainly the British prime minister's intention that the newly crowned Elizabeth II should carry the coronation spirit around the world with her, projecting the prestige of the mother country to an empire that he refused to see in decline. 'It may well be,' declared Churchill sentimentally before her departure, 'that the journey the Queen is about to take will be no less auspicious, and the treasure she brings back no less bright, than when [Francis] Drake first sailed an English ship around the world.' The prime minister

wanted to demonstrate to the leaders of America and Russia, with whom he had worked during the Second World War on equal terms, that the power of the British Crown to command loyalty around the globe made for international heft that still entitled the United Kingdom – and Churchill himself – to a full place at the top table. 'And, if I may, ma'am,' he confides to the Queen as he bids her godspeed at London airport, 'never let them see the real Elizabeth Windsor . . . The cameras, the television. Never let them see that carrying the crown is often a burden. Let them look at you, but let them see only the eternal.'

These were heavy loads to lay upon a mere collection of hats and frocks, but, having designed outfits for royal occasions since the 1930s, Norman Hartnell was well up to the challenge. Royal fashion is not the height of fashion, since the dressing of a queen is a game played by rules that are all its own. Queenly fabrics and styling may bear a surface resemblance to the clothes that the rest of the world is wearing, but actually they indicate the total 'otherness' of the person who is draped in them: the hat, the gloves, the stand-out, bright colours that are only worn by ordinary ladies when dressing up for a wedding – plus the overlarge handbag resolutely carried everywhere, despite the spare hands of a lady-in-waiting. As Hartnell once put it, the Queen's public costume has to be 'totally conspicuous, without being vulgar'. Hartnell had

designed Elizabeth's wedding dress in 1947, as well as her grand coronation robes, and they provided a theme for the dozen Commonwealth destinations she would be visiting that winter. Elizabeth had suggested that her coronation dress be embroidered with the emblem of every realm of which she was Queen – among them the wattle for Australia, the fern for New Zealand and the lotus for Ceylon. So, the quasi-religious dress from the abbey was brought along to be worn at the Opening of Parliament ceremonies in those three countries, while Hartnell – noted for his opulent embroidery – extended the concept to stitch a local wild-flower emblem into at least one costume for every country she would visit: Bermuda, Jamaica, Fiji, Tonga, New Zealand, Australia, the

Right: Norman Hartnell with his design for the coronation dress of June 1953. Left: Elizabeth II wears a slim-fitting white outfit designed by Hartnell's rival Hardy Amies in February 1954 in Sydney.

Cocos Islands, Ceylon, Aden, Uganda, Malta and Gibraltar. The designer also had to cope discreetly with the practical challenges of so many warm-weather destinations – the hazard of lightweight dresses that might blow upwards in the wind. That meant a separate slip for modesty, with small lead weights sewed into the hems of both slip and skirt.

'Her hat has to be off her face so her picture can be taken,' explained Hartnell in a later interview with the *New York Times*, 'and it can't be so big that she has to hold it to keep it from blowing away. After all, a Queen needs one hand for accepting bouquets and another for shaking hands . . . The Queen and the Queen Mother do not want to be fashion setters. That's left to people with less important work to do.'

The essential *un*-fashionability of royal dressing was a favourite theme of the up-and-coming Hardy Amies, chosen by Elizabeth to share and compete with Hartnell in the task of designing much of her daywear for the tour (introducing some healthy price competition as well). 'I don't think she feels that chic clothes are friendly,' Amies liked to say. 'There's always something cold and cruel about chic clothes which she wants to avoid.' Eight years younger than Hartnell, Amies was a self-proclaimed snob. 'I'm for elitism and its survival,' he explained, saying that when he reached heaven he was hoping to encounter God in a five-buttoned suit.

A Hardy Amies flared and pleated day dress with a waist belt worn by Queen Elizabeth II at a civic reception in Broken Hill, Australia in March 1954.

But he was deeply respectful when it came to his principal patron. 'I do not dress the Queen,' he once declared. 'The Queen dresses herself. We supply her with clothes – there is a difference.' Amies was credited with livening up Elizabeth's daywear to make the most of her tiny 23-inch waist. His proposals for Australia (some of which were unworn hangovers from the aborted tour of 1952 that had got no further than Kenya) included some sprightly, off-the-peg frocks from Horrockses, the historic Lancashire cotton producer – and Elizabeth herself seemed to enjoy her visits to the Amies workshop. 'The sketches were put all over the floor and the rolls of fabric,' recalled Valerie Rouse, a Hardy Amies *vendeuse*. 'She used to crawl around the floor saying, "Well, I'll have this with that." She absolutely knew she didn't want too many shoulder pads. She didn't want it too short. She did a lot of sitting down and waving.' Never let it be said that Queen Elizabeth II did not thoroughly enjoy the process of choosing – and wearing – her clothes.

Amies did *not* find favour, however, when he inspired a battle of the couturiers against 'Bobo' MacDonald's mass-market taste in handbags and hats. While the dour Scottish dresser yielded dress design to the designers, she insisted that accessories – shoes, hats and handbags – were strictly her preserve, provoking cries of pain whenever she matched some elegantly tailored outfit with a discordant and boxy handbag of her choice. Amies made no secret of his unhappiness, and he started giving the Queen tasteful handbags for Christmas in the hope that she might decide to use one of

them. 'Bobo will give me hell for this,' remarked Her Majesty drily when she knighted her loyal couturier in 1989 (Hartnell had received his knighthood in 1977). Unsurprisingly, Hartnell and Amies saw each other in competitive terms. 'Hardly Amiable' was Hartnell's nickname for his young rival. But together the two designers helped their mistress achieve a signal triumph in her six-month public service marathon around the world through the winter of 1953–54. Royal tours and visits were invented in the nineteenth century to help make the Crown 'truly imperial', in the words of historian Sir David Cannadine, 'and the empire authentically royal', and the success of Elizabeth II's grandiose Commonwealth odyssey could be said to have achieved both goals – if, probably, for the very last time. Churchill could retain Britain's seat at the top table for just a year or so more.

'I want to show,' Elizabeth declared in New Zealand on 25th December 1953, in the first Christmas Day broadcast ever made from outside Britain, 'that the Crown is not merely an abstract symbol of our unity, but a personal and living bond between you and me.' The Queen deeply believed what she said, and the Commonwealth believed her as well. Still, sometime later when she was discussing outfits with Hardy Amies and was congratulating him on a particularly stylish woollen dress that he had made for her, Her Majesty called for a fur coat to round off the ensemble. 'Very good,' she said, standing in front of the mirror and studying the effect with some satisfaction. 'Now, if only someone would ask us somewhere *smart*.'

The Wattle Dress, based on Australia's national flower, designed by Norman Hartnell for the Commonwealth Tour of 1953–54, and photographed by Baron Nahum in the Grand Entrance of Buckingham Palace.

'We are not amused'

It was the Duke of Edinburgh who came speeding out of the chalet first, followed by his tennis racquet and shoes. Then came the Queen in hot pursuit of her husband and shouting furiously at him to come back inside, as if she had already realised that someone might be watching. The royal tantrum depicted in Episode 8 of *The Crown* actually happened – on Sunday 7th March 1954 at the O'Shannassy Reservoir near the small town of Warburton in the Yarra Ranges of Victoria, 50 miles east of Melbourne. It was captured on film by Frank Bagnall, an Australian cameraman who was waiting to shoot a routine sequence of the royal couple relaxing with the local wildlife community of koala bears, but who instead found himself filming a sequence of flying sports equipment and ill-tempered hollering.

We know of the incident thanks to Jane Connors, an Australian broadcaster who wrote her doctoral thesis, *The Glittering Thread*, on Queen Elizabeth II's post-coronation tour of Australia in the early months of 1954, and who interviewed Loch Townsend, the distinguished film director and head of the camera crew who were recording the eight-week odyssey in glorious Ferraniacolor, a new Italian cine film stock. *The Queen in Australia* was Australia's first full-length colour feature film, and it would play to packed cinemas for months to come – sadly, if not surprisingly, without the sequence of the airborne tennis racquet.

Townsend had arrived outside the royal chalet that Sunday afternoon with Bagnall and sound recordist Don Kennedy to take up their positions as instructed by Commander Colville, the formidable royal press secretary whom the British press knew as 'The Abominable "No" Man'. The Australian press contingent had nicknamed him 'Sunshine'. The brief was to film the royal couple at the halfway stage of their tour 'relaxing' in the scrubby bush around the reservoir, where extra koala bears had been imported to enhance the photo opportunities. But the scheduled appearance time came and went. The minutes ticked by, and the crew started to get agitated about the light ('Christ,' Townsend remembered them complaining, 'when are they bloody well coming?'). The camera was in position and focused on the door ready to film the emergence of the royal couple – when the tennis racquet and the speeding Duke came flying out instead.

Frank Bagnall was looking through the viewfinder when the door opened, and his old Fox Movietone instincts took over. He pressed the button and before anyone knew what was going on, he had the whole incident on film, complete with the indignant Queen grabbing

hold of her husband and dragging him back inside the chalet. There followed a moment of stunned silence while Townsend, Bagnall and Kennedy tried to take in what they had just seen – do anointed queens really fling shoes at their husbands?

At this point in Episode 8, 'Pride and Joy', Elizabeth emerges meekly from the chalet to make her personal peace with the camera crew. But as events actually unrolled beside the O'Shannassy Reservoir that Sunday afternoon in March 1954, it was Commander Colville, the Abominable 'No' Man, who next appeared, charging down the lawn and threatening to have the entire camera crew arrested for their impertinence.

Loch Townsend was a Second World War veteran, a man not easily intimidated. 'I said, "Calm down",' he later related to Jane Connors, 'and I went up to Frank [Bagnall].' As supervising director and producer, Townsend started to unscrew the magazine at the back of the film camera. 'What are you doing?' asked Bagnall. '"Exposing the film, Frank," I said. "You may have finished using your balls, but I've still got work for mine, and I'd like to keep them" . . . I'll never forget saying that. And anyway, I unscrewed it and I took it. There was about three hundred feet of film . . . and I said, "Commander, I have a present for you. You might like to give it to Her Majesty".'

Loch Townsend's main worry, he explained to Jane Connors some 40 years later, was that Colville would withdraw royal cooperation from his ambitious film project. The producer felt uncomfortable that privacy had been invaded, and there was no market in those deferential times for footage which would today be flashed around the world on social media. Even the raucous Australian tabloid press would not have touched the story.

So, Commander Colville was able to take the film indoors, and a few minutes later one of the royal aides appeared with beer and sandwiches for the crew – followed shortly by the Queen herself who came out to thank them personally for the gesture. 'I said who I was and introduced Don and Frank,' recalled Townsend, 'and she said, "Oh, thank you very much. I'm sorry for that little interlude, but as you know, it happens in every marriage. Now, what would you like me to do?"'

In Episode 8 Peter Morgan imagines it was the strains of non-stop touring that had produced the spectacular royal bust-up – 'This whole thing is a circus,' Philip complains. 'It is a miserable circus. Trudging from town to town, and we are the dancing bears.' In their two months of travelling through Australia, the royal couple covered 2,500 miles by rail, according to one accounting, 900 miles by car, and 10,000 by plane, listened to 200 speeches (Elizabeth herself delivered a further 102) and stood to attention through at least 162 recitals of the National Anthem. With less than a day's rest per week, they did their valiant bit for the 'glittering thread' that kept Australian hearts loyal and true to the mother country. But it was small wonder, perhaps, that when Loch Townsend led the Queen and her husband from their chalet to pose with the waiting koalas, the couple found it hard to raise a smile.

Sunday 7th March 1954, near Warburton, Victoria. The Queen and her husband do their best to summon a smile for the camera, standing on the verandah across which the Duke's tennis racquet and shoes had gone flying only an hour or so earlier.

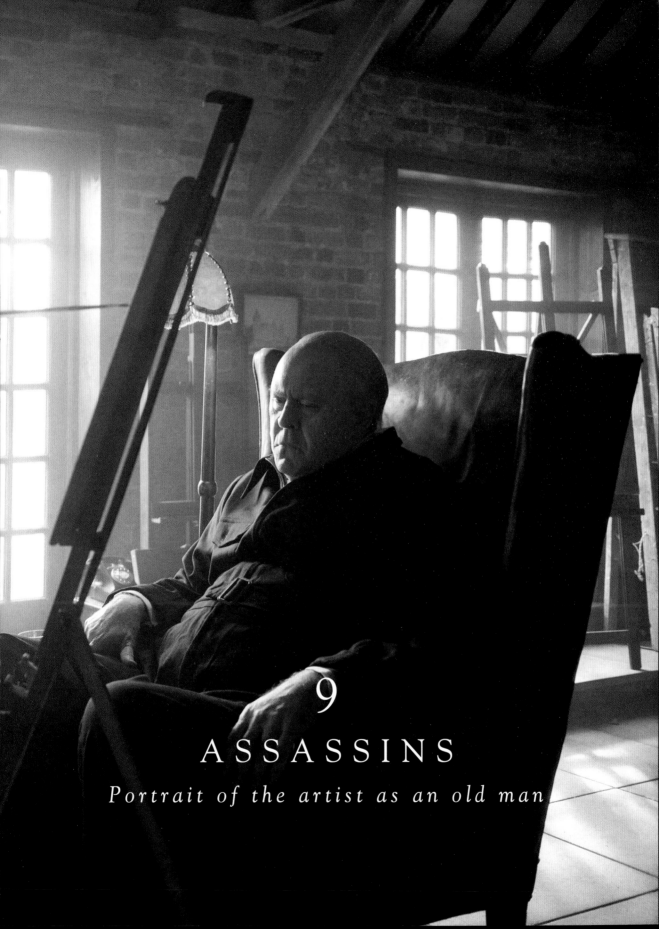

9

ASSASSINS

Portrait of the artist as an old man

9

'A re you going to paint me as a cherub or a bulldog?' asks Winston Churchill at the opening of Episode 9, interrogating Graham Sutherland, the artist commissioned by the Houses of Parliament to paint the great man's portrait to mark his eightieth birthday at the end of November 1954. 'Assassins', the confrontational title of this episode, refers to Churchill's political colleagues who are using the prime minister's advanced age as a reason to force his resignation – so the arrival of Graham Sutherland with his pencils and camera adds another possible assassin to the band. Will this spikey modern artist, so charming to meet, but so notorious for his merciless depiction of his subjects' every weakness, wield a generous brush when it comes to the inescapable physical decrepitude of the ailing statesman? 'Will we be engaged in flattery or reality?' asks Churchill – to which Sutherland answers evasively, 'I imagine there are a great number of Mr Churchills . . . I find in general [that] people have very little understanding of who they are.'

February, 1946. Winston Churchill engrossed in his oil painting at Miami Beach, Florida. 'I know of nothing,' he once wrote, 'which, without exhausting the body, more entirely absorbs the mind.' But his encounter with the artist Graham Sutherland came to absorb his mind in another way . . .

A fine example of Winston Churchill's vivid and swashbuckling brushwork was The Goldfish Pond at Chartwell, *exhibited at the Royal Academy in the summer of 1948. But did his obsessive gazing beneath the surface reflect his grief over the death of his little daughter Marigold?*

And so the duel begins . . .

WSC: 'Perhaps I can implore you not to feel the need to be too accurate.'

SUTHERLAND: 'Why? Accuracy is truth.'

WSC: 'No! For accuracy we have the camera. Painting is the higher art . . .'

The verbal contest between painter and subject draws piquancy from the fact that Churchill himself had been an artist of no little talent and enthusiasm for nearly 40 years. The year 1915 saw the failure of the campaign in the Dardanelles against the Turks, for which Churchill, as First Lord of the Admiralty, was blamed, leading to his ignominious withdrawal from Herbert Asquith's war cabinet and the onset of one of his notorious 'black dog' depressions that laid him low at difficult periods throughout his life. 'I had great anxiety and no means of relieving it,' he later wrote. 'I had vehement convictions and small power to give effect to them … And then it was that the Muse of Painting came to my rescue.' Painting became the disgraced ex-minister's consolation when a chance encounter with some artistic friends inspired him to start work with his own set of equipment – the oil paints, easel, canvas and brushes were a gift from the ever-supportive Clementine – and he never looked back.

'I know of nothing,' Churchill once declared of his painting, 'which, without exhausting the body, more entirely absorbs the mind.' As his longtime friend Violet Bonham Carter remarked, Winston's work with a paintbrush was the only occupation that the great orator ever pursued in total silence. 'I paint all day & every day,' he wrote to his daughter Mary after his crushing defeat in the 1945 election, '& have banished care & disillusionment to the shades.' With the advancing years, the elder statesman's hours in front of the easel came to rival brandy and cigars among his principal consolations. 'I'd like to spend my first million years in heaven painting,' he used to tell his family, according to his granddaughter Emma Soames. 'If Churchill saved Britain during the Second World War,' declared Andrew Marr in his perceptive BBC documentary on Churchill and his more than 500 paintings, 'we can say that it was painting that saved *him*.'

A fine example of Churchill's vivid and swash-buckling brushwork – and of the turmoil at work below the apparently tranquil surface – was *The Goldfish Pond at Chartwell*, which he had painted in the garden of his Kentish home while he was Leader of the Opposition and exhibited at the Royal Academy in the summer of 1948. This pond was a theme to which he frequently returned – we find him painting beside it early in Episode 9, and later

in the same episode Peter Morgan depicts Graham Sutherland complimenting Churchill, painter to painter, on his portrayal of the water, and suggesting a reason why he was so drawn to the subject. 'Beneath the tranquillity and the elegance and the light playing on the surface,' says Sutherland, 'I saw honesty and pain, terrible pain … You wanted us to see something beneath all the muted colours, deep down in the water. Terrible despair. Hiding like a Leviathan. Like a sea monster.' Churchill is dismissive of Sutherland's suggestion, trying to insist that his fascination with the pond is simply 'because it's a technical challenge. It eludes me.' But then he recalls how he and Clemmie had built the pond at Chartwell in the months following the tragic death of their youngest daughter Marigold, aged only two years and nine months, from a sore throat that developed into septicemia. 'I thought

Clementine Churchill with the couple's fourth child, their beloved daughter, Marigold, who died from septicemia when she was less than three years old.

that Clemmie would die from the violence of her grief,' he told his private secretary almost 40 years later, recalling the pain of the tragedy. 'She screamed like an animal under torture.' Nowadays, the little girl would have recovered with a prompt dose of antibiotics. In 1921 her heartbroken father banned all mention of Marigold's existence from family conversation – then got out his brushes, palette and easel to paint the pond at Chartwell for the first of more than 20 times.

Both Churchills enjoyed their conversations with the intelligent and charming Sutherland, who came to Chartwell in the autumn of 1954 for eight 45-minute sittings at which he made charcoal sketches and oil studies, as well as taking photographs, all of which he then took back to work on at his studio at Trottiscliffe, Kent, about 20 miles away. This meant that the Churchills had no means of telling what shape the portrait was taking – though Clementine expressed confidence. She admitted to a soft spot for the eloquent 51-year-old painter and craftsman, who also worked in glass and fabrics and would later design the massive altar tapestry at the rebuilt Coventry Cathedral. 'Mr. Graham Sutherland is a "wow",' she wrote to her daughter Mary after the first three sittings. 'He really is a most attractive man . . . ' – on the basis of which assessment she feels able, quite early in Episode 9, to venture a vote of confidence: 'It's manifestly clear,' Clemmie declares, 'he's a fan … I have the protective instincts of a loving wife, and I can tell you this one is _not_ an assassin.'

But that was early in September. Two months later, at the end of November 1955, just 10 days

'She screamed like an animal under torture.'

before the scheduled presentation, the finished work was finally delivered to Downing Street, a seated life-size portrait nearly five feet high and four feet wide. Churchill hated it immediately. 'It makes me look half-witted . . . ' he would later say. 'How do they paint one today? Sitting on a lavatory! Here sits an old man on his stool, pressing and pressing . . . I look like a down-and-out drunk who has been picked out of the gutter in the Strand.' Physically, the almost square portrait of the seated statesman conveyed an uncanny likeness, but it was the likeness of a decrepit 80-year-old. As Kenneth Clark, the art historian and friend of Sutherland immediately realised, the artist had disregarded the heroic popular stereotypes surrounding the great war leader to focus on the crumbling physical reality. The old warrior was in there to be seen quite clearly – the spark in the eyes and the set of the jaw captured Churchill's defiant spirit brilliantly. But it was a spirit fighting for survival against graphic bodily decay – and that perspective flouted every imagining on Churchill's mental agenda. 'A lot of his time since the end of the war had been spent in arranging and editing the part he will play in history,' wrote his doctor, Charles Moran, 'and it has been rather a shock to him that his ideas and those of Graham Sutherland seem so far apart.'

Next morning an official car left Downing Street for Trottiscliffe, bearing the prime minister's verdict in an imperious letter to Sutherland. 'I am of the opinion,' wrote Churchill, 'that the painting, however masterly in execution, is not suitable as a Presentation from both Houses of Parliament . . .' The ceremony could certainly

CLEMENTINE CHURCHILL

Wife of Sir Winston Churchill

(1 8 8 5 – 1 9 7 7)

PLAYED BY HARRIET WALTER

'Winston may in your eyes . . . have faults,' wrote the 30-year-old Clementine Churchill to Prime Minister Herbert Asquith in May 1915 as the First World War got off to a bad start, 'but he has the supreme quality which I venture to say very few of your present or future Cabinet possess – the power, the imagination, the deadliness to fight Germany.' Asquith totally ignored her plea, sacking Churchill anyway and telling his friends that Clemmie 'wrote me the letter of a maniac'. In May 1940, at an almost identical stage of the Second World War, Clemmie's faith in her husband did not seem quite so mad when he took over as prime minister – with many crediting Churchill's survival over the decades to the sustaining faith of his devoted wife. Only Winston's loving marriage and his painting saved him from his 'black dog' of depression, in their view – and it was Clemmie who had bought him his very first set of brushes and paints. The great war leader's core resolve and conviction, in the opinion of his doctor Charles Moran, started 'in his own bedroom'.

'Winston may in your eyes have faults'

go forward, he wrote, but in the total absence of the portrait. There was no need for anyone to see it, since the parliamentarians had also commissioned 'a beautiful book which they have nearly all signed, to present to me, so that the ceremony will be complete in itself'.

But the wounded Sutherland was not giving in so easily. How could there be an unveiling without a painting? Having consulted Charles Doughty, chairman of the committee of MPs who had commissioned the portrait, he drove down to Chartwell to convey the message that it would offend many MPs if the prime minister rejected their gift, and that Churchill must accept the picture publicly. *The Times* had already published a photograph of the painting, and their art critic had praised it for capturing 'the sitter's character: it is a powerful and penetrating image of the mind whose qualities, here observed without any

excessive or too individual subtlety of interpretation, the world has come to know so well'.

So, the stage was set in Westminster Hall, packed with parliamentarians and their wives, for an eightieth birthday party no one had envisaged – kicked off with a personal tribute from Clement Attlee to whom Churchill hastened to return an elegant compliment. 'The Leader of the Opposition and I,' he declared, 'have been the only two Prime Ministers of this country in the last fourteen years. There are no other Prime Ministers alive. It is not, however, intended to make this a permanent feature of the Constitution.' This political in-joke was a warm-up for Churchill's thanks to the gathering, followed by his one-line dismissal of the painting which Attlee had just unveiled behind him. 'The portrait,' he declared archly, with a pointed failure even to mention the name of the artist, 'is a remarkable example of

30th November 1954, Westminster Hall. 'This portrait,' growled Winston Churchill as he turned his back on Parliament's birthday gift to him of Graham Sutherland's portrait, 'is a remarkable example of <u>modern art</u> . . .' pausing to encourage the derisive laughter from the audience that he wanted.

4 April 1955. On the eve of his resignation as prime minister, Winston and Clementine Churchill entertained Queen Elizabeth II at a full-dress dinner in Downing Street. 'Never,' he declared, 'have the august duties which fall upon the British monarchy been discharged with more devotion than in the brilliant opening of Your Majesty's reign.' He was besotted with his sovereign to the end.

Graham Sutherland, sometimes joined by his wife Kathleen (top right), came to Chartwell for eight sittings at which he made charcoal sketches and oil studies – as well as these photographs of his cantankerous subject from different angles.

modern art . . . ' stressing the words sardonically. Then, having paused to encourage the derisive laughter that accumulated around the hall, he moved on to lavish praise on the 'beautiful' leather-bound book of parliamentary signatures that was the other part of his gift. He said not another word about the painting, but devoted no fewer than 11 effusive sentences to the book, thanking the MPs who had signed it, and even the MPs who had not. 'I shall treasure it as long as I live,' he said, 'and my family and descendants will regard it as a most precious possession.'

The insult could not have been more obvious at the time, but only history would reveal the full extent of Churchillian displeasure. Mortified by her husband's unhappiness, Clemmie had the portrait immediately consigned to the cellars of Chartwell, then spoke in the following months to his latest private secretary, Grace Hamblin. The presentation of the portrait carried no obligation for the painting to be exhibited publicly, nor to

Sutherland was careful never to let either of the Churchills get sight of his portrait while he was painting it. He took all his sketches and photographs back to his studio where, it turned out, he was more interested in depicting what crumbling physical reality had to show than popular heroic stereotypes.

end up one day at Westminster. It was an outright gift for the Churchills to do with as they wished – and Clementine reckoned she knew exactly what her husband wished. She never consulted him, so far as is known, and, having spoken to Hamblin, she herself turned a blind eye to what the efficient secretary did next. Hamblin enlisted the help of her brother, who turned up at Chartwell a few evenings later 'in dead of night' to help spirit away the offending object. 'It was a huge thing,' Hamblin recalled in a taped interview that remained secret for 20 years, 'so I couldn't lift it alone.' Reaching her brother's garden a few miles away, the pair lit a bonfire together out of sight of passers-by and consigned the canvas to the flames. 'I destroyed it,' confessed Hamblin on the tape, 'but Lady C and I decided we would not tell anyone. She was thinking of me.' And thinking most of all, of course, about the morale of her ever more fragile husband, to whom Clemmie had promised that the painting 'would never see the light of day'.

The real issue at stake – the physical and mental decline of the once-great prime minister – proved less easy to send up in smoke. In parliamentary comments that followed the presentation, the Labour MP Henry Usborne mischievously suggested that Graham Sutherland's image had illustrated the look on the prime minister's face 'at the moment when a delegation of his unfaithful cabinet colleagues came to present him with a demand for his resignation' – and they duly came calling. On 22nd December 1955, just three weeks and a day after the ceremony in Westminster Hall, Anthony Eden and Harold Macmillan headed a deputation of seven senior cabinet ministers to Downing Street – a 'hanging jury'. Ostensibly they wanted to discuss the date of the general election that would have to be held at some time before the following autumn, when the current parliament's five-year term would expire. But that raised the question of who would lead the party on the hustings, and Churchill responded angrily, as Eden recorded in his diary, saying 'it was clear we wanted him out. Nobody contradicted him . . . At the end W said menacingly that he would think over what his colleagues had said & let them know his decision. Whatever it was, he hoped it would not affect their present relationship with him. Nobody quailed.' It was 'the most painful affair,' recalled Harold Macmillan.

'Don't you hate it when the show is over?'

Churchill's decline was impossible to avoid. 'He was ageing month by month,' observed Jock Colville in a note written three months later, 'and was reluctant to read any papers except the news-papers or to give his mind to anything he did not find diverting. More and more time was given to bezique [Churchill's favourite, and avidly enjoyed, card game] and ever less to public business. The preparation of a Parliamentary question might consume a whole morning; facts would be demanded from the Government departments and not arouse any interest when they arrived . . .

It was becoming an effort even to sign letters and a positive condescension to read Foreign Office telegrams.' And yet, as the private secretary noted, 'on some days the old gleam would be there, wit and good humour would bubble and sparkle, wisdom would roll out in telling sentences and still, occasionally, the sparkle of genius could be seen in a decision, a letter or phrase.'

Following the December visit from Eden and his 'hanging jury', Churchill was defiant, stomping off for Christmas at Chequers. But when he got back to Downing Street after the holiday, his mood had changed. Perhaps Clementine had spoken to him sternly, for the 80-year-old was now reconciled to stepping down early in April, following Parliament's 1955 Easter recess. He retained the lingering hope that some international development – ideally, a grand, summit peace conference involving America, France and the new leaders of Russia following Stalin's death – might enable him to bow out on a high. But while France was willing to attend such a gathering, President Eisenhower was not, and 5th April became set as the scheduled resignation date. 'Don't you hate it when the show is over?' the prime minister mused unhappily to Sarah, his actress daughter, asking her how she felt at the end of a long-running play.

The old man dabbled with some pet projects during his final months in Downing Street, trying to advance his long-cherished ambition as a Zionist to make the recently independent state of Israel a member of the British Commonwealth: 'Israel,' he explained, 'is a force in the world & a link to the USA . . . So many people want to leave us, it

This troubled study from the years around 1920 is Winston Churchill's only known self-portrait, in a brooding style to which he never returned. He wanted pleasure from his painting, not pain – and sunny landscapes, usually painted on exotic foreign holidays, became his trademark.

might be the turning of the tide.' But his truly memorable contribution was, as ever, oratorical: 'The day must dawn,' he told the House of Commons in a brilliantly sustained 45-minute speech on the hydrogen bomb that proved to be his farewell at the beginning of March 1955, 'when fair play, love for one's fellow-men, respect for justice and freedom, will enable tormented generations to march forward serene and triumphant from the hideous epoch in which we have to dwell. Meanwhile, never flinch, never weary, never despair!' On 4th April 1955, the eve of his resignation, Churchill entertained his Queen and the Duke of Edinburgh to an unprecedented full-dress dinner in Downing Street. 'I have the honour,' he declared, 'of proposing a toast which I used to enjoy drinking during the years when I was a cavalry subaltern in the reign of Your Majesty's great-great-grandmother Queen Victoria . . . Never have the august duties which fall upon the British monarchy been discharged with more devotion than in the brilliant opening of Your Majesty's reign. We thank God for the gift He has bestowed upon us and vow ourselves anew to the sacred cause, and to the wise and kindly way of life of which Your Majesty is the young, gleaming champion.' Then he raised his glass to utter the words for the last time as prime minister – 'The Queen!'

Three days later, on 7th April 1955, as he was boarding a plane for the retirement holiday that he had planned with Clemmie, painting in Sicily, Churchill was given a handwritten letter from the Queen. 'My dear Winston,' she wrote, 'I need not tell you how deeply I felt your resignation last Tuesday, nor how severely I miss, and shall continue to miss, your advice and encouragement. My confidence in Anthony Eden is complete, and I know he will lead the Country

on to great achievements, but it would be useless to pretend that either he or any of his successors who may one day follow him in office will ever, for me, be able to hold the place of my first Prime Minister, to whom both my husband and I owe so much and for whose wise guidance during the early years of my reign I shall always be so profoundly grateful . . . My husband and I enjoyed so much the dinner party at No. 10 Downing St. last Monday – neither of us will ever forget it.

We send our best wishes to you and Lady Churchill for your time in Sicily and we look forward to seeing you on your return and frequently in the future. With my deepest gratitude

for your great services to my country and to myself, I am, yours ever sincerely,

Elizabeth R.'

In the days that followed Churchill read and reread the letter, storing it away when he got home as one of his most treasured possessions, along with a personally inscribed photograph that Elizabeth had given him of her smiling in her carriage on her way to open parliament in November 1952. He also set about the supervision of a new portrait that had recently been commissioned of him as Lord Warden of the Cinque Ports, the ancient union of England's defensive southern harbours – Sandwich, Dover, Hythe, Romney and Hastings – and England's oldest military rank of distinction. Glad of the opportunity to avoid all the mistakes that he felt Graham Sutherland had made, Churchill carefully instructed the artist, Bernard Hailstone, to paint him standing, not sitting; in full ceremonial uniform, not a drab 'parliamentary' suit; in shiny bright hues, not flat mustard-yellow; and with a happy smile, not a malevolent growl, playing across his features. Predictably, the resulting portrait was a mess.

In 1955 Winston Churchill set about supervising a portrait (above) by Bernard Hailstone that had been commissioned of him as Lord Warden of the Cinque Ports. He saw it as his chance to show where Graham Sutherland's portrait (right) went wrong. But maybe it showed precisely the opposite.

At Churchill's request, Queen Elizabeth II gave her first prime minister a signed copy of this photograph of her smiling and waving in her carriage in November 1952 on her way to the Opening of Parliament. He kept it by his bed for the rest of his life.

Elizabeth and her racehorses

In 1953 the Epsom Derby, Britain's premier horse race, was due to be held on Saturday 6th June, four days after the Queen's coronation. The day before the sacred ceremony, on Monday 1st June, one of the Queen's ladies-in-waiting remarked to Her Majesty that she must be feeling very nervous. 'Of course I am,' replied Elizabeth. 'But I really do think that Aureole will win!'

The Queen's love of horses went back to the first ponies of her childhood, and she soon became a proficient rider, quickly mastering the precarious side-saddle posture that she was required to adopt for military parades. But it was not until 1942 that her father took her to the Beckhampton Stables on the Marlborough Downs, where the royal racehorses were trained. Horse racing had continued in Britain during the early years of the war, and that spring the royal stables had two highly fancied prospects: Sun Chariot and Big Game. Both had been bred at the royal studs, and the

Princess was allowed to go up and pat the magnificent Big Game. She later admitted that she did not wash that hand for the rest of the day. It is with her horses that Elizabeth II can be seen most herself, least a queen. She can forget her position sufficiently to leap up and down like any other enthusiast, shouting

21st April 1938. King George VI riding with his daughters in Windsor Great Park on Princess Elizabeth's twelfth birthday.

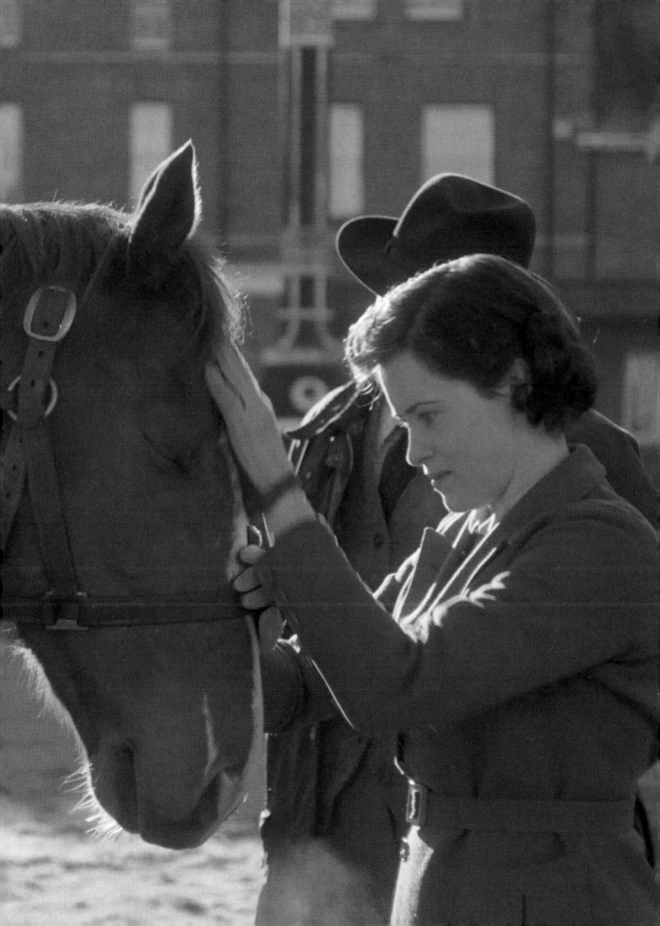

The royal enclosure at Epsom in 1955, from left to right: unknown woman; Queen Elizabeth II; Lord Rosebery; Captain Charles Moore, Manager of the Royal Stud for both George VI and Elizabeth II; Princess Marina, Duchess of Kent, next to her sister Princess Olga (far right). The Duke of Edinburgh stands behind Princess Olga with the Duke of Beaufort, organiser of the Badminton Horse Trials, to his right.

and waving to urge her horse on, and whenever that horse wins you can see reborn the delighted monkey grin of childhood photographs. On the racecourse she comes as close as she possibly can to that most elusive thrill of all – that of being treated just like anyone else (or at least as an equal in an open fraternity). She unashamedly talks to her horses, nuzzling them and losing herself in the spell cast by their inscrutable aristocracy. She revels in the enchantment of rising at dawn to watch the great animals come thundering past her down the dew-covered gallops, and then to walk round the stables afterwards, stroking their glistening sides and talking horse-talk with the nut-brown little men who worship at the same shrine. 'If it were not for my Archbishop of Canterbury,' she once said, 'I should be off to Longchamps every Sunday in my plane.'

The main books beside her desk, according to those who have visited her study, are abstruse volumes of racing pedigrees, for her success at racing is based on her knowledge of bloodstock. It is her grandmother Queen Mary's taste for arcane genealogies turned in another direction, and she has the same royal eye for a well-bred line. It

17th July 1954. Winners' Enclosure. Queen Elizabeth II gives a congratulatory pat to her four-year-old Aureole, after the horse's victory in the prestigious King George VI and Queen Elizabeth Stakes, at Royal Ascot. Aureole went on to a successful and very profitable career at stud, becoming the sire of many winners.

could almost be described as an unfair advantage over non-royal racing owners, but it is the only advantage that Elizabeth II possesses – and this is the basis of the enduring fulfilment she has derived from managing her own racing stables. It is one area of achievement where it is impossible to say that her success is due to her position.

Aureole did not, in fact, win the Epsom Derby in coronation year – he came second – and the Derby remains the only major British race the Queen has never won. But the horse went on to enjoy spectacular success in 1954, winning the Victor Wild Stakes at Kempton, the Coronation Cup at Epsom, the Hardwicke Stakes at Ascot, and Britain's most prestigious all-aged race, the

King George VI and Queen Elizabeth Stakes. In the excitement of victory, Elizabeth despatched a crate of champagne to the press tent so the hacks could join in the celebrations, a generous gesture towards the Fourth Estate that she has never been known to repeat.

HENRY HERBERT, LORD PORCHESTER
'PORCHEY'
(1924–2001)

Racing Manager to the Queen
(also Earl of Carnarvon 1987–2001)

PLAYED BY JOSEPH KLOSKA

'Porchey' was the only person, Princess Anne once said, who could always be sure of being put through to her mother on the telephone at any time, without fail. 'He had the horse news, and that was the news she really wanted to hear.' 'Porchey' was the Queen's hotline to the stables – which mares were in foal, the young stock that looked promising and new race entries that her trainers might be planning. He would ring her on his mobile phone from the sales when he was buying on her behalf, holding it up in the air so she could hear the bidding. The dates made a nonsense of the scurrilous rumour that 'Porchey' fathered Prince Andrew while Philip was abroad – the Duke was in London and Windsor throughout May 1959. But the Queen and her racing manager did devise countless successful racehorse couplings – some of them while staying at 'Porchey's' beautiful Hampshire home of Highclere Castle, familiar to TV viewers since 2010 as the location for Downton Abbey.

'. . . and that was the news she really wanted to hear.'

10
GLORIANA
Love and duty

10

'Your uncle has let us all down,' King George VI tells his two young daughters in December 1936, referring to the recently abdicated Edward VIII at the opening of Episode 10. 'He has put love before family. Now I want you to promise me one thing … that you will never put anyone or anything before one another. You are sisters above all else. And must never let one another down. Understood?' 'Never,' replies the young Princess Margaret, six, nodding gravely. 'Never,' echoes her elder sister Elizabeth, 10, with equal seriousness.

So, as in previous episodes, Peter Morgan opens the drama with an imagined flashback, then leaps forward to historical reality – to Princess Margaret's twenty-fifth birthday on 21st August 1955. Twenty-five was the age when, as explained by private secretary Tommy Lascelles in Episode 6 (two years previously), Margaret could seek to marry the divorced Group Captain Peter Townsend without requiring the permission of her elder sister under the first part of the Royal Marriages Act of 1772 – thus sparing Elizabeth the embarrassments that went with her position as

For an inhibited and traditional man, George VI, shown right at a West End pantomime with the little princesses in the year before his accession, was ahead of his times in encouraging his daughters to be independent. But Princess Margaret would take independence further than he might have wished . . .

Head of the Church (see p. 191). But Lascelles had failed to mention the second provision of the Act – expressly designed by King George III to make life hell for his relatives if they chose to marry spouses of whom he did not approve. Over the age of 25, the Princess no longer needed her sister's consent. But she would now have to give formal notice to the Privy Council of her wish to marry, then wait a full year to see if either House of Parliament chose to raise any objection of their own. Given the agitated nature of national opinion on divorce in 1955, it was hardly likely that some sort of objection would not arise, and with that went the guarantee of 12 months of newspaper coverage and fevered public debate. So, what progress had been achieved by the two-year delay, with all the pain of Townsend's exile in Brussels and the attendant separation and suffering? The young lovers were the victims of a courtier's carelessness – or callousness, more likely.

'Why did no one tell me this at the time?' asks Elizabeth II sharply – then realises that she and Margaret have been played for suckers by the Palace establishment, who had simply wanted to sweep the whole problem under the carpet. It will not be possible for the sisters to fulfil their childhood pledge of total mutual support and loyalty. Grown-up life and love is more complicated.

'The Queen Mother,' explains Lascelles to Michael Adeane, his successor as Private Secretary, at the start of the episode, 'always believed that two years' separation would be long enough for Princess Margaret to lose interest in the Group Captain . . . and the whole thing to go away. But she hasn't. And it hasn't.' So now, if anything, the dilemma for the Queen has become even greater. 'Either she puts her foot down and forbids the marriage – that turns sister against sister,' the former private secretary continues, recapitulating the problem that he himself has made worse, '. . . Or she permits the marriage – setting a collision course with the Church of which she herself is the Head.'

'How can I keep my word [to my sister], after I gave it knowing only half the facts?' Elizabeth asks her new prime minister Anthony Eden, the former foreign secretary who had succeeded Churchill in April 1955. 'Let me take the temperature of the Cabinet,' responds Eden, himself a remarried divorcee. 'We must not forget that times are changing. Morality is changing . . .'

Party girl. With her trademark cigarette holder, Princess Margaret enjoys a glamorous night out at a Parisian nightclub in November 1951.

Well, up to a point, Lord Copper. As Britain in a later decade identified with Diana, Princess of Wales, and her struggles for fulfilment, so Princess Margaret struck a chord in the 1950s with her own personal bid for happiness-against-the-rules. Her apparent willingness to throw over the traces represented the other side of the post-coronation 1950s – the self-obsession of novelist Kingsley Amis's *Lucky Jim* (1954) and the 'Angry Young Men' epitomised by John Osborne and his play *Look Back in Anger* (1956). Margaret might be a princess, but her battle with establishment values resonated with the culture of waywardness that was subverting the goody-goody, dutiful England embodied in her sister. As the Margaret–Townsend romance reached its once-supposed moment of decision – the Princess's birthday on 21st August 1955 – the attitude of the press reflected the new licence. 'Come on Margaret!' exclaimed the *Daily Mirror*. 'Please make up your mind!'

At least they said, 'Please'. Up in Balmoral, more than 300 journalists and photographers appeared for the first recorded instance of what would come to be known as royal 'door-stepping', and when Peter Townsend arrived in London in September, ostensibly on his way to attend the Farnborough Air Show, he was pursued by packs of avid newshounds. Journalists besieged the succession of friends' houses to which the group captain retreated, while Margaret remained up in Balmoral for the time being with the rest of the royal family.

Newspapers stirring up mayhem in the capital, while the royal family kept their heads down at Balmoral, set a fateful precedent, and Elizabeth II did not thank her sister for it. Her feelings had moved far beyond the open-hearted, and somewhat naïve, optimism that had inspired the welcoming *diner à quatre* in the spring of 1953. Now the Queen had grown tired of the fuss. She had not enjoyed having to put this family complication on the agenda with her new prime minister, and she had come to feel that both Margaret and Townsend had imposed on her goodwill and patience. 'She's so instinctively dutiful herself,' says a friend, 'that she can't understand why other people – and particularly her own family – do not just do the right thing.'

By the autumn of 1955 Elizabeth II had no doubt. The obvious and correct course was for Margaret to give up Townsend, but she shrank from imposing that on her sister. As the deadline approached for Margaret to go up to London to be reunited with the group captain at the beginning of October 1955, both sisters avoided the issue. After the final picnic on the Princess's last day in the Highlands, the Queen took her dogs out for a very long walk, carefully arriving back at the castle with time to say no more than a simple goodbye. Her mother was equally evasive.

She was 'ostriching', to employ an expression from the royal repertory of animal catchphrases. The Queen Mother had come to feel quite certain that Margaret should not marry Townsend. It stirred memories of the abdication. She was furious with her younger daughter for provoking such vulgar publicity at the beginning of Lilibet's reign, and she also shared the family's aversion to thrashing things out face-to-face. Meals at Clarence House, where the two women were confined together, were marked, Princess Margaret later remembered, by long and frosty silences 'for weeks on end'. The Queen Mother, however, now 55, did share her feelings with her old friend 'Bobbety' Cecil, fifth Marquess of

The prime minister was himself a divorced man

Salisbury, who was never scared of a scrap, as he had demonstrated in his attempts to elbow out the ailing Winston Churchill. An annual guest at Balmoral, where he had not held back from crossing swords with the young Prince Philip, 'Bobbety' was a pious churchman, as well as a senior and powerful voice in the government of Anthony Eden – and in the middle of October 1955 he made a decisive cabinet intervention.

If Princess Margaret persisted with her plans to marry a divorcee, Salisbury told his colleagues, he would resign from the government rather than acquiesce in a subversion of the Church's teaching. Not wishing to deny the couple personal happiness, he would be agreeable to marriage, but that would have to be subject to a special Bill of Renunciation that would strike the Princess and her heirs from the Civil List – the schedule of royal expenses and allowances – and from the succession. It would be too much to suggest that 'Bobbety' was doing the Queen Mother's dirty work. He felt very strongly about the decay of old-fashioned standards. A few years later he would again threaten to resign in protest against Britain's negotiations with Archbishop Makarios, the terrorist-supported Cypriot leader, stalking out of the cabinet when he did not get his way. But as he made his stand in 1955, the principled marquess knew that one very senior figure in the royal family would sigh regretfully and remind both her daughters that it was not possible to cross the will of an elected government.

Prime Minister Anthony Eden was a divorced and re-married man. But he was not prepared to fight to give Princess Margaret and Peter Townsend the freedom from which he had benefitted.

THE
PRIME
MINISTER
WILL SPEAK

WORKING
FOR PEACE

RKING
PEACE

Anthony Eden had tried to keep himself out of the argument. The prime minister was himself a divorced man who had remarried. But Salisbury had forced the issue on a generally uncensorious cabinet. Though Princess Margaret was by now 25, with the possibility of escaping from the scope of the Royal Marriages Act, she was in receipt of £6,000 a year from the Civil List which would rise to £15,000 when she married. The Civil List was paid from government funds. Even if Eden were willing to accept a cabinet split, he was faced with having to stand up in Parliament and justify, as a matter of government policy, taxpayers' money going to support the divorced Group Captain and the new Mrs Townsend – along with her prospective stepchildren, Townsend's two sons, whose inconvenient existence was seldom brought into the matter. In political terms, the battle was simply not worth fighting, and Eden regretfully informed the Queen that the price of Margaret's marriage would be the Bill of Renunciation as proposed by Salisbury. If the royal family wished to endorse divorce, it would have to do so at its own expense.

Anthony Eden went to convey the unpalatable news to the Queen as part of his weekly royal audience on the evening of Tuesday 18th October. Neither Eden nor his colleagues said it or implied it, but one conclusion was becoming inescapable. If Princess Margaret did marry Peter Townsend, she would have little choice but to leave the country for several years, if not permanently – thus creating *two* sets of exiled Windsor victims of Anglican divorce dogma.

On Friday 21st October came another reminder of the past when the royal family, the Buckingham Palace household, the prime minister and cabinet, along with the leaders of the opposition and representatives of the Church and Commonwealth, gathered on the steps of Carlton Gardens halfway down the Mall for a poignant ceremony to unveil William McMillan's fine-featured bronze statue of King George VI (a scene depicted by Peter Morgan at the opening of Episode 8). 'Much was asked of my father in personal sacrifice and endeavour,' declared Elizabeth II in her moving speech at the unveiling, highlighting 'personal sacrifice' in a way that some felt carried an extra meaning. 'He shirked no task, however difficult, and to the end he never faltered in his duty to his peoples.'

By now, recalled Townsend – who had, pointedly, *not* been invited to the ceremony commemorating the monarch whom he had served with such devotion – 'We were both exhausted, mentally, emotionally, physically. We felt mute and numbed at the centre of this maelstrom.' The couple separated for the weekend – Margaret to stay with her sister and husband at Windsor, Townsend to remain at 19 Lowndes Square, the Knightsbridge apartment of Margaret's friends the Marquess and Marchioness of Abergavenny. 'That Sunday night,' he recalled in his memoir *Time and Chance*, 'I had hardly slept. My mind had turned incessantly on the sadness of the Princess. In just over a week the smile had vanished from her face, her happiness and confidence had evaporated. Events had put us to a rude test and the clamour, louder than ever, still continued about us …'

On the morning of the following Wednesday, 26th October 1955, *The Times* broke silence in a monumental editorial. The paper made no personal criticism of Peter Townsend, describing him as 'a gallant officer with nothing to his disadvantage except that his divorced wife is still living'. Nor did it criticise public interest in the love of the Princess for the group captain. 'The enormous popular emotion that has been generated by the

EXTRA

COMPLETE RACES

Los Angeles Examiner

CHARACTER · QUALITY · AMERICA FIRST! · ENTERPRISE · ACCURACY

AN AMERICAN PAPER FOR THE AMERICAN PEOPLE · THE GREAT NEWSPAPER OF THE GREAT SOUTHWEST

Reg. U.S. Pat. Off.

Examiner Building, 1111 S. Broadway, Zone 54   Examiner Telephone Richmond 8-1212

VOL. LII—NO. 325   LOS ANGELES, TUESDAY, NOVEMBER 1, 1955   PCC   Four Sections—Section I—TEN CENTS

'I Will Not Marry Capt. Townsend'

PRINCESS GIVES UP LOVE FOR DUTY!

ROMANCE ENDS—"I have been strengthened by the unfailing support and devotion of Group Capt. Peter Townsend," stated Princess Margaret (above) yesterday as she announced she'd not marry him.
—Associated Press wirephoto

Church Opposition Influences Decision

Margaret Declares Townsend's 'Devotion, Support' Aided Her

LONDON, Oct. 31.—(P)—Princess Margaret told the world tonight she has renounced her hope of marrying divorced Peter Townsend. She spoke like a girl with a broken heart who has put duty ahead of love.

"I would like it to be known that I have decided not to marry Group Capt. Peter Townsend," she announced.

"I have been aware that subject to my renouncing my rights of succession it might have been possible for me to contract a civil marriage.

"But, mindful of the church's teaching that Christian marriage is indissoluble, and conscious of my duty to the commonwealth, I have resolved to put these considerations before any others."

Strengthened by Devotion

"I have reached this decision entirely alone and in doing so I have been strengthened by unfailing support and devotion of Group Capt. Townsend.

"I am deeply grateful for the concern of all those who have constantly prayed for my happiness."

The 113-word announcement, signed simply "Margaret," was issued at Clarence House, her home, only an hour after she and Townsend met for perhaps the last time in the privacy of her own apartment.

Townsend—who is 40 and 15 years older than the Princess—left the stately mansion alone and drove away toward the seclusion of the English

(Continued on Page 2, Cols. 5-7)

OUT—Group Capt. Peter Townsend (above), his romance with Princess Margaret ended, left London.
—Associated Press wirephoto

RUSSIA TRAVEL BAN LIFTED

By Pierre J. Huss

GENEVA, Oct. 31.—(INS)—Secretary of State Dulles dramatically announced today the United States is removing restrictions that had prevented American citizens from traveling in the Soviet Union and Communist-ruled satellite states.

Dulles told the Big Four foreign ministers' session restrictions were removed starting today in the hope of improving East-West relations.

"Hereafter," he said, "American passports will be valid for the Soviet Union and all countries in eastern Europe

(Continued on Page 4, Cols. 1-2)

Jury to Get 'Mistake' Woodward Death Case

NEW YORK, Oct. 31.—(INS)—The mystery-laden "mistake" killing of millionaire socialite-sportsman William Woodward Jr., by his beautiful wife will be given to a grand jury for investigation, it was announced late today.

Nassau County District Attorney Frank Gulotta said he will let a jury decide whether the shotgun killing of the owner of the racehorse Nashua was a criminal or accidental case.

The decision was made as a protective medical curtain was thrown around the emotionally-shattered blonde former model, barring her temporarily from being questioned about the circumstances surrounding the Sunday morning slaying in the Woodward's palatial Oyster Bay

Cove estate outside New York City.

At the same time, authorities disclosed they are closely checking reports Woodward, 35, and his 32-year-old wife had led a stormy marital life. They stressed, however, that up to the present no factual information has been received to verify such reports.

Among those who will be questioned, Nassau Chief of Detectives Stuyvesant Pinnell said, are Woodward's mother, Mrs. William Woodward Sr., and the Duchess of Windsor. The Duchess was guest of honor at a plush Long Island "gold cast" party just before Woodward was shotgunned to death.

Gulotta told newsmen:

"I expect to bring all the

(Continued on Page 6, Cols. 1-4)

SMOG GREEN

FOR TODAY

SMOG GREEN: Light or no smog forecast.

You can operate your backyard incinerator from 6 to 10 a. m. or from 4 to 8 p. m., in the City of Los Angeles and County unincorporated areas. Hours vary among other cities and in foothill areas; for information on these, call your Fire Department or City Hall.

(Open fires are now banned whether there is smog or not, throughout the county, including in cities, with a few exceptions which do not generally apply to householders.

TODAY'S INDEX

Boy Meets Girl, p 11, Sec. I.
Classified, pgs 5-17, Sec. III.
Comics, p 7, Sec. IV.
Crossword Puzzle, p 4, Sec. III.
Darling, p 1, Sec. III.
Editorials, p 20, Sec. I.
Editorial Contributions, p 21, Sec. I.
Fashions, p 4, Sec. II.
Financial, pgs 2-3, Sec. II.
Fortune Finder, p 18, Sec. III.
Fulton Lewis Jr., p 21, Sec. I.
Horoscope, p 4, Sec. II.
Health Column, p 21, Sec. I.
Livestock, Farm Products, p 3, Sec. II.
Labor News, p 5, Sec. II.
Looking Around, p 5, Sec. I.
Louella O. Parsons, p 7, Sec. II.
Movies, pgs 5-7, Sec. II.
Pegler, p 21, Sec. I.
Pictures, p 3, Sec. I.
Prudence Penny, p 5, Sec. II.
Radio, pgs 17-18, Sec. II.
Society, pgs 1-5, Sec. II.
Sports, pgs 1-6, Sec. IV.
Television, pgs 17-19, Sec. II.
Vital Statistics, p 3, Sec. III.
Weather, p 3, Sec. III.

Fire Chief Alderson Quits Over Integration

Fire Chief John H. Alderson, involved in a controversy over Negro integration in the fire department, yesterday announced his resignation to take effect "not later" than January 1, 1956.

His voice choked with emotion, the chief admitted that his resignation is the result of the racial integration problem within the department.

His decision came after a four and one-half hour meeting at the Jonathan Club with three members of the Board of Fire Commissioners — President G. William Shea, Vice President Ray H. Sheldon and Victor M. Carter.

At the "first press conference I have ever called," Alderson issued the following statement:

"It is very apparent to me that I've lost the confidence of the Board of Fire Commissioners. I have explained to the board the conditions under which I accepted the position of Chief Engineer of the Department. I can see no other man to be placed in the position that I was placed in when I was appointed as emergency, and eventually permanently, to the position of Chief Engineer of the department.

"It is my intention to retire not later than January 1, 1956. The reason I am encountering this decision is that your honorable board may have an

(Cont. on Page 12, Cols. 4-5)

American newspapers had first broken the Townsend-Margaret story in June 1953, ahead of the more reticent British press, and they maintained their interest to the end of the saga.

recent happenings is in itself perfectly healthy . . . It proceeds from genuine affection for the Royal Family which they have inherited and continue to deserve and which is a principal guarantee of the stability of Kingdom and Commonwealth.'

Interestingly, it dismissed Elizabeth II's position as Governor of the Church as being of real concern only to 'that southern part of the United Kingdom in which the Church of England is established'. This meant little, said *The Times*, to the vast majority of people in the Commonwealth. But (and here was the rub) the vast majority of the rest of the Commonwealth clearly cared about whether or not Princess Margaret married Peter Townsend, and this was for the highest reasons. Whether she liked it or not, Princess Margaret was the sister of the Queen, 'in whom her people see their better selves reflected, and since part of their ideal is of family life, the Queen's family has its own part in the reflection. If the marriage which is now being discussed comes to pass, it is inevitable that this reflection becomes distorted. The Princess will be entering into a union which vast numbers of her sister's people, all sincerely anxious for her lifelong happiness, cannot in conscience regard as a marriage.

'There is no escape from the logic of the situation,' continued the paper. 'If the Princess finally decides, with all the anxious deliberation that clearly she has given to her problem, that she is unable to make the sacrifice involved . . . then she has a right to lay down a burden that is too heavy for her.' But, said *The Times*, this would be 'a blow at all that the royal family had traditionally stood for.' And the parting thrust was sharper still. Whatever decision Margaret's conscience might settle on, 'Her fellow subjects will wish her every possible happiness – not forgetting that happiness

in the full sense is a spiritual state and that its most precious element may be the sense of duty done.'

It was an overwhelming onslaught, and even if the *Daily Mirror* retorted two days later that *The Times* spoke 'for a dusty world and a forgotten age', and suspected that its editor would have preferred the Princess to marry 'one of the witless wonders with whom she has been hobnobbing these past years', the editorial of 26th October 1955 made clear that something serious was going on. *Punch* had been running cartoons of counting peas on a plate – 'Tinker, Tailor, Soldier, Group Captain' – and a comedian had mimicked the news bulletins on the BBC: 'They had tea together again today.' But until *The Times* spoke many people had remained convinced that the crisis was the concoction of the popular media.

Even if Peter Townsend was seeing Princess Margaret – and *The Times* itself had chronicled starkly such visits as he had made to Clarence House – it seemed to many people to be a totally private matter, for she could not seriously be contemplating a marriage which would flout the teaching of the Church and the traditional royal attitude towards marriage vows. It now became clear, however, that she was.

The Chairman of the Methodist Conference, Dr Leslie Weatherhead, felt the time had come to pronounce on his church's behalf. 'Princess Margaret and Group Captain Townsend are popular young people in love with one another,' he declared. But, even if the Princess were to renounce her income and rights to the throne, to many 'her example does not make it easier to uphold the ideal of Christian marriage in a land in which divorce is already too lightly regarded, homes too readily broken up, and children too thoughtlessly deprived of the mental security of having two united parents, a security which is surely part of God's plan.'

Peter Townsend had, in fact, already decided. During the morning of the day *The Times* editorial appeared, he later recalled, 'I had sat mechanically dictating thanks to the scores of letters pouring into No. 19 Lowndes Square. With rare exceptions, they were simple, touching expressions of sympathy; whether "for" or "against", I felt they all deserved acknowledgements.' Ever the perfect equerry, the group captain politely answered every letter.

'I felt so played out,' he wrote, 'that I tried to snatch a few winks of sleep before leaving to see the Princess at 4 p.m. But sleep evaded me. I was obsessed by the thought that the Princess must tell the world there would be no marriage. Words, broken phrases turned in my head. Of a sudden, I rolled off the bed, grabbed a piece of paper and a pencil. The words now came to me with clarity and fluency and I began to write: *"I have decided not to marry Group Captain Townsend … It may have been possible to contract a civil marriage. But mindful of the Church's teaching …"'*

Peter Townsend had, in fact, already decided.

Less than an hour later, Townsend was with the Princess inside Clarence House. 'She looked very tired,' he recalled, 'but was as composed and affectionate as ever. I told her quietly, "I have been thinking so much about us in the last two days, and I've written down my thoughts, for you to say if you wish to." I gave her the rough piece of paper and she read. Then she looked at me, and very quietly, too, she said, "That's exactly how I feel." Our love story had started with those words. Now, with the same sweet phrase, we wrote *finis* to it.'

Margaret told her sister and mother at once, then went to see the Archbishop of Canterbury next day in a scene engraved in the popular imagination by Winston Churchill's son, Randolph. 'The Archbishop,' wrote Churchill, 'supposing that she was coming to consult him, had all his books of reference spread around him carefully marked and cross-referenced. When Princess Margaret entered, she said, and the words are worthy of Queen Elizabeth I, "Archbishop, you may put your books away; I have made up my mind already."' Dr Fisher was indeed surprised that the Princess's decision had already been reached so unambiguously, and was delighted by the path of duty she had chosen. But he was still more surprised when he read this account of the crucial meeting since, as he later told his biographer, William Purcell, 'I had no books of any sort spread around. The Princess came and I received her, as I would anybody else, in the quarters of my own study. She never said, "Put away those books," because there were not any books to put away.' The following Monday, the BBC broke into its evening radio programming to broadcast the statement. 'This is a great act of self-sacrifice,' wrote Harold Nicolson in his diary, 'and the country will admire and love her for it. I feel rather moved.' Most of the editorials of 1st November 1955 bore him out. 'All the peoples of the Commonwealth will feel gratitude to her for taking the selfless, royal way which, in their hearts, they expected of her,' declared *The Times* with ill-concealed satisfaction.

Once the decision was made, Peter Townsend could eventually escape back to Belgium to live in relative anonymity. But for Princess Margaret there was no escape. She had to stay in the spotlight in Britain

But the *Daily Mirror* declined to join 'in the suffocating chant of "good show!"', while the *Manchester Guardian* prophesied that Margaret's decision 'will be regarded by great masses of people as unnecessary and perhaps a great waste. In the long run, it will not redound to the credit or influence of those who have been most persistent in denying the Princess the same liberty that is enjoyed by the rest of her fellow citizens . . . That odd piece of inconsistency may be typically English, but it has more than a smack of English hypocrisy about it.'

Hypocrisy was the theme that Noël Coward picked up in his diary three days later, hoping that Margaret would not now 'become a frustrated maiden Princess [and] that they had the sense to hop into bed a couple of times' – though he privately doubted this. 'It would have been an unsuitable marriage anyway . . .' mused The Master. 'She cannot know, poor girl, being young and in love, that love dies soon and that a future with two strapping stepsons and a man eighteen years older than herself would not really be very rosy.' As Margaret's occasional confidant Kenneth

Rose would knowingly put it, the Princess could not have long survived the bottom-line reality of 'life in a cottage on a Group Captain's salary'. Elizabeth's younger sister had not been raised to be anything other than a princess, and marriage to Townsend would have meant surrendering her lifestyle, her status and, in many ways, her very identity. 'Let me tell you from bitter experience,' remarked the former Princess Patricia of Connaught, Queen Victoria's granddaughter, who nobly surrendered her HRH status on her marriage to the naval officer Captain Alexander Ramsay in 1919, and was to spend 55 happy but obscure years as Lady Patricia Ramsay, 'It's not a good idea to give up being a princess.'

'We are half people . . .' declaims the Duke of Windsor philosophically in a telephone call that Peter Morgan imagines Elizabeth making to her Uncle David at the height of Margaret–Townsend crisis. 'I understand the agony you feel and I am here to tell you, it will never leave you.'

The irony of the Princess Margaret–Peter Townsend crisis of October 1955 was that it was the supposedly wayward Margaret, the younger sister, and not the dutiful Elizabeth II, who took action to protect the Crown with her act of personal sacrifice – and that, sadly, that sacrifice did not count for very much in the long run. Within 40 years, the marriages of three of the Queen's four children would end in divorce, not to mention Princess Margaret's own marriage to Lord Snowdon; and, looking to the next reign, the future King Charles III, due to be solemnly crowned and consecrated one day with holy oil, is a divorced man who is married to a divorced woman. What price now the Church's teaching?

Peter Townsend quietly made his escape back to Belgium, to live the rest of his life safely removed from the twin perils of the British press and the British royal family, while Princess Margaret continued to ruminate on exactly what – and who – had denied her happiness. Her greatest, and most understandable, complaint was that the obstacles of the Royal Marriages Act that were placed in her way in 1955 had all existed back in 1953 when she first committed herself to Townsend. She and Peter had wasted two painful years planning life and love on false pretences, and she focused her particular resentment on Tommy Lascelles, since it was Lascelles who had kept the truth from both herself and from her sister, taking the excuse to exile Peter to Brussels, while attributing spurious hope to her twenty-fifth birthday. Everyone had taken their cue from the private secretary.

In later years, Margaret came to be a neighbour of Lascelles in his grace and favour retirement apartment in Kensington Palace, and she described the moment one morning when she saw his grey and stooping frame trudging across the pebbles in front of her car. The Princess who had made such sacrifice for the sake of her Christian faith happily confessed to a most un-Christian impulse – to command her chauffeur to step on the accelerator and crunch the former private secretary into the gravel.

*Final encounter. Peter
Townsend, surrounded
by crowds, press and police
on 1st November as he
leaves his London lodgings
following the announcement
of Princess Margaret's
decision not to marry him.*

Princess Betts

TRAINEE MECHANIC

'She's a bit throaty, I'm afraid,' says Queen Elizabeth II as she leads Anthony Eden towards an old green Land Rover during his autumn visit to Balmoral in 1955. 'We've been having trouble with the fuel pump.' The prime minister wants to discuss the Suez Canal and his problems with the fiery Egyptian leader, Gamal Abdel Nasser.

But the Queen is happier talking about fuel pumps and cylinder heads – fond memories of her most sustained spell in the outside world, when she studied as a trainee mechanic on an army vehicle maintenance course as a member of the women's Auxiliary Territorial Service, the ATS, at the end of the Second World War: 'No. 230873, Second Subaltern Elizabeth Alexandra Mary Windsor. Age: 18. Eyes: blue. Hair: brown. Height: 5 ft. 3 ins.'

The Princess had enrolled for wartime youth service as soon as she was eligible, on her sixteenth birthday in April 1942, but her parents had been reluctant to let her 'out into the world' at such a young age. George VI felt his elder daughter should concentrate on her formal studies with Henry Marten, her constitutional tutor, as well as with her governess Marion Crawford. But both the governess and the Princess herself felt that the King was being overprotective. 'I ought to do as other girls of my age do,' complained Elizabeth, and she had to fight a long-running campaign to get her father to change his mind.

'After exercising all her persuasion,' in the diplomatic words of Dermot Morrah, Elizabeth finally won permission to join the ATS while she was still just 18. She was fitted for her hard-won khaki uniform, and for six weeks in the spring of 1945 she was driven over daily from Windsor to Aldershot, the traditional home of the British Army in Surrey, to pursue the ATS course on vehicle maintenance – working on, in and underneath motor cars and lorries. She learned how to read a map, how to drive in convoy and how to strip and service an engine. It was the first time in history, her 11 fellow students were told, that

'I ought to do as other girls of my age do'

During her six-week training course at Aldershot in 1945, 'Princess Betts' learned how to change a tyre, how to strip and service an engine, how to drive in convoy and how to read a map.

Royal recruit to the Auxiliary Territorial Service: No. 230873, Second Subaltern Elizabeth Alexandra Mary Windsor. Age: 18. Eyes: blue. Hair: brown. Height: 5 ft. 3 ins.

a female member of the royal family had ever attended a course with 'other people'. They were under strict instructions not to reveal her identity and were bursting with curiosity to see what she looked like. Noted Corporal Eileen Heron in her diary, 'Quite striking. Short, pretty, brown, crisp, curly hair. Lovely grey-blue eyes, and an extremely charming smile, *and* she uses lipstick!' The Princess was equally eager to get to know her course mates, but that proved difficult. While they slept in huts

at Aldershot in the all-female base, Elizabeth was chauffeured the 22 miles back home to Windsor, where her earnest discourses on pistons and cylinder heads over dinner became something of a family joke. When the course broke for lunch, the Princess was 'whisked away' by the officers to eat in their mess, and at lectures she was placed in the middle of the front row, with a protective sergeant on either side. But she did her best in the circumstances. 'When anyone is asked a question,' noted

Eileen Heron, 'she turns round to have a good look at the person concerned. It is her only opportunity to attach names to the right people.' And by the end of her course, Elizabeth had managed to escape from her overprotective mentors and take tea with the other girls. According to one report, her more familiar companions referred to her as 'Betts'.

When the King and Queen visited the depot to observe 'Betts' taking her final test, they found their daughter in greasy overalls with black hands and a smudged face peering out from under a car 'looking very grave and determined to get good marks and do the right thing'. As a measure of her proficiency at the end of the course, the Princess drove her company commander up from Aldershot through the thick of London afternoon traffic into the courtyard of Buckingham Palace

– 'though whether the fact that she found it necessary to drive twice around Piccadilly Circus on the way was due to high spirits or to a less than absolute mastery of the round-about system,' wrote Dermot Morrah, 'has not been determined by competent authority'.

The experience ended all too quickly for Elizabeth. '[She] says she will feel quite lost next week,' noted Corporal Heron, 'especially as she does not know yet what is going to happen to her as a result of the course.' The Princess told Eileen that she was hoping to join ATS headquarters later that summer as a junior officer, where she would have worked in an office with the other young women on transport organisation. But it was not to be. Less than a month later, on 8th May 1945, came VE (Victory in Europe) Day. There was ATS work aplenty in the months of demobilisation that followed, but George VI wanted his daughter back home on more prominent public duties. On the evening of VE Day itself, after the family had appeared for the umpteenth time on the balcony of Buckingham Palace to the cheers of the enormous crowds, the King detailed a group of young officers to take his daughters quietly out of the Palace to mingle with the throngs of merrymakers revelling in the almost forgotten experience of brightly lit streets and buildings. The Princesses were swept along in the mass rejoicing. 'Poor darlings,' wrote George VI in his diary, 'they have never had any fun yet.' The King had already forgotten his elder daughter's vehicle maintenance course at Aldershot. But Elizabeth never did.

26th May 1945. The 'Princess Mechanic' poses for a different sort of glamour shot on the cover of Illustrated *magazine.*

Annigoni and Beaton
Royal Portraits

In the spring of 1955 the Florentine artist Pietro Annigoni was preparing to display his huge and unashamedly 'chocolate box' portrait of Queen Elizabeth II at the Royal Academy's Summer Exhibition. More than five feet tall, the painting was the painstaking product of no fewer than 14 sittings, and its strikingly representational, almost photographic image boldly upheld the painter's defiance of 'modern art'. No Graham Sutherland, Annigoni had joined with six other Italian artists in 1947 to proclaim a manifesto of 'Modern Realist Painters' in defiance of abstract art, protesting against the various non-figurative movements that were gaining favour in Italy in the post-war years.

In fact, the artist's towering, three-quarter-length study of the Queen was not totally traditional. While meticulously detailed in the early Renaissance style to which Annigoni adhered, its symbolism had a Surrealist feel, with Elizabeth dressed in her dark blue Garter robes, floating in a cloudless sky above a bleak landscape of windswept trees, with a mysterious lake in the distance.

The portrait caused a sensation when it was unveiled at the Academy's summer show. It appealed to both the eye and to the heart. Crowds queued for hours and they clustered around the painting up to 10 deep. One critic compared the precision of the imagery to Hans Holbein's

portrait of Jane Seymour, Henry VIII's favourite wife, and Annigoni took pride in the comparison. In documentary terms, his painting displayed a monarch who had come of age – self-assured and in command, a royal portrait and no mistake.

The most plausible explanation of its enigma was offered by the artist himself, an endearingly diminutive and chatty Italian no more than five feet tall, who had cajoled the Queen into talking about her experiences as a child – in French, since his English was faulty and her Italian non-existent. Elizabeth told him how, as a little girl, she had spent hours looking out of the Palace windows, wondering about the cars and the passers-by and the reality of the lives they led, trying to put herself in their place and imagine where they were going and what they were thinking. In the eyes of Annigoni, Elizabeth II was both remote from her people and very engaged – and that was the paradox his painting sought to convey.

'Chocolate box' was the reaction of the fiercer critics, but that did not discourage Cecil Beaton, about whose photographs the very same has been said. Invited to photograph the Queen in the autumn of 1955, he decided to do an Annigoni of his own, photographing her in her Garter robes against another of his painted backdrops – this time of Windsor Castle from the Thames. He painted in the backdrop of the sky himself *in situ* at the Palace on the morning of the sitting, to make quite sure it had the tone he was aiming at.

In later years, royal photographers would bring along teams of make-up artists as if for a fashion shoot, but this afternoon in the Blue Drawing Room Beaton had to make do with the powder and lipstick that Elizabeth had applied herself – with no mascara. The lighting did not work for him to start with; it seemed too harsh. But he persevered through several poses, and he played on his familiarity with his subject and their shared memory of the epic session with the maids of honour after the coronation, two summers earlier.

'Luckily, it seems that the Royal Family have only to get a glimpse of me for them to be convulsed in giggles,' he wrote in his diary. 'Long may that amusement continue, for it helps tremendously to keep the activities alive. Throughout the afternoon I found it was very easy to reduce the Queen to a condition of almost ineradicable *fou rire* and this prevented many of the pictures being sullen and morose.' Beaton tried the monarch standing and the monarch seated, and by the time he got to the Garter photographs he felt he had finally got his subject relaxed. 'Now I knew how to arrange the lights,' he wrote, 'and to get the Queen three-quarter face with the head turned sufficiently back for the cheek bone to be clear and flattering. I was excited . . .'

At the end of Episode 10, Peter Morgan rides on that excitement to round off the episode. 'All hail, sage Lady, whom a grateful Isle hath blessed!' exults Beaton as he shoots the final frame, reverting to archaic, *Faerie Queene* language to match the style of his Windsor fantasy. 'Not moving! Not Breathing! Our very own Goddess!' So, Season 1 of *The Crown* ends on a photographic crescendo, with Elizabeth starring as Gloriana – on canvas, at least, as well as on the silver nitrate plate.

✻⊱──•─•─ ♛ ─•─•──⊰✻

Queen Elizabeth II in her Garter robes, photographed against a backdrop of Windsor Castle by Cecil Beaton in the autumn of 1955.

As Season 2 of The Crown *approaches, however, Elizabeth II and her country face challenges on many fronts, particularly in the Middle East. We have watched the tensions developing in this final episode as Anthony Eden seeks to confront and fails to pacify Egypt's Colonel Nasser over the ownership of the Suez Canal. It seems a minor colonial annoyance in 1955.*

But by the end of 1956, the folly and tragedy of Suez will come to stand for far more – an historic watershed after which Britain's place in the world will never be the same again. The shock and disillusionment will strike harshly at many aspects of British life, and not least at the crown and the woman who wears it. The gloriously robed monarch who smiles into Cecil Beaton's camera in the autumn of 1955 is, to all appearances, an eternal figurehead, as classic and serene as her portrait by Annigoni. But that was then. Have we – has she – seen the best of it?

PHILIP, DUKE OF EDINBURGH

PLAYED BY MATT SMITH

'What kind of marriage is this?
What kind of family?

You've taken my career from me,
you've taken my home.

I thought we were in this together.'

♔

QUEEN ELIZABETH II

PLAYED BY CLAIRE FOY

'I am aware that I am surrounded by people who feel they could do the job better.

Strong people with powerful characters, more natural leaders . . .

But, for better or worse, the Crown has landed on my head.'

ROYAL TIMELINE

1947–1955

1947

19 November – King George VI ennobles Lieutenant Philip Mountbatten as His Royal Highness the Duke of Edinburgh, Knight of the Garter. Princess Elizabeth and Philip are married next day in Westminster Abbey.

1948

5 July – National Health Service is launched by Clement Attlee's Labour Government.

14 November – Prince Charles is born.

1949

Autumn – Philip leaves for Malta as first lieutenant of the destroyer HMS *Chequers*.

1950

16 July – Philip is promoted to lieutenant commander and given command of the frigate HMS *Magpie*.

15 August – Princess Anne is born.

1951

July – Philip ends his naval career and returns from Malta.

23 September – King George VI's lung is removed in an operation inside Buckingham Palace.

26 October – The Conservatives defeat Labour in the General Election. Clement Attlee resigns. Winston Churchill becomes Prime Minister.

December – King George VI spends his last Christmas with his family at Sandringham.

1952

31 January – Princess Elizabeth and Philip stand in for her father and leave on their Commonwealth Tour, starting in Kenya.

6 February – King George VI dies in his sleep at Sandringham. The new Queen Elizabeth II hears the news of her father's death at the Sagana Lodge in Kenya and flies back to London.

15 February – Funeral of King George VI.

April – The Coronation Commission meets for the first time, with the Duke of Edinburgh as Chairman.

Summer – Queen Elizabeth the Queen Mother sees and decides to purchase and restore the Castle of Mey in northern Scotland.

5 – 9 December – The 'Great Smog' brings London to a standstill. Several thousand die.

1953

February – The end of British sweet rationing, first imposed in July 1942.

24 March – Queen Mary dies, aged 85.

2 June – The Coronation of Queen Elizabeth II. British television ownership rises from 400,000 in 1950 to 1,100,000 in 1953.

7 June – A report of romance between Princess Margaret and Peter Townsend is published in the *New York Journal American*.

10 June – Anthony Eden has abdominal surgery in Boston, Massachusetts.

23 June – Winston Churchill suffers a stroke at Downing Street.

3 July – London newspapers report the romance between Princess Margaret and Peter Townsend.

15 July – Peter Townsend leaves for Brussels to begin his new position as Air Attaché to the British Embassy.

31 July – Anthony Eden returns to London following his surgery in America.

Summer – Sir Alan 'Tommy' Lascelles retires as Private Secretary to Elizabeth II. Michael Adeane succeeds him.

12 August – Soviet Union explodes the hydrogen bomb at the Semipalatinsk test site, Kazakhstan.

24 November – Queen Elizabeth II and the Duke of Edinburgh set off on their round-the-world tour of the Commonwealth, starting in Bermuda.

1 9 5 4

15 May – Queen Elizabeth II and her husband return, having travelled more than 40,000 miles and visited Bermuda, Jamaica, Fiji, Tonga, New Zealand, Australia, Cocos Islands, Ceylon, Aden, Uganda, Malta and Gibraltar.

4 July – British food rationing ends when restrictions on the purchase of meat and bacon are lifted.

17 July – Queen Elizabeth II's horse Aureole wins the King George VI and Queen Elizabeth Stakes at Ascot.

August – Graham Sutherland begins painting his portrait of Winston Churchill.

30 November – Parliament presents Winston Churchill with Sutherland's portrait in Westminster Hall on his 80th birthday.

1955

February – Anthony Eden returns to London after meeting with Colonel Gamal Abdel Nasser in Cairo, Egypt.

4 April – Winston Churchill entertains Elizabeth II for a farewell dinner in Downing Street.

5 April – Winston Churchill resigns and Anthony Eden becomes prime minister.

10 October – Peter Townsend returns to London from Brussels.

21 October – Elizabeth II unveils the statue of King George VI in the Mall.

31 October – A statement by Princess Margaret announces that she will not pursue her plans to marry Peter Townsend.

4 November – Townsend returns to Brussels to resume his position as Air Attaché to the British Embassy.

November – Cecil Beaton photographs Elizabeth II in her Garter robes in front of a painted back-drop of Windsor Castle.

CAST

THE ROYAL FAMILY

Queen Elizabeth II	Claire Foy
Philip, Duke of Edinburgh	Matt Smith
Queen Mary	Eileen Atkins
'David', Duke of Windsor	Alex Jennings
Wallis, Duchess of Windsor	Lia Williams
King George VI	Jared Harris
Queen Elizabeth, the Queen Mother	Victoria Hamilton
Princess Margaret	Vanessa Kirby
Lord Louis Mountbatten	Greg Wise
Young Princess Elizabeth	Verity Russell
Young Princess Margaret	Beau Gadsdon
Prince Charles	Billy Jenkins
Princess Anne	Grace & Amelia Gilmour
Prince Ernst of Hannover	Daniel Betts

Mike Parker	Daniel Ings
Duke of Norfolk	Patrick Ryecart
Lord Chamberlain	Patrick Drury
Cecil Mann, Crown Jeweller	John Surman
Margaret MacDonald, 'Bobo'	Lizzy McInnerny
Marion Crawford, 'Crawfie'	Sara Vickers
Chief Telephonist	John Rowe
Duke of Edinburgh's Valet	Chris Gordon
Equerry (Buckingham Palace)	James Hillier
Page (Buckingham Palace)	Jonathan Newth
Page (Clarence House)	Thomas Padden
Princess Margaret's Dresser	Angela Sims

THE WORLD OF THE COURT

Alan Lascelles, 'Tommy'	Pip Torrens
Michael Adeane	Will Keen
Martin Charteris	Harry Hadden-Paton
Mary Charteris	Jo Herbert
Peter Townsend	Ben Miles

MOVING IN ROYAL CIRCLES

Henry Porchester, 'Porchey'	Joseph Kloska
Jean Wallop	Andrea Deck
Baron Nahum	Julius D'Silva
Billy Wallace	Nick Hendrix
Colin Tennant	David Shields

Commander Vyner	David Yelland
Lady Doris Vyner	Caroline Goodall
Johnny, Earl of Dalkeith	Josh Taylor
Judy Montague	Abigail Parmenter
Cecil Beaton	Mark Tandy
Norman Hartnell	Richard Clifford

👑

THE WORLD OF POLITICS

Winston Churchill	John Lithgow
Clementine Churchill	Harriet Walter
Clement Attlee	Simon Chandler
Anthony Eden	Jeremy Northam
Clarissa Eden	Anna Madeley
Lord Salisbury, 'Bobbety'	Clive Francis
John Colville, 'Jock'	Nicholas Rowe
R. A. Butler, 'Rab'	Michael Culkin
Walter Monckton	George Asprey
Harry Crookshank	Nigel Cooke
John Foster Dulles	Garrick Hagon
Gamal Abdel Nasser	Amir Boutrous

👑

HISTORICAL CHARACTERS

Archbishop of Canterbury	Ronald Pickup
Archbishop of York	John Woodvine
Henry Marten, Vice-Provost of Eton	Michael Cochrane

Lord Moran	Nicholas Jones
Sir John Weir	James Laurenson
Graham Sutherland	Stephen Dillane
Mlle. De Bellaigue	Héléna Soubeyrand
Captain F. B. Imbert-Terry	John Standing
Eric Sherbrooke Walker	David Clatworthy
Governor General of Kenya	Wayne Harrison
Chief Kungu Waruhiu	Yule Masiteng
Chief Pelipel	Treasure Tshabalala
Kathleen Sullivan	Amelia Bullmore

👑

FICTITIOUS CHARACTERS

Venetia Scott	Kate Phillips
Chief Sironka	Dan Sitoe
Bill Matheson	Paul Thornley
Collins	Jo Stone-Fewings
Mary	Samantha Baines
Mrs Wills	Catherine Lamb
Nancy Lewis	Clare Foster
Professor Hogg	Alan Williams
Thurman	Anthony Flanagan
Tony Longdon	Ed Stoppard
Newspaper Editor	Peter Wight
Newspaper Proprietor	Clive Arrindell
Chief Scientist (Met Office)	Simon Poland
Director (Met Office)	Stephen Chance
TV Producer	Ryan Early

CREW

Creator and Writer	Peter Morgan		Duncan Macmillan
Executive Producers	Peter Morgan	Script Executives	Oona O Beirn
	Stephen Daldry		David Hancock
	Andy Harries	Story Editor	Edward Hemming
	Philip Martin	Head of Research	Kerry Gill-Pryde
	Suzanne Mackie	Specialist Researcher	Annie Sulzberger
	Matthew Byam Shaw	Asst. Producer to P. Morgan	Tanya Von Moser
	Robert Fox	Dialect Coach	William Conacher
	Tanya Seghatchian	Historical Consultant	Robert Lacey
	Nina Wolarsky	Protocol Advisor	Major David Rankin-Hunt
	Allie Goss	Asst. Production Coordinator	Charlotte Michel
Series Producer	Andrew Eaton	Jnr. Production Coordinator	Rachel Linehan
Producers	Faye Ward	Production Secretary	Rebecca Warren
	Michael Casey	Crowd 2nd Asst. Director	Gary Richens
Directors	Stephen Daldry	Supervising Art Director	Mark Raggett
	Philip Martin	Key Production Assistant	Sarah Childs
	Julian Jarrold	Production Assistant	Jesse Algranti
	Benjamin Caron	Rushes Runner	Toby Robinson
Co-Producer	Andy Stebbing	Producers Assistant	Dominique Summers
Production Designer	Martin Childs	Directors Assistant	Akaash Meeda
Directors of Photography	Adriano Goldman		Joe Madden
	Ole Bratt Birkeland		Tom McCormack
Casting Directors	Nina Gold	Art Directors	Hannah Moseley
	Robert Sterne		James Wakefield
Costume Designer	Michele Clapton	Standby Art Directors	Lizzie Kilham
Make-up and Hair Designer	Ivana Primorac		Louise Lannen
Main Theme Music	Hans Zimmer	Assistant Art Director	Damian Leon Watts
Music by	Rupert Gregson-Williams	Draughtsman	Thomas Turner
Music Supervisor	Sue Crawshaw	Art Department Assistant	Georgie Carson
Editors	Pia Di Ciaula	Set Decorator	Celia Bobak
	Luke Dunkley	Production Buyer	Lucinda Sturgis
	Mark Eckersley	Assistant Set Decorators	Alison Harvey
	Stuart Gazzard		Sophie Coombes
	Kristina Hetherington	Assistant Buyer	Rachel Corbould
	Úna Ní Dhonghaíle	Drapes Master	Tony Szuch
	Yan Miles	Graphic Designer	Neil Floyd
1st Assistant Directors	Martin Harrison	Graphics Assistant	Victoria Reynolds
	Finn McGrath	Clearance Coordinator	Joanna Garrard
	Richard Styles	Property Master	Craig Cheeseman
2nd Assistant Directors	Andy Mannion	Standbys Props	Mark Brooks
	Charlie Waller		Stuart Headley-Read
3rd Assistant Director	Matt Bensley	Prop Storeman	Owen Harrison
Production Manager	Eve Swannell	Prop Chargehands	Stuart Frift
2nd Unit Production Manager	Harriet Worth		Peter Wood
Financial Controller	Alistair Thompson	Dressing Props	Joe Gallagher
Post Production Producer	Nicki Mousley		Sean Board
2nd Unit Director	Justin Martin	Props/Set Dec. Coord.	Jenny Hawes
Production Coordinator	Carrie Banner		
Casting Assistant	Kate Bone		
Additional Material	Nick Payne		
	Tom Edge		

Camera Operator/Steadicam	Stuart Howell	Costume Workshop Supervisor	Christine Atkinson
Camera Operator	Iain Struthers	Make-up and Hair Artists	Gemma Hoff
1st Assistant Camera	Tim Battersby		Sarah Spears
	Jason Walker		Amy Riley
			Michele Davidson-Bell
2nd Assistant Camera	Phoebe Arnstein	Make-up and Hair Trainee	Natasha Klipp
	Kriss Dallimore	Crowd Make-up Supervisor	Fiona Rogers
Camera Trainee	Ruy De Carvalho	Crowd Make-up/Hair Artist	Sophie Ashworth
Digital Image Technician	John Paxton	Crowd Make-up/Hair Trainee	Liv Barningham
Digital Image Tech Assist.	Liam Beard	Security	Ray Cummins
Video Operator	Guy McCormack	Transport Captain	Mark Crowley
Video Assistant	Luke Haddock	Production Accountant	Lita O'Sullivan
Gaffer	Andy Lowe	Assistant Accountants	Linda Tootill
Best Boy	Chris Stones		Munawar Ahmad
Rigging Gaffer	John Antill	Cashier	Giles Barnett
HOD Electrical Rigger	Steve Fitzpatrick	Accounts Assistant	Renata Pavelka
Sound Mixer	Chris Ashworth	Accounts Trainee	Rajneet Jabbal
Boom Operator	James Harris	Head Chef	Chris Blyth
2nd Boom Operator	Duran Darkins	Chef	Paul Creasey
Key Grip	Ronan Murphy	Director of Publicity	Ian Johnson
Grips	Michael Wacker	Asst. to Director of Publicity	Allie Elwell
	James Ray-Leary	Stills Photographer	Alex Bailey
Trainee Grip	Steve Wells	Producer South Africa	Genevieve Hofmeyer
Supervising Location Mngr	Pat Karam	Line Producer South Africa	Angela Philips
Location Managers	Peter Gray	Location Mngr South Africa	Robert Bentley
	Mark Walledge	Archive Producer	Victoria Stable
	Andrew Ryland	Music Supervisor	Sue Crawshaw
	Chris Johnston	VFX Supervisor	Ben Turner
Asst. Location Managers	Adrian Hubbard	Colourist	Asa Shoul
	Ian Lumsden	Online Editor	Gareth Parry
Unit Manager	Nathan Flaher	Supervising Sound Editor	Lee Walpole
Location Assistant	Olivia Grant	Dialogue Editor	Iain Eyre
Script Supervisors	Karen Jones	ADR Supervisor	Kallis Shamaris
	Janice Schumm	Sound Design	Andy Kennedy
SFX Supervisor	Chris Reynolds	Re-Recording Mixers	Stuart Hilliker
SFX Floor Supervisor	Mat Horton		Martin Jensen
Construction Manager	Gene D'Cruze		Lee Walpole
HOD Carpenter	Danny Margetts	Titles	Elastic
HOD Painter	Marc Beros	1st Assistant Editor	Dan Gage
Standby Carpenter	Steve Carling	2nd Assistant Editor	Ruth Antoine
Standby Painter	Nick Bowen		Izabella Curry
Costume Supervisor	Kate O'Farrell	Post Prod. Coordinators	Becky Page
Asst. Costume Designer	Alex Fordham		Leonie Bleasdale
Crowd Costume Supervisor	Gordon Harmer		Natasha Lauder
Costume Design Assistant	Emma O'Loughlin	Post Production Secretary	Senait Ghezzehey
Wardrobe Mistress	Barbara Harrington	Business Affairs Executive	Henry Buswell
Costume Coordinator	Rebecca Tredget	Head of Business Affairs	Charlie Goldberg
Principle Costume Standbys	Jade Armstrong	Finance Director	Grace Wilson
	Gabriella Morpeth	Director of Production	Marigo Kehoe
	Oliver Southall	Head of Production	Hilary Benson
Crowd Costume Standby	Ashleigh Lennox		

RECOMMENDED READING

BIOGRAPHIES OF QUEEN ELIZABETH II

Bradford, Sarah. *Queen Elizabeth II: Her Life in Our Times*. London: Viking, 2012.

Brandreth, Gyles. *Elizabeth and Philip: Portrait of a Royal Marriage*. New York: W. W. Norton & Company, 2004.

Hardman, Robert. *Our Queen*. London: Arrow Books, 2012.

Lacey, Robert. *Majesty: Elizabeth II and the House of Windsor*. London: Hutchinson, 1977.

Marr, Andrew. *The Diamond Queen*. London: Macmillan, 2011.

Pimlott, Ben. *The Queen: Elizabeth and the* Monarchy. London: HarperPress, 2012.

Smith, Sally Bedell. *Elizabeth the Queen: The Life of a Modern Monarch*. New York, Random House, 2012.

ROYAL BIOGRAPHIES AND STUDIES

Bloch, Michael. *The Secret File of the Duke of Windsor*. London: Transworld, 1988.

Bogdanor, Vernon. *The Monarchy and the Constitution*. Oxford: Clarendon Press, 1995.

Boothroyd, Basil. *Prince Philip: An Informal Biography*. New York: McCall, 1971.

Bradford, Sarah. *George VI*. London: Weidenfeld and Nicolson, 1989.

Buxton, Aubrey. *The King in His Country*. London: Longmans, Green, 1955.

Eade, Philip. *Prince Philip: His Turbulent Early Life*. London: HarperPress, 2011.

Heald, Tim. *The Duke: A Portrait of Prince Philip*. London: Hodder & Stoughton, 1991.

Menkes, Suzy. *Windsor Style*. London: Grafton, 1987.

Pope-Hennessy, James. *Queen Mary, 1867–1953*. London: George Allen and Unwin, 1959.

Rose, Kenneth. *King George V*. New York: Alfred A. Knopf, 1984.

Rose, Kenneth. *Kings, Queens & Courtiers*. hLondon: Weidenfeld and Nicolson, 1985.

Shawcross, William. *The Queen Mother: The Official Biography*. New York: Vintage Books, 2010.

Vickers, Hugo. *Elizabeth, the Queen Mother*. London: Hutchinson, 2005.

Warwick, Christopher. *Princess Margaret: A Life of Contrasts*. London: André Deutsch, 2002.

Ziegler, Philip. *King Edward VIII*. London: Collins, 1990.

Ziegler, Philip. *Mountbatten*. London: Collins, 1985.

MEMOIRS AND DIARIES

Brown, Anthony Montague. *Long Sunset: Memoirs of Winston Churchill's Last Private Secretary.* Great Britain, Podkin Press, 1995.

Hartnell, Norman. *Silver and Gold.* London: Evans Brothers, 1955.

Moir, Phyllis. *I Was Winston Churchill's Private Secretary.* New York: Wilfred Funk, Inc., 1941.

Nel, Elizabeth. *Winston Churchill by His Private Secretary.* New York: iUniverse, Inc., 2007.

Nicolson, Nigel. *The Harold Nicolson Diaries, 1907–1964.* London: Phoenix, 2005.

Rhodes James, Robert. *'Chips': The Diaries of Sir Henry Channon.* London: Phoenix, 1996.

Shawcross, William. *Counting One's Blessings: The Selected Letters of Queen Elizabeth the Queen Mother.* New York: Farrar, Straus and Giroux, 2012.

Soames, Mary. *Speaking for Themselves: The Personal Letters of Winston and Clementine Churchill.* London: Doubleday, 1998.

Soames, Mary. *A Daughter's Tale: The Memoir of Winston Churchill's Youngest Child.* New York: Random House, 2012.

Townsend, Peter. *Time and Chance.* London: Collins, 1978.

BIOGRAPHIES AND HISTORIES

Bew, John. *Citizen Clem.* London: Quercus, 2016.

Clarke, Peter. *Mr. Churchill's Profession.* New York: Bloomsbury Press, 2012.

Gilbert, Martin. *Churchill: A Life.* New York: Henry Holt and Company, 1991.

Hennessy, Peter. *Having It So Good: Britain in the Fifties.* London: Penguin, 2007.

Hennessy, Peter. *The Prime Minister: The Office and Its Holders since 1945.* London: Penguin, 2001.

Jenkins, Roy. *Churchill: A Biography.* New York: Plume, 2002.

Lough, David. *No More Champagne: Churchill and His Money.* New York City: Picador, 2015.

Manchester, William and Paul Reid. *The Last Lion: Winston Spencer Churchill, Defender of the Realm, 1940–1965.* New York: Bantam Trade Paperbacks, 2013.

Purnell, Sonia. *Clementine: The Life of Mrs. Winston Churchill.* New York: Penguin Books, 2015.

Roberts, Andrew. *Eminent Churchillians.* London: Phoenix, 1995.

Soames, Mary. *Clementine Churchill: The Biography of a Marriage.* Boston: Houghton Mifflin Company, 2003.

Strong, Roy. *Cecil Beaton: The Royal Portraits.* New York: Simon and Schuster, 1988.

Vickers, Hugo. *Cecil Beaton: The Authorized Biography.* London: Weidenfeld and Nicholson, 1985.

P eter Morgan is the inspiration of *The Crown*, and he is also the inspiration of this book, *The Inside History*, which has been raised upon the solid foundations of his drama. The book has been piloted by Peter's purpose to lay out the historical evidence on which the drama is based – and from which, on a few occasions, he unashamedly departs. History, as Hilary Mantel has recently reminded us, is our imperfect way of organising our ignorance of the past. Imagination is our way of understanding it, and Peter has supplied both imagination and understanding in abundance.

Thank you also to Andy Harries of Left Bank Pictures for his whole-hearted support and encouragement – along with his colleagues Marigo Kehoe, Suzanne Mackie, Charlie Goldberg, Ian Johnson, Robert Fox and Matthew Byam-Shaw. In writing the book, I have benefitted hugely from the historical delving and documentation of Left Bank's *Crown* script and research team: Kerry Gill-Pryde, Annie Sulzberger, Edward Hemming, David Hancock and Oona O'Beirn. What happened to King George VI's severed lung? Left Bank discovered the secret.

The pre-ordained protocols of modern publishing can drain the fun and creativity out of old-fashioned, hands-on book production. But not the lively and creative team at Blink, with whom it has been such a pleasure to work: Ben Dunn, Beth Eynon, Oliver Holden-Rea, Emily Rough, Vivien Hamley and Richard Collins. Thank you for your hope and brightness, your taste and style, your original thinking and your problem-solving sensitivities which have added so much to every page. And thank you too, Michael Foster, for your own push and problem-solving at some difficult moments, and for the unfailing support of Jonathan Pegg.

On some specific points of history, I have benefitted from the collegial advice of Michael Bloch and William Shawcross, as well as from Dr Jane Connors and Dr Yvonne Ward in Australia. On questions of literary balance, I have relied on the immaculate instincts of my old friend Ben Dyal with his sharp-eyed partner Mrs Norris. Robert Donnelly supplied the elegant family tree. Roy and

Zoe Snell brought their precision to fuzzy pictures. And thank you to Lesley Baker, Jane Turner and Emma Anstock for their professional secretarial back-up.

Susan Link Camp, my California-based Nancy Drew, has been my indispensable colleague in checking the facts and discovering original documents and photographs, many of them reflecting her particular flair for fashion history. This book has been written, designed and produced in a miraculously short length of time, and if the nimble Blink team can take credit for the editorial end of things, it is Susan's tireless hours of support and research that have made it possible for me to fulfil my end of the bargain.

I have never forgotten the morning of 2nd June 1953, when my family trooped next door to watch the coronation of Elizabeth II on the newly acquired television of our neighbours, Mr and Mrs Ronny Gleave, in Westbury-On-Trym, Bristol. Little did I imagine that Jane Stewart, the Maid of Honour carrying the train just behind the Queen's left shoulder, would one day bring such happiness into my own life. But here we are in a new century, with dear Jane's love and laughter bringing such joy to an author's weariness.

Robert Lacey, July 2017

IMAGE CREDITS

INDEX

Facing page: Elizabeth II pictured by Dorothy Wilding on 26th February 1952, just twenty days after her accession, in her first formal portrait session as Queen, wearing a black taffeta strapless 'cabbage leaf' dress by Norman Hartnell. The purpose of the session was to produce the portraits to be used on the coins, banknotes and stamps of the new reign. One of the 58 photos from the session was selected as the official portrait to hang in every British embassy around the world. Another was the silhouette image used on the front and back covers of this book.

THE
CROWN
SEASON ONE

COMPLETE THE COLLECTION
ON BLU-RAY AND DVD